ROUTINE VIOLENCE

Cultural Memory

in

the

Present

Mieke Bal and Hent de Vries, Editors

ROUTINE VIOLENCE

Nations, Fragments, Histories

Gyanendra Pandey

STANFORD UNIVERSITY PRESS

STANFORD, CALIFORNIA

2006

Stanford University Press
Stanford, California

Printed in the United States of America
on acid-free, archival-quality paper

Library of Congress Cataloging-in-Publication Data

Pandey, Gyanendra.
 Routine violence : nations, fragments, histories / Gyanendra Pandey.
  p. cm. — (Cultural memory in the present)
 Includes bibliographical references and index.
 ISBN 0-8047-5263-x (cloth : alk. paper)
 ISBN 0-8047-5264-8 (pbk. : alk. paper)
  1. Political violence. 2. Minorities. 3. Discrimination. 4. Toleration.
 5. Political violence—India. I. Title. II. Series.

JC328.6.P36 2006
303.6—DC22

2005013564

Original Printing 2006

Last figure below indicates year of this printing:
15 14 13 12 11 10 09 08 07 06

For Ruby

Contents

Acknowledgments

This book has benefited greatly from the generous and critical comments of several friends who read all or part of the manuscript: Jane Bennett, Bill Connolly, Peter Geschiere, David Hardiman, Pamela Reynolds, Romila Thapar, and especially (for their close reading and detailed observations) Talal Asad, Ajay Skaria, and Ruby Lal. Dipesh Chakrabarty, Partha Chatterjee, Homi Bhabha, Shahid Amin, Sudhir Chandra, Nayanjot Lahiri, Nicholas Dirks, and Suresh Sharma have continued to be important interlocutors and well-wishers.

Hent de Vries kindly suggested that *Routine Violence* might be included in Stanford's series Cultural Memory in the Present. Penny Harris, independent and innovative Baltimore photographer, generously offered an extraordinary photograph for the cover.

My mother and sisters in Delhi, Nishad and Ruby in their (or our) movement through many places, have been a source of endless support.

To all of them, my deepest gratitude.

Parts of the book have appeared before, in different forms and different forums. They have been substantially rewritten, recast, and rearranged here to make the larger argument of this study. Chapter 2 is a revised version of "In Defense of the Fragment: Writing about Hindu-Muslim Riots in India Today," published in *Economic and Political Weekly* 26, no. 11–12 (March 1991), and *Representations* 37 (Winter 1992). Earlier versions of parts of Chapter 4 appeared in "The New Hindu History," *South Asia* 17 (1994); of Chapter 5 in "Which of Us Are Hindus?" published in Gyanendra Pandey, ed., *Hindus and Others: Questions of Identity in India Today* (New Delhi: Viking, 1993); and Chapter 6 in "Can a Muslim Be an Indian?" published in *Comparative Studies in Society and History* 41, no. 4 (October 1999). The appendices to Chapters 2 and 4 are unrevised versions of articles published in the Delhi journals *Sunday* (19–25 January 1992) and *Seminar* (December 1989), respectively.

ROUTINE VIOLENCE

1

Introduction: Negotiating the Boundaries of Political Violence

This book is about minorities, and hence majorities. It investigates how these categories are constituted in the modern political community. How are minorities identified by the notional mainstreams of our societies? What are the conditions of their being recognized and accommodated, the conditions of their *being*?

There is a violence written into the making and continuation of contemporary political arrangements, and into the production and reproduction of majorities and minorities, which I have called *routine violence*. The present study is concerned with the routine violence of our history and politics. It is about the enabling conditions of what is commonly seen as violence, but suggests that these conditions—political stipulations, history writing, the construction of majorities and minorities, the education of marginalized and subordinated groups and assemblages—are themselves shot through with violence.

It will help to begin with some discussion of the received understanding of the last term. In an important sense, violence remains a premodern category in contemporary usage. It functions also as a residual one. *Premodern* in that it has to do, supposedly, with what happened before rational thought and organization governed society, and what still happens when these are at a discount. *Residual* in that every act of aggression, destruction and intimidation for which we cannot find an approved, scientific name (that links it to the natural, rational human pursuit of progress and development)—war, mutiny, punishment, insurgency and counterinsurgency operations, for instance—can be described with the word.

The premodern character of the violent condition is very clearly signaled in Hegel's commentary on the absence of history in many parts of the world. Take one example: "Not only does India have ancient religious texts and brilliant works of poetry, but ancient codes of law—the very thing that was set down just now [by Hegel] as a precondition in the formation of history—and yet it has no history. The organizing impulse that led to social differentiation was immediately ossified into caste distinctions interpreted as determinations of nature. . . . Due to the unfreedom arising from the natural permanence of the caste system, the cohesion of society is nothing but wild arbitrariness—fleeting activity or rather blind rage—without any goal for progress or development."

Much has happened in that country, the philosopher goes on to say, "without giving rise to history: the rich and immense growth of families into tribes, of tribes into nations; their consequent spread, along with so many complications, wars, revolutions, decline—all occurring with much noise and clamor, although all has remained in effect silent and has passed by stealthily, unnoticed."[1]

What we have here—and even more crudely in his comments on Africa[2]—is "noise and clamor," "fleeting activity" and "blind rage," which however pass by "stealthily, unnoticed"—all of it unrelated to any "goal of progress or development." That is probably as good a statement of the popular sense of violence as any we will come across.

In the same discussion, Hegel suggests that it is the state itself "which first presents a subject matter that is entirely appropriate to the prose of history; indeed the state creates it as it creates itself."[3] Is the first *it* the "subject matter" or "the prose" of history? Or is it, as I am inclined to suggest, both? The state creates history, the subject matter and the prose of history. Everything that lies outside the state belongs to prehistory, and (I am suggesting) to the order of violence. It is hard to describe the violent condition precisely, for the state has not provided us with the vocabulary for it.

A quick checklist of some acts of destruction and intimidation that are widely counted as violence, along with some that are not, may be instructive here:

—Hindu-Muslim riots in India and black-white riots in Britain (both of which themselves cover a whole variety of evils), but not World War I and II in many journalistic and academic accounts;

—suicide bombings in Palestine and Iraq, but not the razing of civilian homes and entire villages by Israeli and American tanks and missiles from the air;

—warlordism in Afghanistan, but not American interrogations in Guantanamo Bay.

It may help to underline some of the implications. The actions of politically disadvantaged, or unrepresented, people are commonly labeled violent; the acts of those in power, the authorities and the arms of the state, less frequently so. Thus one may add to our checklist:

—Natives in northern India killing English women and children (and armed men, including civilian administrators and military personnel) in 1857 are guilty of violence, but not the English torching whole villages and localities, and hanging dozens of untried inhabitants of suspected areas;

—crime in the inner cities figures as violence, but not always the brutality of the Los Angeles police;

—so does public beheading, but not the electric chair.

Let us take a quick look too at what counts as brutality or excess in the use of force:

—suicide bombs (obviously and appropriately), but not precision bombing and Daisy Cutters;

—Japanese Kamikaze pilots flying their fanatical missions during World War II, but not those who dropped enough firebombs to destroy 51 percent of Tokyo and kill 100,000 of its inhabitants in one night;

—Cambodia and Rwanda and Bosnia-Herzegovina, but not (until late in the day) the American destruction of Vietnam;

—machetes and hatchets, but not guillotines (in the time when they were thought to be the most scientific and painless way of administering the death penalty) or (today) the electric chair;

and dare one say it,

—Muslim fanaticism, but not Christian wars of religion (medieval or modern).

Even such a brief checklist may suffice to show that there are three kinds of indicators that go into our understanding of what constitutes violence, or excess—which may amount to the same thing. The first is organization and scale. (If these are large and developed enough, the acts do not qualify as violence, which is why the state is often exempt.) A second is technology. (If this is sophisticated enough . . .) The third is race, which of course incorporates class, gender, and culture. (The black in the United States is always a man, although there is an insidious if now subterranean discourse about the black woman as well, whereas the white—though a man—is implicitly, and now more and more explicitly, accompanied by a woman and children; just as the Muslim in India is a man, with the women and children barely visible, whereas the Hindu is a family, and usually an extended one.) The importance of each of these will, I hope, become clearer in the chapters that follow.

The Violence of the Modern

I am aware of what Marx and, following him, writers like Frantz Fanon and Jean Suret-Canale had to say about the violence that marked the advent of modernity, especially in its colonial moment; and again of what thinkers like Hannah Arendt and Zygmunt Bauman have written about the modernity of modern evil, and the rational bureaucratic procedures that lie behind some of the worst examples of violence in recent history.[4] Fanon provides a paradigmatic comment: "The violence which has ruled over the ordering of the colonial world, which has ceaselessly drummed the rhythm for the destruction of native social forms and broken up without reserve the systems of reference of the economy, the customs of dress and external life, that same violence will be claimed and taken over by the native at the moment when, deciding to embody history in his own person, he surges into the forbidden quarters [of the colonial ruling class]." The practice of violence binds the colonized population together, he goes on to say, although he might have added that such violence can be easily deflected onto a group's own most vulnerable segments, particularly women and children. "Each individual forms a violent link in the great chain, a part of the great organism of violence which has surged upward in reaction to the settler's violence." The two groups "recognize each other" in and through the violence.[5]

Recent events in America and Europe have perhaps bucked the trend, and served to (re)establish other strains in Western political discourse. Until this happened, the violence of the colonial state—the French in Southeast Asia and North and West Africa, South Africa under apartheid, and so on—was fairly widely recognized as violence. It was the violence of the illegitimate state, comparable to the violence of the failed state: the state without control over its territory and institutions, the state without civil society and nation, the warlord and mercenary state—Sudan, Congo, Afghanistan. Much of the critical, oppositional scholarship of our own time has continued to focus on such acts of illegitimate violence: in Abu Ghraib, as in Hiroshima, Nagasaki, or Vietnam.

What remains unacknowledged are two dimensions of modern politics and history. First, the violence of the legitimate state, a state that had the backing of something called a nation and could speak in the name of the people. Secondly, the fact that violence was not merely transitional, a birthmark or a departure, but a much more general and continuous aspect of modern life.

For older writers on the subject, violence was temporary, occasional, even abnormal. For Fanon it was a kind of purge; for Marxist historians more generally, a colonial intermezzo. Similarly, Abu Ghraib and the excesses of Vietnam are still widely seen as just that: aberrations, excesses, deviations from the norm. Perhaps our apprehension of violence and terror has changed a little over the last couple of decades, as the violence has come home—to Europe and to the suburbs of the elites in the ex-colonial world. One may still ask, however, whether the understanding of violence as interruption has altered very significantly.

In a review published in summer 2004, David Herman cites Orlando Figes's 1996 history of the Russian Revolution, *A People's Tragedy*; Adam Hochschild's 1998 account of Congo in the early twentieth century, *King Leopold's Ghost*; Antony Beevor's account of the fall of Berlin (*Berlin: The Downfall, 1945*), published in 2002; and even Simon Schama's earlier study of the French Revolution, *Citizens* (1989), to make the point that the study of violence and terror has now moved to centerstage.[6] One might add to his list: W. G. Sebald's clinical study of the devastation of German cities in the latter phase of the Second World War, *On the Natural History of Destruction* (1999); Achille Mbembe's exploration of the grotesquerie of power and subjectivity in postcolonial Africa, *On the Postcolony* (2001); the plethora of new studies focusing on the massive violence of Partition and Independence in the Indian subcontinent in 1947;[7] and much more.

Historians are creatures of their times. The Indian writings on Partition were clearly influenced by the public spectacle of arson, murder, rape, and looting that took place on the streets of Delhi, Bombay, and other Indian cities in 1984, 1992–93, and on other occasions during this period: "the worst riots since Partition," as they were described time and time again, in the press and in common conversations. Similarly, the works on

Europe and Africa mentioned above were conditioned by the destruction, genocide, and ethnic cleansing that occurred in Rwanda, Bosnia, and Kosovo, not to mention Nazi Germany. Historians of the new generation (nearly all born after 1945) "have none of the optimism or reticence of their illustrious predecessors," writes David Herman. "They have been drawn to the darkest episodes of modern European [and African and Indian] history, in their most terrible details. The result is history of the highest standard: compelling, humane and without illusions."[8] That may be overstated, but the proposition about scholars paying closer attention to the details of violence is valid.

Herman compares E. H. Carr's academic account of the violence of the class war and civil war of 1917–23 in his impressive three-volume history of the Bolshevik Revolution with that of Orlando Figes. Carr refers to a number of mass killings, and states that "bald records . . . conceal horrors and brutalities . . . [which] are the invariable concomitants of war and revolution waged with . . . fanatical desperation." By contrast, Figes foregrounds the "horrors and brutalities" committed on all sides, in order to come to terms with the violence of modern history. Of the savage war between Russian peasants and Bolsheviks in 1920, he writes at one point: "Thousands of Bolsheviks were brutally murdered. Many were the victims of gruesome (and symbolic) torture: ears, tongues, eyes were cut out; limbs, heads and genitals were cut off; stomachs were sliced open and stuffed with wheat; crosses were branded on foreheads and torsos; Communists were nailed to trees, burned alive, drowned under ice, buried up to their necks and eaten by dogs or rats, while crowds of peasants watched and shouted."

Nor was the savagery reserved to the peasantry. "In Kharkov they [the Cheka, or Russian Secret Police] went in for the 'glove trick'—burning the victim's hands in boiling water until the blistered skin could be peeled off. . . . The Tsaritsyn Cheka sawed its victims' bones in half. In Voronezh they rolled their naked victims in nail-studded barrels. In Armavir they crushed their skulls by tightening a leather strap with an iron bolt around their head[s]. In Kiev they affixed a cage with rats to the victim's torso and heated it so that the enraged rats ate their way through the victim's guts in an effort to escape."

Sebald writes of the wooden crosses that still stood, after 1950, on "piles of rubble in towns like Pforzheim, which lost almost one-third of its sixty thousand inhabitants in a single raid on the night of February 22,

1945," and points out that "when we think of the nights when the fires raged in Cologne and Hamburg and Dresden, we ought also to remember that as early as August 1942, when the vanguard of the Sixth Army had reached the Volga and not a few were dreaming of settling down after the war on an estate in the cherry orchards beside the quiet Don, the city of Stalingrad, then swollen (like Dresden later) by an influx of refugees, was under assault from twelve hundred bombers, and that during this raid alone, which caused elation among German troops stationed on the opposite bank, forty thousand people lost their lives."[9]

Schama refers to "the wholesale destruction of an entire region of France. Nowhere as much as in the area of the Vendée . . . did the Terror fulfill Saint-Just's dictum that the 'republic consists in the extermination of everything that opposes it.'" Jean-Clement Martin suggests that nearly a quarter of a million people, one-third of the entire population of the region, died in the Vendée and the neighboring departments of Loire-In-férieure and Maine-et-Loire, in addition to the tens of thousands of Republican soldiers who lost their lives in the war.[10] Suret-Canale describes the incalculable scale of the depopulation of Benin and the Congo, Gabon and other parts of West and Central Africa, on account of slave raids and wars and the slaughter caused by colonialism, including the breakup of families and the spread of new diseases and famine.[11] Indian historians suggest that in the course of Partition violence anywhere between half a million and one million people were killed, and twelve to fourteen million uprooted and transformed into long-term refugees.[12]

None of this information is altogether surprising or new. Nevertheless, given how short and selective human memory is, it does no harm to rehearse it again and to interrogate the deep-rooted belief that our civilized times have been overwhelmingly benign. The fact is that violence has been endemic to the advance of the modern, it has reappeared in constantly new forms, and it has occurred on all sides. Yet a history of modern political violence can hardly stop at that point. It is important to view violence not as an isolated act, or a series of isolated acts, but rather as what the anthropologist Marcel Mauss called a *total social phenomenon.* I turn to this proposition in the following section.

Violence as a Social Fact

Mauss was writing about the gift, a universal idea that is readily seen as a singular, isolated event and generally counterposed to the market, exchange, or commerce. For Mauss, the gift was (and is) always part of a cycle of social obligations: the idea of a pure, free gift is a contradiction. The gift embraces "an enormous complex of facts," and "involve(s) the totality of society and its institutions" or, at least, a large number of them. It gives expression to all kinds of institutions—juridical, political, economic, religious, and even (says Mauss) aesthetic and morphological—"at one and the same time."[13]

There can be little doubt, it seems to me, that examples of collective violence—and indeed most cases of individual violence—constitute a complex social fact in this sense, with important religious, economic, political, and moral implications. Hence, the antecedents, the enabling conditions, the cycle of violence that a violent act initiates or continues, the forms that it takes, the wide sections of society that it involves, the consequences that it has both near and far—all these must form part of the study of violence.

There is one other step that we must take if we are to appreciate violence as a social fact: we must recognize violence not only in its most spectacular, explosive, visible moments, but also in its more disguised forms—in our day-to-day behavior, the way we construct and respond to neighbors as well as strangers, in the books and magazines we read, the films we see, and the conversations and silences in which we participate. It is through such reasoning that I came to the object of investigation taken up in the following chapters—the routine violence involved in the construction of naturalized nations, of natural communities and histories, majorities and minorities. I need to say a word about these routine procedures, revealed in the construction of nationalism in particular, before I return to further remarks on the study of violence.

Michael Billig has drawn attention to the qualities of innocence and intolerance built into the ideology of nationalism, an ideology that is now "so familiar that it hardly seems noticeable."[14] One may observe, with him, that nationalist prejudice is daily reinforced by school textbook and media stories, by box office hits and the no longer noticed vocabulary of everyday national politics, shared by the Left and the Right alike. The newspapers that address readers as members of the nation, and sports commentators who take special pride in the achievements of our nationals (in individual as well as team events, in highly paid professional tournaments as well as in periodic World Cup and Olympic competitions between national teams), are part of the same subconscious process of mobilization of nationalist pride. Nationalist consciousness and pride is reproduced too in the ways we construct ourselves and interact with others in daily life. The stars and stripes prominently displayed on office desks and car windows, in restaurants and private homes in the United States, and the image of Uncle Sam on T-shirts, notebooks, and food packages, attract no special attention. They are natural, proper, and peculiarly invisible.

As early as 1960, Elie Kedourie drew a distinction between "patriotism"—"affection for one's country, or one's group, loyalty to its institutions, and zeal for its defence"—which was good and explicitly identified with Britain and the United States, and "nationalism," which was bad.[15] The mood has spread in the succeeding decades. The political leaders of the West, whether from France, the United States, Britain, or New Zealand, do not now parade themselves as nationalists. The term is no longer so fashionable, although it appears to be making a comeback, with growing anti-immigrant feelings in Western, Central, and Southern Europe. For some time prior to this, it was largely reserved for separatists in Quebec, the extreme right wing in France and Germany, East European militants, and of course political tendencies in the Middle East and Asia in general. Yet, as Michael Billig suggests (citing examples such as those given in the previous paragraph), the United States, France, Britain, and others are "daily . . . reproduced as nations and their citizenry as nationals."[16] He cites the writings of the American philosopher Richard Rorty to drive home the point: "Most of us, despite the outrage we may feel about governmental cowardice or corruption, and despite our despair over what is being done to the weakest and poorest among us, still identify with our country," Rorty writes. "We take pride in being citizens of a self-invented, self-reforming, enduring constitutional democracy." And further, "A left that refuses to take pride in its country will have no impact on that country's politics, and will eventually become an object of contempt." Billig notes that the naturalness of nations is assumed in Rorty's *New York Times* article, where these sentences appear. "'Society,' 'nation' and 'country' are used as synonyms. 'Our society' might give a raw deal to some, but the left, by campaigning against this, is helping to reform 'our country.' 'We' should take pride in being citizens of a democracy, and should identify with America's traditions."

Rorty is no romantic, conservative nationalist. His nationalism is of a "banal, low-key" kind. The philosopher posits an implicit distinction between patriotism and nationalism, reminiscent of Kedourie. The former is good and gentle, although it too can go wrong. The latter tends to be "bellicose," "arrogant." "The denial of 'our' nationalism is nationalist," comments Billig, "for it is part of the common-sense imagining of 'us,' the democratic, tolerant and reasonable nation, rightfully inhabiting 'our' homeland." Thus, "a global American hegemony is rhetorically constructed in Rorty's texts, as he suggests that the pragmatic, non-ideological voice of America should be the voice of 'us all.'"[17]

Far from being an "intermittent mood," nationalism is the "endemic condition," even in advanced, established nations. Billig calls the daily reproduction of the nation, the routine invocations of nationalist pride, "banal rehearsals for the extraordinary times of crisis, when the state calls upon its citizenry, and especially its male citizenry, to make ultimate sacrifices in the cause of nationhood."[18] For him, that last—the crisis of war, so often trumped up and unnecessary—is the moment of violence, the moment we must guard against.

I want to develop the argument a little differently, by suggesting that the violence of nationalism is in fact rather more insidious and unremitting than the focus on international war allows. I emphasize that nationalism continuously constructs social and political hierarchies, privileged languages, and relations of dominance and subordination, not only outside but *within* the natural modern political community and state. These hierarchies and languages signal other political problems to which we need to attend: the problem of minorities, of hyphenated (and sometimes second-class) citizens, of homogenized histories and national cultures that all the inhabitants of a particular land are expected to accept and cherish, and so on. And they raise other issues in the study of violence.

The Boundaries of Violence

One issue is the important tactical question: what do we gain, or lose, by extending the boundaries of the phenomenon called violence beyond the obviously bloody and physically (or psychologically) devastating? There is much to be said for maintaining the narrower sense of the term, for—if nothing else—it makes communication and debate somewhat easier. I will, perforce, continue to use the term in this narrower sense. Yet, it will hardly do to suggest that there is some sharp line of demarcation between the state of violence and that of its absence, between war and peace. Achille Mbembe makes the point well in relation to the history of colonialism.

The colony, he writes, following Fanon, is "a place where an experience of violence and upheaval is lived, where violence is built into structures and institutions. It is implemented by persons of flesh and bone, such as the soldier, the . . . administrator, the police officer, and the native chief. It is sustained by an imaginary—that is, an interrelated set of signs that present themselves, in every instance, as an indisputable and undisputed meaning. The violence insinuates itself into the economy, domestic life, language, consciousness. It . . . pursues the colonized even in sleep and dream." What one has here, he suggests, is the "*spirit of violence.*" This spirit "makes the violence omnipresent; it is presence—presence not deferred (except occasionally) but spatialized, visible, immediate, sometimes ritualized, sometimes dramatic, very often caricatural."[19]

Things are different, but not altogether so, in the postcolonial regime. "Through the harshness of the exactions required, the redeployment of constraints, and the new forms of subjection imposed on the most deprived segments of the population, this form of government forces features belonging to the realm of warfare and features proper to the conduct of civil policy to co-exist in a single dynamic."[20] Perhaps, one might add, that condition is not the result of some particular flaw in the postcolony alone. As Donald Carter notes in relation to Sudan, in an implicit critique of Mbembe, "The Sudanese state cannot be separated from the interlinking system of powerful states that shadow its every move. . . . The African postcolonial state . . . in the so-called global age is a crossroads, an operating theatre for more powerful states, NGOs and other international organizations."[21]

The prehistory of the more glaring and visible acts of political violence can be traced, it seems to me, in the exercise of particular kinds of violence—upon the poor, upon marginal groups, upon trade unions and women and other subordinated sections of society—as a routine, everyday and unremarkable practice. Jonathan Glover makes a significant suggestion regarding the rising threshold of what is considered legitimate use of force in war, brought about by an ever escalating employment of more and more brutal and devastating weaponry and forms of attack. As he puts it, the blockade of Germany at the end of World War I, which caused nearly

800,000 deaths, "made it easier to embark on area bombing [during the second]. In turn, the raids on Hamburg, Darmstadt and Dresden meant there was relatively little outcry when the American Air Force embarked on the fire-bombing of Tokyo. And that in turn eased the way to Hiroshima and Nagasaki."[22]

One might make the same kind of point in relation to other forms of political violence today, such as terrorism and racial and religious conflict. It is not simply that we become inured to the horror of suicide bombing or mass rape when these become more or less regular features of the political and military landscape; rather, there is a way in which hostile (quotidian) attitudes toward the poor, and toward women and minorities, translate into a tolerance of organized collective violence against them. The routine, ordinary practice of violence—for instance, the beating, rape, and indeed burning of women, in homes, in village squares and barely secluded parking lots, and their general humiliation on the streets, in public buses, in films, and so on—gives rise to a considerable tolerance (not to say celebration) of such violence, even when carried out on a frightening scale in mass campaigns of ethnic cleansing and the destruction of people who were formerly neighbors. Although not a dimension of the prehistory of violence that I address at length in the following pages, the point is implicit in much of what I have to say, and I hope my study will underline the need for closer investigation of the pervasiveness of the spirit of violence.

The Aims of This Book

In a 2001 book on Partition, I tracked the debates on a moment of extraordinary violence in the recent history of the Indian subcontinent. I sought thereby to portray something of both the enormity of Partition violence and the impossibility of describing it. The present volume extends that inquiry by focusing on the enormity of the violence of ordinary times—a violence that we hardly notice, let alone attempt to describe. The self-imposed silence about the destruction of Partition and events like it that many have sought to confront, in India, South Africa, Germany and elsewhere, is also found in relation to this routine violence—more emphatically so, precisely because the violence is so routine, and so much more invisible.

"How ought . . . a natural history of destruction to begin?" W. G. Sebald asks, early in his account of the destruction of Germans and German cities in *On the Natural History of Destruction.* "With a summary of the technical, organizational, and political prerequisites for carrying out large-scale air raids? With a scientific account of the previously unknown phenomenon of the firestorms? With a pathographical record of typical modes of death, or with behaviorist studies of the instincts of flight and home-coming?"[23]

I want to turn Sebald's question to my purposes and ask, what would a natural—that is to say, elementary, fundamental—history of routine destruction be? Or should we say of routine construction, which necessarily implies destruction? To be seen, for example, in the history of far-flung African communities and peoples, disrupted, uprooted, and reconstituted by the trans-Atlantic slave trade, in the lives of African-Americans (ex-slaves) in the United States, or of ex-untouchables in India, or immigrants and minorities forced to live on the brink in so many late modern societies.

Where would we begin a natural history of such routine violence? There is surely no one *correct* answer. However, a plausible way is to analyze how we write and think about recurrent violence between communities defined as majorities and minorities, or natural citizens and hyphenated ones, autochthones and allochthones;[24] how we narrate the history of the modern political community and its constituent elements; how we construct notions of community, and majority and minority; and debate appropriate policies for a pluralistic society (which all societies in the world are, and probably have long been).

This book takes its material from the history of twentieth-century India, the land of Gandhi and of effective nonviolent resistance to British colonial rule, and the world's largest democracy. It asks questions about the histories that are claimed as the real histories of India, the construction of the normalized nation, its (mainstream) culture and politics, and its collective amnesia. More specifically, it asks how such amnesia is produced.

Note that even today—after the experience of February and March 2002, when the entire Muslim population, urban and rural, of Gandhi's home province of Gujarat was attacked and terrorized by large crowds of Hindus drawn from a very wide section of the society, including the well-to-do middle classes—Hindu middle-class Gujaratis continue to speak of the peaceful character of their community and province.[25] Just as, for decades after Partition, with its unprecedented looting and destruction accompanied by a massive "ethnic cleansing" in large parts of the northwest and northeast of the subcontinent, the Indian middle classes continued to claim that Indians were an especially peaceful people—as demonstrated by the nonviolent national movement against the British.

I make the point that communal violence (as violence between people belonging to different religious denominations is called in India) has long been seen by Indian intellectuals and commentators as an aberration, or a break from normalcy, and is still described by many in terms of the sociological category of the riot. The representation of violence as an aberration deflects attention away from the way the construction of a normal India sets different populations—the Muslims, and sometimes other communities—against the authentic nation. The use of the category "riot" similarly makes the violence an event with a closure. In that perspective, we can forget communal violence because it is episodic and momentary, a closed chapter as soon as it is over.

It is for this reason that I stress the importance of investigating such violence as a social fact. There is a violence involved in the unrelenting construction of enemies of the nation, and the concomitant denial of equal rights or respect to the latter. The violence is unceasing, if partly unconscious and often disguised. It may be noticed in the practice of administrative and police surveillance, in history books, films, and the media, which reinforce widely held beliefs and attitudes that are expressed commonly in graffiti in all kinds of public places, and by people standing at railway ticket counters or sitting in tea stalls and in our drawing rooms. It is implicit in the insistent construction of permanent majorities and minorities, based usually on supposedly immutable racial, religious, or ethnic differences, and in the construction of particular, special kinds of minority (the Jews in Europe, the Asians in East Africa, the Tamils in Sri Lanka, the Muslims in the world today).

These are unlike other minorities because of the threat they supposedly pose to the mainstream of the natural political community, or more accurately to its ruling classes. Sometimes, this sense of peril follows from the presence of particular groups in sizable numbers, which threatens the balance of a population—and hence of power. More often, and often enough to make this a very worrying pattern, it is because the mainstream *imagines* the emergence of such a demographic and political challenge.[26] In given historical situations, then, certain minorities constitute a danger almost by definition. Their *being* is a threat—and the consequences are predictable.

In examining the writing on Hindu-Muslim violence, and on recent Indian history more generally, I also put forward the notion of the fragment in an attempt to modify, or at least clarify, our understanding of historical amnesia. The fragment in this usage is an interruption in the narrative, a recalcitrant element, the hint of another vision—now frequently irrecoverable. It is in that sense an index of power relations. The emphasis on the fragment allows me to suggest, also, that the forgetting of violence is not so much that of closure as that of trauma—something which, even when apparently forgotten, cannot be forgotten, a suggestion of horror or of shame that returns to haunt even the mainstream that pretends to have little or nothing to do with it.

The routinization of violence occurs, I am suggesting, not only in the unashamed display of spectacular and brutal acts of aggression, nor yet in the mundane, banal, everyday exercise of power over women and children, politically disadvantaged communities, and the poor. It occurs also in the construction and naturalization of particular categories of thought, in history and in politics. What is it that counts as history, as historical event and historical (or legal) evidence? Whose word counts, and how much? What are the terms in which we are to understand the distribution of a population, and therefore of its political demands and needs? What do we describe as violence?

This book seeks to investigate the ideological and political conditions that allow, and indeed sanction, the undisguised political violence of our times. It is concerned with the regnant demands of nationalism and of history writing, and the unity and uniformity that these insist upon. What is striking about these statist demands is their *internal* inducement to violence, since something "sacred" is protected by it.

This sacred was once called civilization. In the modern world, it is called the nation—and, increasingly once again, civilization too. (The civilized nation is civilization. Liberal democracy—one person one vote, more or less—is civilization, with scant regard for other factors that go into the making and distribution of political power.) The sacred political community has been presented to us, and long been defended, in the form of the (natural) liberal nation-state. I wish to ask what space this self-satisfied notion of the politically indispensable leaves for an understanding or even a recognition of the violence that we now live with as a "normal" condition of political life.

2

In Defense of the Fragment

The present chapter focuses upon one instance of massive intercommunity violence in India and the question of writing about it. I have chosen to begin with a discussion of this single instance of strife between Hindus and Muslims because it allows me to delineate many of the themes I explore in the rest of this book: the naturalization of nationhood, the representation of a small section of society as the national mainstream, the call for conformity to the mainstream culture, the drive toward homogenization in the nation's history and politics, and not least, the refusal to face up to the consequences and implications of large- and small-scale violence.

The statement presented in this chapter is very general, the bare outline of a larger argument about the nature of evidence and the modes of analysis and representation employed in historical discourse. I proffer it in this form in the hope that it will focus some points for consideration in a way that a more detailed statement might not. But I do so with some hesitation. One reason for hesitation is that the formulations presented here are as yet far from being sufficiently well worked out; by the nature of things, they may never be adequately worked out. I hesitate also because my criticism of some of the most significant writings on recent social and political conflict in India may appear ungenerous, especially in respect to scholars and activists who have come out boldly against the sources of oppression and exploitation in our state and our society.

The argument I put forward in the chapter arises in large part out of the experience of the Bhagalpur riots of 1989, which figure in some detail in its later part, and I make considerable use of personal impressions and insights gathered as part of a ten-member team sent under the aegis of the People's Union for Democratic Rights (PUDR), Delhi, to investigate the situation in Bhagalpur. I can only add that the kind of criticism (and self-criticism) presented here would have been impossible but for the pioneering investigations and studies of individuals like Asghar Ali Engineer and organizations like the People's Union for Civil Liberties (PUCL) and the PUDR.[1] It is possible that my criticism of their writings on contemporary politics and strife will appear academic and of little immediate relevance. I would like to believe, however, that there is some dialogue between the "academic" and the political, and that some of the propositions in these pages will contribute in a small way to the continuing debates on vital political issues that affect all of us.

Writing about Sectarian Strife

Let me restate a point I made in the introduction and suggest another aspect of it. The matter of collective violence has been treated in the historiography of colonial and postcolonial India as *aberration* and as *absence*. Aberration in the sense that violence is seen as removed from the general run of Indian history: a distorted form, an exceptional moment, not the real history of India at all.[2] Violence also appears as an absence—and here the point applies more emphatically to a field wider than Indian history—because historical discourse has been able to capture and represent the moment of physical or psychological violation only with great difficulty. The history of extreme violence is, therefore, almost always about context—about everything that happens around violence.[3] The acts of violation themselves are taken as known. Their contours and character are simply assumed: their presence and their anticipation (which has perhaps become a more continuous part of our being than ever before) need no investigation.

Consider the writings on the history of sectarian strife in the subcontinent. Indian historiography has long functioned here in a political context in which the rhetoric of nationalism is of central importance. In recent times, especially the last couple of decades, this rhetoric has taken on a new tone and a new level of belligerence. The highly centralized state power that now goes by the name of the Indian nation-state has spoken more and more brazenly on behalf of a get-rich-quick, consumerist middle class and its rural (rich peasant) allies. In furthering the ambitions of this sectional interest, the state has displayed its willingness to mark any opposition to its goals as "antinational"—whether this opposition is located in the industrial working class, among the rural poor, in other regional and local movements, or even among historians critical of the policies of the national government.

The fragments of Indian society—the smaller religious, caste, and tribal communities, industrial workers, unemployed slum dwellers, and activist women's groups, all of which might be said to represent minority cultures and practices—have been expected to fall in line with the mainstream (Brahmanical Hindu, consumerist) national culture. The culture of this mainstream, which represents but a small section of the society, has been flaunted as *the* national culture. "Unity in Diversity" is no longer the rallying cry of Indian nationalism. On the contrary, all that belongs to any minority other than the ruling class, all that is challenging, singular, or local—not to say all difference—appears threatening, intrusive, even foreign to this nationalism.

Writings on Indian politics need to foreground this state-centered drive to homogenize and normalize, and the deeply contested nature of the territory of nationalism. Part of the importance of the fragmentary point of view lies in this: that it resists the drive for a shallow homogenization and struggles for other, potentially richer definitions of the nation and the future political community.

I do not wish to suggest that resistance by the minority always, or even usually, functions consciously in this way. But the historian, social scientist, or political activist who stands back to analyze the conditions of Indian society will perhaps agree that this is often an important part of what is happening. There is a historiographical issue involved here, too. The narrow and diminishing view of nationalism described above has been bolstered not only by a reference to current world trends in the economic and political practice of states nor only by those who speak of ancient India as the cradle of civilization and the storehouse of all that is good and valuable in the contemporary world, but also by a modern and avowedly secular nationalist historiography that has reinforced these notions of a natural Indian unity and an Indian national essence.

This historiography has elevated the nation-state—or rather, the contingent form of the nation-state found in India today—to the end of all history, so much so that History in schools, colleges, and universities in

India still ends for the most part in 1947. It has also created for us the neat binary categories that we have worked with for a long time now: secular/communal, national/local (in both of which the second term is readily represented as being antinational or at least antimodern), and pro-gressive(economic)/reactionary(cultural). These are categories that histori-ans have only recently begun to seriously question.[4]

Even today, after decades of powerful and sophisticated history writ-ing by left-wing as well as nationalist and other liberal scholars, the view from the center remains the required vantage point for any meaningful re-construction of Indian history. The official archive (government records, the papers of leading political parties and other institutions recognized by the state, the private papers of leading individuals, and for an earlier period, the records of various courts) remains the primary source for this historical re-construction. This historiographical practice fails to stress the provisional and changeable character of the objects of our analysis: India as well as Pak-istan, the Hindi heartland and the Bombay presidency, the Hindu and the Muslim community, the nation, nationalism, communalism.

By attributing a natural quality to the particular unity called India, and adopting its official archive as the primary source of historical knowl-edge pertaining to it, the historian has adopted the view of the established state. With the emphasis placed on the unity of India and the unity of the struggle to realize its independence, the history of India since the early nineteenth century has tended to become the biography of the emerging nation-state. It has also become a history in which the story of Partition, and the Hindu-Muslim and Muslim-Sikh violence that made it what it was, has been given short shrift.

The history of sectarian strife in general, and of what is called com-munalism in India,[5] has been written up as a secondary story, entirely sub-sidiary to the main drama of India's struggle for independence from colo-nial rule. Hindu politics, Muslim politics, and Hindu-Muslim strife have appeared as minor elements in this drama, associated usually with the machinations of the colonial ruling class. Histories of Partition, too, are generally written up as histories of communalism.

These are not histories of confused struggle and mutilated bodies, sacrifice and loss; of the tentative forging of new identities and loyalties; or of the rise among uprooted and embittered people of new resolutions and new ambitions. Instead they have tended to be accounts of the origins or causes of Partition, investigations of the political mistakes, the accidents, or the less amenable social and economic developments that supposedly brought about this terrible event. For all its tragic consequences, moreover, the tragedy appears in this account as one that, miraculously, left the course of Indian history unaltered. In spite of the emergence of two, now three, independent nation-states as a result of Partition, India, this historiography would seem to say, stayed firmly (not to say naturally) on its secular, democratic, nonviolent, and tolerant path—at least until the rise of the Bharatiya Janata Party and associated Hindu right-wing groups in the 1980s and 1990s.

Bipan Chandra's *Modern India*, perhaps the best textbook on the colonial period available to high school graduates and junior university undergraduates, illustrates these points very well indeed:

On August 1947, India celebrated with joy its first day of freedom. The sacrifices of generations of patriots and the blood of countless martyrs had borne fruit. But the sense of joy . . . was mixed with pain and sadness. . . . [For] even at the very moment of freedom a communal orgy, accompanied by indescribable brutalities, was consuming thousands of lives in India and Pakistan.[6]

There is "pain and sadness" at what can only be seen as the hijacking of an enormously powerful and noble struggle. We read on:

The symbol of this tragedy at the moment of national triumph was the forlorn figure of Gandhiji—the man who had given the message of *nonviolence, truth and love and courage and manliness* to the Indian people. . . . In the midst of national rejoicing, he was touring the hate-torn land of Bengal, trying to bring comfort to people who were even then paying through senseless communal slaughter the price of freedom. (p. 306, emphasis added)

The identity of those responsible for the violence is not explicitly stated at this point, although other pages make it clear that Hindu and Muslim communalists, political reactionaries, and of course the British were the culprits.[7] This hijacking of the movement leads to senseless slaughter, with hundreds of thousands of lives lost as "the price of freedom." Something is elided here, however. Which people pay? For whose freedom? Rather than ask these questions, Bipan Chandra's textbook goes on to record how Gandhi died, assassinated in January 1948, "a martyr to the cause of unity," and how the people of India, "with confidence in their capacity and their will to succeed . . . now [after August 1947] set out to build the just and the good society" (pp. 306–307).

Here Gandhi and the people become symbols of a nationalist

essence, the Indian spirit, symbols that may be easily substituted for one another. Gandhi clearly stands in for the people in the secular nationalist account of India's anticolonial struggle. With Gandhi gone, "the people" apparently take over Gandhi's work and march forward, unaffected by Partition, riots, refugees, and the like, to build "the just and the good society."

Sumit Sarkar's more critical textbook, meant for advanced undergraduates and graduate students, puts forward a different argument but arrives at much the same conclusion about the secular path of the Indian people. The author writes movingly of "the Mahatma's finest hour" from 1946 until his death in January 1948, when he labored almost single-handedly to restrain the passions leading to the slaughter of Hindus, Muslims, and Sikhs all over northern India. The futility of such "isolated personal effort" was, however, evident, Sarkar suggests. "One might still argue," the historian writes, "that the only real alternative lay along the path of united militant mass struggle against imperialism and its Indian allies."[8] He goes on to describe the continuing potential for such struggle in fairly optimistic terms:

Despite the obvious disruption caused by the riots, this possibility was by no means entirely blocked even in the winter of 1946–47. Five months after the August riots [the "Great Calcutta killings" of 1946], the students of Calcutta were again on the streets on 21 January 1947 in "Hands Off Vietnam" demonstrations against the use of Dum Dum airport by French planes, and all communal divisions seemed forgotten in the absolutely united and ultimately victorious 85-day tram strike under Communist leadership which began the same day. (pp. 438–39)

Sarkar refers also to the strike wave of January–February 1947 in Calcutta, Kanpur, Karachi, Coimbatore, and elsewhere, only to add: "The strikes . . . were all on purely economic demands: what remained lacking was a sufficiently influential and determined political leadership" (p. 439).

Partition was, for the majority of people living in what are now the divided territories of northern India and Pakistan, *the* event of the twentieth century—equivalent in terms of trauma and consequence to World War I (the "Great War") for Britain or World War II for France and Japan.[9] The experience of the First and the Second World Wars was commemorated in Western Europe and Japan through the erection of major national and civic monuments. There is, not surprisingly, no equivalent for Partition in India. However, the erasure of memory goes further in this case. There has been no movement for the establishment of a Partition archive, in spite of several individual efforts to collect memories, documents, and photographs; no movement for acknowledgment of collective guilt; no expression of regret or shame at any organized official or unofficial level. Neither has there been any equivalent to the 1960s debate among historians in Germany,[10] although the recent emergence of much new research and writing on Partition marks an important first step.[11]

I have quoted from two of the best general books on the history of colonial India and the Indian national movement, both from scholars writing within the Marxist tradition, to emphasize my point about the quite remarkable dominance of the nationalist paradigm in the historiography of Partition and Independence: only recently has a serious challenge to this trend emerged.[12] This historiography was of course part of a larger nationalist discourse, which also found powerful expression in films, journalism, and literature.

As in history writing, so in films and fiction, Indian intellectuals tended for a long time to celebrate the story of the Independence struggle rather than dwell on the anguish of Partition. This statement requires considerable qualification. There has been a great deal of writing on Partition and the open violence of 1946–47 in Punjabi, Urdu, and Hindi.[13] But Partition literature of the early period—of which Sa'adat Hasan Manto's devastating stories are the outstanding example—was largely confined to the strife-torn areas of Punjab and its environs in the decade or so after Partition.[14] The violence of the times does not appear to have become a central motif in the Bengali literature of the post-Partition period. One study notes that while the famine of 1943 deeply moved Bengali writers, "the Partition of Bengal [dividing East Bengal, which became part of Pakistan in 1947, from West Bengal, which remained part of India] that . . . conclusively changed all erstwhile socio-economic configurations in and after 1947, never became a dominating theme of Bengali fiction even during the 1950s or shortly thereafter."[15]

In cinema, the great Bengali director Ritwik Ghatak produced a series of unparalleled filmic statements about the pain, despair, and hopes of those dispossessed and displaced by Partition: *Komal Gandhar* (1959), *Subarnarekha* (1962), *Titash ekti nadir nam* (1973), and somewhat more indirectly, *Meghe dhaka tara* (1960). But Ghatak remained an exception—and not only because of his brilliance. In Bengali cinema generally, as in the huge Hindi-Urdu film industry centered in Bombay, and in the large number of documentary films produced by the Films Division of India, filmmakers of the 1950s and 1960s paid relatively little attention to the rape and bloodshed of Partition.

Since then, there has been a new wave of creative writing and film-making on this theme. The best of the Partition literature that has come out of northern India during this later period conforms pretty much to the secular nationalist problematic—in which Partition was a history gone wrong, a puzzling and in effect inexplicable failure—but is no less impressive for that. The classic in this genre was probably Rahi Masoom Raza's *Aadha Gaon* (1966). Among Hindu/Urdu films, the example that stands out from this period is M.S. Sathyu's *Garam Hawa*, a remarkable statement of the early 1970s that sensitively portrayed the collective insanity, the uprooting, the meaninglessness of existence, and the fear-laden searches for new meaning elsewhere that was the lot of so many people in the aftermath of Partition.

The more recent television serial *Tamas*, based on Bhishma Sahni's eponymous novel published in 1972, acquired a special importance because of the wide audience it reached. However, the story marked a return to a less subtle nationalist statement in which agents provocateurs and mysterious evil folk, pulling the strings from behind the scenes, misled an innocent and bewildered but brave people. At the same time, Partition was represented here in the likeness of a natural disaster, far removed from the run of daily life, in which human actions in fact played a smaller part than inexplicable fate. All of this is in line with what professional nationalist historians have offered up in the past.

The reasons for this turning away from the ugliness of Hindu-Muslim violence in India's national history are not hard to find. Differences and strife between Hindus and Muslims persisted in India after Independence, and in relating the history of such strife there was always the danger of reopening old wounds. Beyond the inadequate explanation that all this was a result of British machinations (and, to a lesser extent, "Muslim evil"), there was little agreement about the implications of Partition. Indian leaders and thinkers appear to have had no means of accounting for the losses, nor of pinning down—let alone accepting—responsibility. Consequently, Indian nationalist historiography, journalism, and filmmaking tended to generate something like collective amnesia. Consciously or otherwise, they represented Partition and all that went with it as an aberration. The day of Pakistan's establishment, 14 August 1947, became a historical accident, a mistake, one for which not we but others were responsible.

It is my contention that the analyses of politics and strife in contemporary India have run pretty much along the same lines. The following pages seek to demonstrate this through an examination of the historiography of Hindu-Muslim violence since 1947. There is another benefit that may flow from such an examination. Recent events and the writings upon them reveal, by their immediacy and uncertainty, many of the hazards of evidence-gathering and of representation to which historians of earlier periods sometimes believe themselves to be immune. The difficulties encountered here seem to me, however, to point to the folly of using accounts of, say, fifty or a hundred years ago as if they were somehow transparent— biased reports to be sure, but reports that may be balanced by setting them one against another, by appropriate additions and subtractions, to give a more or less adequate reconstruction of history.

Narratives of a Riot

It became routine in the India of the 1980s and 1990s to describe one instance of strife and then another as "perhaps the worst since 1947," such was the magnitude and brutality of sectarian violence of the period.[16] Bhagalpur was another devastating example of this kind of extreme violence. This particular round of aggression and bloodshed began in the last week of October 1989. Arson, looting, and murder spread from the city to the surrounding countryside and raged practically unchecked for several days. The situation was then brought under some sort of control by military and paramilitary forces, but an atmosphere of fear and terror remained for months afterward.[17]

Given the scale of the riots and the infamous role of the local administration in encouraging the attacks and suppressing evidence, it was impossible to establish the facts of this occurrence—what traditional historians like to call the nuts and bolts of the story. Possibly as many as a thousand people were killed in the course of the violence, most of them Muslims, but estimates of the casualties vary greatly.[18] During the first days of the riots, trains were stopped repeatedly in Bhagalpur and its neighboring districts; on several occasions, Muslim travelers were dragged out and lynched. No one could say for certain how many were killed in this way, even in particular incidents—not even disturbed travelers who were on these trains and saw people being pulled from their own carriages. In the major attacks, in the rural areas as well as in the city, neither old people nor infants, neither women nor children were spared. There was a widespread suspicion that women had been abducted and raped on a large scale, but none of the survivors was willing to talk about rape; the five specific cases recorded by the PUDR team that conducted investigations in Bhagalpur in January 1990 were incidents that Muslim women informants had heard about.

It was, however, beyond question that the extent and ferocity of the attacks was completely unexpected, even for a district that had seen much sectarian strife in the past, including major riots in 1946. At the worst stage of the violence, in October–November 1989, some forty thousand people left their homes and lived in makeshift relief camps. Destruction and looting of property occurred on a massive scale, continuing for weeks. The fear generated in the heavily outnumbered minority community was such that a great many were unwilling to return to their homes even three months after the initial outbreak of open violence; an estimated ten thousand were still in relief camps toward the end of January 1990, apart from those who had moved in with relatives or friends in safer places in or outside Bhagalpur district. At this time many Muslims were pressing for the permanent retention of military or paramilitary forces in the vicinity of their villages or wards (*mohallas*) as the only trustworthy means of protection, and some were demanding that they be given arms by the government. The air was still thick with rumors, and isolated attacks and looting continued to occur; one such incident was reported as late as March 1990.

How do we write the history of such an event? In Bhagalpur, the state's archives—those official sources that generations of historians and social scientists have treated as core sources, more comprehensive than any other record—are largely missing. Like historians generally, the teams of independent investigators visiting Bhagalpur were eager to obtain the official account in order to establish some overall picture in the midst of an otherwise confusing investigation.[19] But the view from the center had largely been destroyed in this instance, at any rate concerning the first few absolutely critical days of the riots. A *Sunday Mail* (Delhi) report of 11 February 1990, made after a two-week-long investigation into the Bhagalpur carnage and its aftermath, summed up the situation in this manner:

Crucial records of the period, especially those from the tables of [the] then district magistrate [DM] and superintendent of police [SP] are missing.

Evidence strongly suggests that [DM] in all probability destroyed the log book of the Central Control Room in which the many SOS received in the fateful week were recorded. The fresh log book that has been placed in the office strangely makes no mention of the incidents. . . .

[SP at the time], who has since gained notoriety, too has left his successor . . . without a clue to work [with?]. His records too show a single joint report on the Chanderi massacre [one of the worst incidents in the countryside], just because Patna High Court had issued a notice.

Even the joint report of the DM and the SP on the first incident at Tatarpur Chowk [in Bhagalpur city] on October 24 that had lit the fuse is among the papers not traceable.

The fact, incredible as it may sound, is that there is no statement of facts available in either the DM or the SP's office.

This kind of destruction or removal of records is not entirely new: the British practiced it on a large scale in India after 1937, when popular Indian ministries took office in many of the provinces, and no doubt there have been many other instances since Independence. What is less frequently noted, however, is the destruction entailed in the systematic *construction* of evidence on all sides, official and unofficial, when an event of this kind occurs. Extreme violence produces the necessity of evidence gathering, of uncovering hidden processes and contradictions that we might normally prefer to ignore, but such violence also wipes out evidence and even, to a large extent, the possibility of collecting it in a manner and form that is deemed acceptable in the social sciences. Let me illustrate this with reference to the PUDR team's work in Bhagalpur.

In spite of the size of this team and the very long hours we put in during our eight-day visit to the district, our investigation was subject to severe constraints.[20] The majority of the people we spoke to in Bhagalpur were Muslims. They were the primary victims of the riots; they were in the relief camps; they were the people who were willing to and perhaps needed to talk. Hindus in many of the worst-affected areas met us with studied silence, if not hostility.[21] The Hindus we could speak with easily were from a narrow stratum: middle-class intellectuals, political activists, professionals, and officials with established opinions (or theories) about what had occurred.

In addition, when we met victims of the aggression or other eyewitnesses, we were confronted with the problem of what questions to ask and how. Our questions suggested particular answers, and there were particular answers that we were more ready to hear than others. This is a point to which I will return. But we faced a further difficulty at the outset. Faced with the victims of such barbarism—the father and son, or the mother and four little children, who survived because one was away and others managed somehow to hide in the fields, where they could see elders and young ones, kith and kin and neighbors, women and infants in arms, everyone who was found in the Muslim quarter of their village being slaughtered—how does one ask such people for details of what they saw?

And yet one asks, because investigators are bound to ask. And sometimes the victims, survivors, and other bystanders begin to talk without even being asked, because they have been asked so many times already or because there is need for a public narrative of their suffering. However, this narrative soon assumes a set form. It appears as a practiced account, a collective memory or record that has been generated on behalf of the entire community—Yadavs, Muslims, or Hindus. The standard practice in the affected *mohallas* and villages we visited was for us to be taken to a central spot where many people gathered, and the elders or the educated gave us what might be called the authorized statement about local happenings.

The teams of three or four members that went to any one place tried to get around this screening by breaking up and talking to different groups separately. But in several places women and youth were prevented from holding independent conversations with us; in one village some of the inhabitants (especially women) turned somewhat aggressively upon one of our female colleagues and upon those village women who had continued to talk in spite of earlier signals to stop. Even when women, youths, or children spoke up independently, revealing differences of emphasis and priority, their accounts still emerged as part of a collective statement. The broad outlines of what occurred appeared to be known to everyone in the same way, and the concerns were common: the suffering of the collectivity, the need for protection and compensation, the identification of those who had proved to be friends in need (mainly religious organizations and, in places where the Left had a presence, left-wing activists and associations).

The PUDR team went to Bhagalpur three months after the beginning of these attacks, and it is possible that the ritualized nature of these collective accounts was more firmly set by then. Yet I have little doubt that collective memory, in a set form, comes into being very soon after the events it describes. This has to do with the living conditions of the local communities, the history of past strife, and the difficult relations with the state. But it has to do with another factor as well: that the purpose of the public narrative is at least in part to impress a particular point of view on the state and its agents.

The situation produced by any large-scale outbreak of violence deepens the divisions that always exist between privileged people and common folk in India. Such situations work to level communities and make entire groups that are under suspicion a part of the commoners. At these times, the informants—distant villagers, illiterate artisans, faceless members of a makeshift relief camp, and even the elite of a community, such as medical practitioners and university professors—tend to become part of a collective subject that approaches the investigator as "a person of influence" and appeals to her or him for relief, justice, mercy, or simply understanding.

Consequently, much of our conversation with local people in Bhagalpur had to do with minute details of property losses, injuries, and deaths that we did not necessarily consider central to our investigation. We were asked repeatedly to go just a little farther, to the next village, to see for ourselves the destruction of this house, to make a note of those names, too. We were asked also to record "First Information Reports"[22] and evidence where the police had failed or refused to record these, or at least to help in getting them recorded because, as a number of informants said, "We are under constant threat and may well be killed before anyone bothers to take down our evidence." In other places, we encountered the bare response, "We don't know anything. We were not here."

Sometimes, as the denial of all knowledge of what occurred in a particular place indicates, the collective accounts we heard partook of the character of preemptive narratives. They were constructed, more or less consciously, in order to falsify particular theories or explanations of the course of events. Hindus, who were accused of forming an armed procession that adopted extremely aggressive tactics during its course through the city of Bhagalpur, thus igniting the attacks of 24 October, declared that the procession was an ordinary religious one, like any other on important festive occasions, and that it was accompanied by large numbers of women and children singing devotional songs and playing musical instruments. Muslims, who were accused by the local administration and others of making preparations for a riot long before 24 October, declared all over the district and almost without exception that they had never had any quarrel with the Hindus and had no reason to fear a riot, that perfect amity had always existed between the Hindus and Muslims of the district and that, "even in 1946–47," while the rest of northern India burned, there had been no trouble in Bhagalpur.

Even where the defense of the immediate group or collectivity was not an issue, as when we spoke to urban professionals and intellectuals, the defense of something larger and more intangible was sometimes at stake:

the good name of the city or community, for example, or the very possibility of Hindus and Muslims living together in the future—as indeed they must. It was this kind of thinking that led many people to stress the importance of letting bygones be bygones. A similar thought process perhaps lay behind the pronounced tendency to lay the blame for the strife on "outsiders": political leaders in Patna and Delhi, "criminal gangs," or a corrupt and spineless administration. The theory of "criminal" instigation and conduct of the riots was especially popular. It was asserted that "criminal castes" from across the Ganges (which flows west to east through the district, just north of the city of Bhagalpur) came into the city and other strife-torn places in large numbers, that these castes (designated criminal by the erstwhile colonial regime) are the cause of much of the lawlessness in Bhagalpur even at normal times, and that criminal gangs making free use of these outside elements were largely responsible for the unprecedented violence of 1989.

The difficulties of evidence gathering are, however, only part of the problem of reconstructing the history of extreme violence. Writing about such proceedings is equally hazardous. There is an obvious danger of sensationalizing events, and thus rendering such strife and its consequences extraordinary, aberrational. And there is at least an equal danger of surrendering to the demands of an academic discourse that sanitizes, and thereby makes more bland and palatable, what is intensely ugly and disorienting. This kind of academic writing also tends to push the moment of violence into the realm of the exceptional and aberrant, as I will show.

Discussions of sectarian strife in India typically balance an account of Hindu atrocities with some account of Muslim (or Sikh) ones. So, a few weeks after our visit to Bhagalpur, the chief minister of Bihar made a public announcement on the steps being taken to restore normalcy, enumerating Hindu temples and shrines that were destroyed in the district along with large numbers of Muslim holy places. This was, in fact, against all available evidence, for no investigating team had reported a single Hindu temple or shrine damaged or destroyed.

Similarly, a documentary film on the Bhagalpur events made by an independent and enterprising filmmaker, Nalini Singh, and shown on national television in March 1990 equated Jamalpur (the one Hindu village to be attacked in the course of the riots) with Logain (the site of one of the worst massacres of Muslims), implying that the attacks and casualties were of the same order. However, the most reliable estimates suggest that seven people were killed and some seventy houses and huts burned and looted in Jamalpur, whereas 115 were killed and the entire Muslim *basti* looted, burned, and destroyed in Logain. More to the point, the looting and killing in Logain was part of the general terrorizing of the Muslim population of the district, which went on as I have mentioned for several weeks, whereas the attack on Jamalpur was part of a much more isolated and fitful retaliation. The equation of the two thus made for poor history.[23]

The professedly liberal demand to document and present "both sides of the case" frequently accompanies the social scientist's search for those "outside forces" and "exceptional circumstances" that always lie, in this view, behind such acts of collective violence. In the case of Bhagalpur, journalists and other investigators pointed a finger at "criminal" elements, at the local administration, and at the vicious propaganda of the Vishwa Hindu Parishad (World Hindu Council, VHP) and other militant Hindu organizations. As a newspaper report of 19 November 1989 had it:

Is it possible that people who live together [have always lived together] and share each other's daily concerns—about food and drink, the marriage of daughters, and electoral politics—should become enemies overnight? . . . What have these people to do with the Babari Masjid and Ram Janmabhumi controversy? But the criminal elements of both communities saw their opportunity and very quickly indeed they filled the minds of the people with a poisonous insanity.

That the task of poisoning the minds of the people could be accomplished so quickly does not seem to have raised any questions for the writer. We are simply told that "the Bhagalpur riots are not so much the product of sectarian [communal] feelings as a calamity brought about by the criminals."[24]

The moral of the story, which carries over from nationalist accounts of the pre-Independence period, is that the people are essentially secular. The same newspaper report goes on to say:

The criminals are armed with rifles, guns, bombs, axes, choppers, spears, and the blessings of [powerful] political leaders. The unfortunate public is helpless. [*Bechari janta kare to kya kare?*] The members of both [Hindu and Muslim] communities wished to live together in peace and friendship but the criminals ultimately succeeded in spreading the poison among them.[25]

Explanations of extreme violence in terms of larger historical processes are not as far removed from this kind of analysis as might first appear. Instead of focusing on the activities of VHP propagandists and criminal elements or on dereliction of duty on the part of local officials, these explanations invoke the "criminalization" of politics, the "communalization" of Indian public life, not excluding the administration, and long-term economic changes, such as the rise of the "backward castes," the emergence of new trading groups, unionization, and labor troubles. The PUDR's careful and detailed report on the Bhagalpur riots, for instance, makes an elaborate—if somewhat confusing—statement regarding the complex of circumstances surrounding the outbreak of open violence:

A common simplification of the riots has consisted in placing the responsibility for them on criminals. We feel it may be more accurate to say that it was the sum of relations between criminals, the police administration, politicians, the dominant elite and the economy which are responsible and, at any given time, one or all of these—along with some local people—were significant factors and agents in the riots.[26]

Too often, however, the statement of complex long-term historical processes leaves little room for human agency and responsibility and becomes a statement about the essential and unchanging (secular) character of the majority of the people concerned. A segregated economic dimension commonly emerges as the villain of the piece. Two examples from the work of Asghar Ali Engineer, perhaps the most prominent writer on the causes of sectarian violence in independent India, will serve to illustrate the point. On the fighting between Hindus and Muslims in Jabalpur in 1961, he wrote:

The apparent cause was the "elopement" of a Hindu girl with a Muslim boy. However, although it brought the powerful religio-cultural prejudices between the two communities into play . . . it was not the real reason. The *real reason* lay elsewhere. The Muslim boy was the son of a local *bidi* magnate who had gradually succeeded in establishing control over the local *bidi* industry. His Hindu competitors were very sore over this development. It was not insignificant that the *bidi* industry belonging to the Muslims in Jabalpur suffered heavily during the riots.

And on the Bhiwandi conflict in 1970:

[Bhiwandi] is a thriving centre of the powerloom industry, with quite a few Muslims owning powerlooms and a large number of Muslim artisans working as weavers on these looms. . . . Also, being on the Bombay-Agra National Highway, Bhiwandi receives a large amount of revenue by way of octroi from the passing trucks. Its municipality thus has a handsome income. Local municipal politics, therefore, assumes [a] great deal of importance. Different parties and political groups vie with each other to wrest control of the Municipal Council. A section of Muslims with their increased prosperity due to the loom industry developed greater political aspirations, challenging the traditional leadership and this led to communal tension.[27]

In its more extreme versions, this economistic viewpoint tends to reduce all history to a fight for land and profit. Here is a journalist's account of the "economy of communalism" in Bhagalpur: "It would be simplistic to dismiss the recent Bhagalpur communal riot as a manifestation of the ugly face of our civilization. Attention must be focused on [the] ruined economy, dying industry and the decadent feudal agrarian structure of the area which provides food [fuel?] to such an event." Further: "Religion is no consideration among the buyers and sellers [of firearms]. Profit is the overwhelming motive. They have a vested interest in keeping the communal tension going. . . . Another factor that keeps it going is [the] profitability of relief camp operations."[28]

Obviously it is not my submission that economic interests and conflicts are unimportant. However, more than a narrowly conceived material interest is involved in the history even of our times. Unfortunately, some of the most sophisticated writing in the social sciences continues to reduce the lives of men and women to calculations of financial profit and loss or to large impersonal movements in economy and society over which human beings have no control. The thrust of this writing is to say that the real battle lies not where it sometimes appears—say, in matters of history or notions of honor, or in the centrality of religion or people's attachment to particular cultural and religious symbols—but in the question of immediate material interests, and especially those of the elite.

Let me reiterate what I have already said. The point is not that land and property are of no importance in bringing about or perpetuating sectarian strife. Rather, the emphasis placed upon such factors often leaves little room for the emotions of people, for changing feelings and perceptions, for mediation and politics—in short, little room for affect and agency.

The mass of the people have counted for little in most analyses of collective violence in India. It is economic interests, land struggles, the play of market forces, and frequently elite manipulation that make riots occur. The people find their place, once again, outside history. This is one means of preserving their innocence and purity.[29] The message of much of the writing on riots in the country since 1947 is the same as that found in the nationalist histories of the pre-Independence period: events like Bhagalpur

1989 do not represent the real flow of Indian history; they are mere glitches, the result of an unusual conjuncture of circumstances. This writing pretends that the occurrence of riots on the scale and with the frequency that we have seen since the 1980s still leaves untouched the essential secularism of the people and the cherished national traditions of nonviolence and peaceful coexistence.

The Construction of the Other

This is, to my mind, an unacceptable history. It is unacceptable not only because it is reductionist and because it continues to ply a tired nationalist rhetoric, but also because it essentializes communalism, communal riots, and the religious communities, making these out to be substantial and immutable entities around which circumstances and context alone somehow change. In the rest of this chapter, I will dwell a little more on the inadequacies of history writing in this vein.

Contrary to what such a historiography would have us believe, the scars of intercommunal conflict and bloodshed are all too evident in the popular construction of Indian history *and* in the construction of those brutish (or pious) characters that pass for the Hindu, the Muslim, or the Sikh, often with deadly consequences. I will not try here to analyze in any detail the changing self-image of the different religious communities and their constructions of the other.[30] However, a reference to some aspects of the image of Hindus and of Muslims, as it appears in recent Hindu propaganda, may help to illustrate the importance of the question.

Many observers have pointed to the new heights reached by Hindu militancy and propaganda over the last two decades. Plainly this has had a great deal to do with the increased frequency and scale of Hindu-Muslim strife since the 1980s. It is not sufficiently stressed, however, that the violent slogans and demands of organizations like the VHP and the killing sprees, looting, and destruction they have sparked do not poison the minds of the people only for a moment. On the contrary, given the colonial and postcolonial constructions of India's history, the very different scale of resources available to small secular groups and the growing communal forces in the country, the opportunism of the major political parties, and the continued and repeated outbreak of collective violence, the most extreme suggestions about the evil, dangerous, and threatening character of the other community (or communities) have become established as part of a popular dogma.

Only this kind of deep-rooted prejudice can explain the kinds of atrocities perpetrated in recent instances of sectarian strife: the call to leave not a single Muslim man, woman, or child alive, which was acted upon in several places in Bhagalpur; the massacre of all eighteen Muslim passengers, along with the Hindu tempo-taxi driver, when they were stopped on a major country road two-and-a-half weeks after the cessation of widespread rioting, and their burial in a field that was then planted with garlic; chopping off the breasts of women; spearing infants and children, and twirling the spears with impaled victims in the air to the accompaniment of laughter and shouts of triumph.[31]

What lies behind this incredible brutality, I suggest, is the conviction that the victims are real or potential monsters who have done all this and worse to "us" or will do so if given half a chance. In many cases, the alleged atrocities for which these actions are supposed to be just recompense are believed to have occurred "last month" or "the other day," in "the city" or a neighboring district or farther away. In Bhagalpur, the rumor that set off the major Hindu attacks in the countryside was that the Hindu students living in Muslim-owned boardinghouses in a part of the city near the university (many of whom came, of course, from the villages of Bhagalpur) had been massacred on the first two days of the riots.[32] In other instances, revenge is sought for what "they" have done to "us," generally in the past: the enslavement of the Hindus by the Mughals, the destruction of temples and the construction of mosques in their stead. The point to be underscored is that what appears to many of us as rabid and senseless Hindu propaganda is widely accepted.

A familiar example is the view, shared by a very large number of middle-class Hindus, that all Muslims in India are Pakistanis. Witness, we are told, their response in the course of any cricket match between India and Pakistan. The argument follows that local Muslims are out to create another Pakistan, in one place after another—in Bhagalpur, in Moradabad (where another serious clash between Hindus and Muslims occurred in 1980), or in Meenakshipuram, Tamilnadu (where a large number of Dalits chose to convert to Islam in the early 1980s).[33] By this juncture we are well into that realm where "Muslims" are seen as inherently turbulent, fanatical, and violent: a hundred million Osamas or Saddams.

Aggression, conversion, unbounded sexuality—these are the themes that make up the history of the spread of Islam as told by the Hindu historians and propagandists: "Wherever Muslim communities exist, there will inevitably be a 'dance of annihilation' in the name of Islam." It is the "religious duty of every Muslim" to "kidnap and force into their own religion non-Muslim women." Several pamphlets and leaflets distributed by militant Hindu organizations in places where strife has lately occurred show a Hindu husband and wife with two children (*Ham do, hamaare do,* "We two, our two") by the side of a Muslim family—a man with four wives and numerous children accompanied by the self-explanatory slogan *Ham paanch, hamaare pacchis* ("We five, our twenty-five").[34] Thus a whole new common sense develops, relating to the marital and sexual practices of the Muslims (here, as elsewhere, referring only to Muslim men), to their perverse character and their violent temperament.

It will perhaps suffice to illustrate the tenor of right-wing Hindu propaganda and beliefs about the Muslims if I reproduce here the substance of just one leaflet that was distributed in Bhagalpur sometime between the last quarter of 1989 and January 1990. Entitled "Hindu Brothers Consider and Be Warned," the leaflet asks:[35]

1. Is it not true that the Muslim population is increasing, while that of the Hindus is decreasing?

2. Is it not true that the Muslims are fully organized [prepared] while the Hindus are fully disorganized [scattered]?

3. Is it not true that the Muslims have an endless supply of weapons while the Hindus are completely unarmed? . . .

5. Is it not true that the Congress has been elected to power for the last forty years on a mere 30 percent of the vote—in other words, that the day the Muslims become 30 percent of the population they will gain power?

6. Is it not true that the Muslims will become 30 percent of the population in twelve to fifteen years' time—in other words, within twelve to fifteen years the Muslims will easily become the rulers of this country?

7. Is it not true that as soon as they gain power, they will destroy the Hindus root and branch, as they have done in Pakistan?

8. Is it not true that when destroying the Hindus, they will not stop to think which Hindu belongs to the Lok Dal, who is a Socialist and who a Congressman, who belongs to the "Forward" castes, who to the "Backward," or who is a *Harijan* [untouchable]? . . .

11. Is it not true that after the conceding of Pakistan, the land mass that remained was manifestly that of the Hindus? . . .

13. Is it not true that Hindus are prohibited from buying land or settling in Kashmir, whereas Kashmiri Muslims are free to buy land wherever they want in the country? . . .

16. Is it not true that Christians have their own "homeland"[36] or country, Muslims also have their own "homeland" or country, where they feel secure in every way, but Hindus have not been able to retain their country because under the banner of secularism it has been turned into a *dharmshala* [hospice]?

17. Is it not true that while Hindus are in power, Muslims can live safely, but as soon as the Muslims come to power, life will become difficult for the Hindus—that is, they will be destroyed? . . .

21. Is it not true that those Muslim women who have been divorced by their husbands are supported through the Waqf Committee[37] by the government, with funds taken from the government treasury; which means that for the maintenance and joy- [or lust-] filled lives of the Muslims, the majority Hindu community has to bear an additional tax burden?

If these things are true, then, Hindu brothers, you must immediately awake—awake while there is still time. And vow to sacrifice your wealth, your body, your all for the protection of the Hindu people and nation and for the declaration of this country as a Hindu nation.

What follows from all this is a profound anxiety about the Muslim and the call to disarm him—by disenfranchisement and deculturization. Muslims must adopt "our" names, "our" language, "our" dress. What follows is the demand that if the Muslims wish to stay in India, they should learn to live like "us"—the invisible mainstream that does not need to be identified: "*Hindustan mein rahna hai, to hamse milkar rahna hoga* [If you wish to live in Hindustan, you will have to live like us]"; "*Hindustan mein rahna hai, to Bande Mataram kahna hoga* [If you wish to live in Hindustan, you will have to cry Victory to the Mother]."[38]

Alongside is sometimes found the paradoxical argument that "we" will certainly provide justice to the Muslims and other minorities because they are overwhelmingly local converts and it is "Hindu blood (that) flows in their veins."[39] But the central message remains: "Live like us" or, its blood-curdling corollary, face annihilation: "*Babar ki santan—jao Pakistan ya kabristan* [Descendants of Babar, Pakistan or the grave]," a slogan that appears to have been taken literally by large sections of the police and the local Hindu population in Bhagalpur in 1989, in Gujarat in 2002, and in other places on other occasions.

The obverse of this vilification of the Muslim is the promotion of a rather different image of the Hindu from that which has most commonly been advertised from colonial times to today. The emphasis in militant Hindu propaganda is not so much on the nonviolent, peaceful, tolerant character of the Hindus—although astoundingly, even that proposition remains. It is rather more on how the Hindus have been tolerant for too long; they are still too timid; the need of the hour is not tolerance but courage. The Hindus must now claim—are now finally claiming—what is rightfully theirs. If Christians and Muslims have their nations, why should the Hindus not have their own nation and their own state in the only territory they inhabit, where they form an absolute majority, and where they have lived for thousands of years? For too long Hindus have been asked to make concessions on the grounds of their tolerance and on the plea of secularism; they must no longer allow themselves to be bullied, they must make no further concessions. "*Garva se kaho ham Hindu hain* [Announce with pride that you are Hindus]" and "*Hindu jaaga, desh jaagega* [The Hindus awaken, the nation will awake]," the walls of Delhi and other Indian cities have proclaimed loudly over the last two decades.

That there is nothing changeless or sacrosanct about the traditions, values, images, and self-images associated with particular communities is strikingly demonstrated by this new construction of the Hindus.[40] Indeed the statement applies not only to ordinary Hindu men and women, but also to some of the most popular Hindu deities, who are supposed to represent the divine spirit in various earthly forms. Thus, in a fine study of the new iconography of Ram produced in the context of the movement to destroy a sixteenth-century mosque allegedly erected on the site of his birth in Ayodhya, Anuradha Kapur shows how the great god-hero of the *Ramayana* here takes on the aspect of a Hindu crusader—complete with martial gear and the muscular body of a well-exercised modern adult male, neither of which he required in the traditional epic, since God is axiomatically more powerful than any opponents. At least for the duration of this political campaign, then, this crusading deity sheds his character as never angry, ever gracious, serene and benign.[41]

What I have noted about the malleability of Hindu images and traditions is true for the traditions, images, and self-images of other communities too.[42] The observation may also be applied to acts of open violence between men and women belonging to different religious denominations in India. These have for a hundred years now been designated simply as communal riots. One needs to stress, on the contrary, that these are not neatly bracketed events that happen periodically; further, there is no well-established and recurrent form of violence called the riot around which only the historical circumstances and actors change. The changing character and modes of sectarian strife over the twentieth and early twenty-first centuries themselves need study.

New Thresholds of (Acceptable) Violence

Sectarian violence in South Asia appears to have taken on new and increasingly ugly forms in recent times. Strife between people belonging to different religious denominations is no longer typified by pitched battles on the streets between crowds armed with sticks and stones, or cloak-and-dagger attacks and murders in side lanes, which were the chief markers of riots in, say, the 1920s and 1930s. The worst instances of recent violence—Gujarat in 2002, Bombay in 1992–93, Bhagalpur in 1989, Meerut in 1987, the anti-Sikh riots in Delhi in 1984, the anti-Tamil riots in Colombo in 1983, the Hindu-Muslim riots in Moradabad in 1980, and so on—have amounted to pogroms, organized massacres in which large crowds of hundreds or thousands have attacked the houses and property and lives of small, isolated, previously identified members of the "other" community.[43]

As a local leader of the Communist Party (Marxist) observed in Bhagalpur in January 1990, if just one or two deaths occur in an incident now, it is not even considered a riot.[44] Attacks on young and old, the blind and the maimed, and women, children, and infants; the physical destruction of lives, property, tools for work, and standing crops with the intent of wiping out the enemy; the open participation of the police; the lynching of enemy people found on trains or buses passing through the affected area—all these have become standard features of today's communal riot.

When the lynching of railway passengers first occurred on a large scale in 1947, it was remarked that the country had just been divided: two new states were coming into being, the armed forces and police had just been split, and the new regimes needed time to consolidate their positions; confusion, serious crime and open violence were only too likely. When such actions were repeated in 1984, in the anti-Sikh pogrom that followed the assassination of Indira Gandhi by her Sikh guard, it was said that a world leader and enormously popular prime minister had been gunned down and that when a colossus falls some upheaval, some exceptional reaction, is only natural. Now it has become unnecessary to plead exceptional circumstances when people are lynched or burned alive in the course of sectarian strife; newspapers report these occurrences, sometimes in their inner pages, without special comment.[45]

Clearly, all this is not unrelated to other kinds of physical violence in the society, which also pass quickly from the domain of the exceptional and noteworthy to that of the banal. Two small examples from 1990, when an early version of this chapter was first written, will serve to illustrate the point. The first is a cursory report on the deaths of five peasant volunteers from Bihar, who were among the tens of thousands who streamed into Delhi to attend a rally organized by the Indian People's Front. These five volunteers were run over and killed by a three-wheeler truck while they were sleeping on a pavement on the night of 8 October 1990. Their deaths provoked no editorial comment, and no calls for investigation, only a three-line statement of fact.[46]

At around the same time, the newspapers were full of reports of attempted self-immolations by school and college students from the upper castes, protesting the reservation of government jobs for people from "Backward Classes."[47] Yet, even here, after their first manipulative and sensationalizing appearance in a press that was openly on the side of the upper castes, national daily newspapers fairly quickly consigned news of such acts to the local news on pages 3 and 5.

The discourse on violence brands events of this kind "extraordinary," and yet treats them as completely ordinary, inconsequential, and unworthy of attention in the long run. It is in this context that I turn, finally, to another fragment from Bhagalpur that provides a somewhat different perspective on this concentrated and massive violence, and a different commentary on the meaning of communal riots today.

A Fragment

I present this fragment here not as another piece, or even another kind, of evidence. I propose it, instead, as the suggestion of another subject position arising from a certain experience (and understanding) of sectarian strife, one that may say something about the parameters of our own subject positions and understandings. And one that provides a commentary on the limits of scientific history and the scientific historian's search for truth.

The fragment in question takes the form of a collection of poems written by a college teacher in Bhagalpur, a resident in a mixed Hindu and Muslim lower middle-class locality that was not the scene of the worst outrages in the Bhagalpur attacks of 1989, but was nevertheless attacked repeatedly, traumatized, and scarred forever. In Manazir Aashiq Harganvi's poems, written for the most part during the first five days of the violence, we get some sense of the terror and desolation that so many people in Bhagalpur experienced at this time. The poems speak of darkness, of long nights, and of those days and nights that seemed to run into one another without meaning and without end. They speak of the hysterical screaming that marked that time, screams for help that were drowned out by the laughter and shouts of the attackers:

Jaan leva hansi	Blood-curdling laughter
Bhayanak kahkahe	Terrifying shouts
Bachao ki awaazen	Cries for help
Balwaiyon ke beech	Lost among the attackers
phansi rah gayeen[48]	

We have pictures of fields and corpses, and the impossibility of counting them:

Ek ... tin ... sattar	One ... three ... seventy
Sau ... do sau ... dhai sau	One hundred ... two hundred ... two hundred and fifty
Yeh ginti paar nahin lagegi	This counting will never end
Inhen ginne se pahle hi	For before it has ended
Tum aa jate ho	You come again
Bam aur goli lekar	With bombs and bullets
Ginti ki tadad badhane	To increase the numbers to be counted.
Lamhe ki rupahli tasveer	If only someone could come and see
Koi dekhe aakar!	The beauty of this moment!

We have a representation of the wake, waiting for the darkness to end and the light to begin to appear, but also—and more dreadfully—waiting simply for the attackers to come again:

Dangai phir aayenge	The rioters will come again:
Aisa hai intezar	We wait for them.

Among these poems there are many that talk about rape: a metaphorical statement of the humiliations suffered by a community, or a literal description of events that occurred?

Mar gaye bete mere	My sons have been killed
Biwi mari	My wife is dead
Aur yeh beti jise tum saath	And this daughter, whom you observe out of
mere kankhiyon se dekhte ho	the corner of your eye, sitting by my side—
Beshumar hathon ne loota hai ise	How many have plundered her?

Like the verse just quoted, there are others that are addressed to neighbors and friends—or people who were once neighbors and friends. Neighbors turned killers, people—known and unknown—running away from one another, and people ("all of us") afraid to look in the mirror for fear of what they/we will see. We have in them appeals and accusations. We have figures of emptiness:

Kuch bhi nahin rah gaya hai kahin	Nothing is left anywhere
Aadmi bahut hi bauna ho chuka hai	Man has become a midget
Apni lambai ka jhootha ahsas bhi	Unable any longer even to delude himself
baki nahin bacha	about his height
Ham behad khokhle ho gaye hain	We have been emptied [of meaning]
Aadhe-adhure log	Half people, incomplete people

And the endless search for ourselves, our loved ones, our friends:

Khud apne aap ko dhoondte hue	In search of yourself
Ab tum us kinare par khade ho	You have now reached that shore
Jahan se koi nahin lauta	From where no one has returned
Koi nahin laut-ta dost	No one ever returns, my friend
Ab to tum bhi nahin laut paoge	Now you, too, are lost forever

Yaad ki sirf ek shart rah jayegi	There remains but one condition
	of memory
ki jab bhi kahin	that whenever, wherever
Fasad hoga	A riot occurs
Tum bahut yaad aaoge	I will remember you.

It is a fragment that tells us a great deal about the Bhagalpur riots of 1989, and tells us also how much of this history we will never be able to write.

Standard historiographical procedure in the nineteenth century required the acceptance of a prescribed center (a state formation, a nation-state) as one's vantage point and the official archive as one's primary source for the construction of an adequate history. The power of this model can easily be seen in the writing of Indian history. This is a procedure that is not easily discarded, both because states and nations are central organizing principles of human society as we know it, and because the historian must necessarily deal with periods, territories, social groups, and political formations constituted into unities or blocs. However, the fact of their constitution into such unities or blocs—by historical circumstance and by the historian—should not be too quickly forgotten. The provisionality and contested character of all such unities (the objects of historical analysis) needs to be borne in mind.

I would like to suggest, in opposition to this established procedure, that for all their apparent solidity and comprehensiveness, what the official sources give us is still (in a Gramscian sense) but a fragment of history.[49] And that what I have called the fragment—a weaver's diary, a collection of poems by an unknown poet (and to these we might add all those literatures of India that Macaulay condemned, creation myths and women's songs, family genealogies and local traditions of history)—is of central importance in challenging the state's construction of history, in thinking other histories and marking those contested spaces in which some unities are constituted and others destroyed.

If the contingent nature of our units of analysis and our archives needs stressing, so does the provisionality of our interpretations and our theoretical conceits. While claims to total and objective knowledge are no longer as common as they once were among social scientists and historians, the temptations of totalizing discourses are nevertheless considerable. The yearning for the definitive statement, which says it all, will remain an important and necessary part of the social scientific endeavor. At the same time, however, it would be well to acknowledge the provisionality of our findings, their own historicity and location in a specific epistemological and political context, and their consequent privileging of particular forms of knowledge and particular tendencies to the exclusion of others.

At the present juncture in India, however, the totalizing standpoint of a seamless nationalism seems particularly counterproductive. The dominant nationalist historiography that insists on this standpoint needs to be challenged not only because of its interested use of categories such as "national" and "secular." It needs to be challenged also because of its privileging of the so-called national over the local, the mainstream over the marginal, the rational over the affective. In relation to that last pair, it is especially important that students of sectarian politics and strife pay closer attention to the visceral aspect (and apprehension) of collective violence and try in some way to make it part of their analyses.

Attention to this "visceral register of subjectivity and intersubjectivity," as William E. Connolly has described it,[50] may help us not only to think through the conditions that provoke fear, hatred, and violence, but also to understand better how moments of extreme violence transform people's sense of self, community, and history. Attention to these subliminal layers of our being may also help us see how the ordinary violence of our day-to-day existence is connected with these examples of massive, and apparently extraordinary, violence. Let me cite just one brief, and common, example.

A detailed newspaper report on the rape of two nuns teaching at a convent school in Gajraula, Uttar Pradesh, noted that the three rapists, wearing nothing but undergarments, addressed one another as *ustad* and *guru* (literally, "teacher" and "guide," here used roughly for "boss," "partner") while they held the nuns at gunpoint.[51] This is the kind of brag regularly associated with young louts found teasing women and girls on Delhi buses and in Bombay films. It is worth pondering how large the step is from this kind of molestation of women to the kind of violent assault involved in rape, and from the taunting of members of the minorities and lower castes in normal times to the attacks they suffer in the more publicized acts of collective violence.

The PUDR team of which I was a member was in Bhagalpur on the eve of India's Republic Day, 26 January, in 1990. On the evening of 25 January, we heard extracts from the Indian Constitution recited on national television: "We, THE PEOPLE OF INDIA, having solemnly resolved to

constitute India into a SOVEREIGN, SOCIALIST, SECULAR DEMO-
CRATIC REPUBLIC and to secure to all its citizens: JUSTICE, social,
economic and political; LIBERTY of thought, expression, belief, faith and
worship . . . "[52] The remoteness of Delhi struck us on that occasion in a
way that is hard to recapture in writing. During the preceding days, we had
seen men, women, and children, with little bundles of their belongings,
fleeing their villages for fear of what might happen on 26 January. It was
strongly rumored that on that day of national celebration, Muslims—"trai-
tors," as always—would hoist black flags (or even the Pakistani flag) on
their religious buildings and there would be another riot. We had seen
heated altercations among Muslim villagers and townsfolk, between those
who said that running away only added to the alarmist rumors and the
dangers, and others who accused them of foolhardiness given all that had
happened. We had been asked in a relief camp to take down "First Information Reports" and evidence because the police, who should have done
this, were themselves the guilty party and, in many cases, were still ensconced in office. The words *justice* and *liberty* rather stuck in the throat at
this time.

The remoteness of Delhi that I have mentioned is not just a function
of physical distance, or felt only in times of crisis. I have no doubt that
many have felt the same remoteness—periodically, or indeed continuously
at certain times—in Bombay and in Jammu and Kashmir, in Meham and
Maliana (Meerut), in Shahdara, across the river Jamuna from the capital of
India, and indeed inside the old city of Delhi itself—where, too, talk of
"justice" and "liberty" must often appear callous. We must continue to
search for ways of representing that remoteness in the histories we write. It
is in this spirit that I pursue my critique of the procedures of nationalist
history writing in the next chapter.

Appendix to Chapter 2:
Reply to a Right-Wing Journalist

A prominent right-wing journalist used his column in one of India's leading weekly news magazines to critique the essay that forms the substance of the above chapter, when it was first published in 1991 under the title, "In Defense of the Fragment: Writing about Hindu-Muslim Riots in India Today." In a two-page review, he condemned the writing of such politically interested histories. I reproduce below what I wrote in response to his charge. I believe it lays out fairly well the terms of the debate about politics and history that many of us have been engaged in over the last decade and more, and indicates the concerns that provoke the reflections contained in the present volume.

A journalist of right-wing persuasion, Mr. S. D., has devoted two pages in a popular weekly to my piece entitled "In Defense of the Fragment." In the course of these two pages, he accuses me and others who defend minority rights and the plurality of cultures in India of a "thinly-veiled secessionism" and support for the "emotional balkanization" of this country. "The defense of the 'fragment' is a defense of the fragmentation of India," he writes. Mr. D.'s position needs to be "confronted politically" (to use his own phrase), for an air of neutral, objective journalism should not be allowed to hide the real thrust of his politics and of his support for the Hindu Right.

Let me first make it clear, as Mr. D.'s critique perhaps does not, that my article on the fragment is concerned primarily with the way we write history—more specifically, with the problems faced by historians in writing the history of sectarian violence. One of my central arguments is that, given the conditions and manner in which historical evidence is gathered and compiled, and the enormous difficulties involved in historical representation, there is need for greater circumspection and provisionality in our statements than historians have allowed in the past. Yet while many historians are now more willing than before to question their own historical practice, some journalists seem to have appropriated the seat of the almighty or the omniscient.

Mr. D. compliments me on my history writing, but finds serious fault, and grave danger, in my politics. "Tragically," he says, "the activist" gets the better of "the historian" at some point in the article. It would be possible to return the compliment, simply substituting the words "the propagandist" and "the reviewer." But there is a prior difficulty here, which is that it is not always possible to distinguish between the two. Mr. D.'s writing provides clear illustrations of this difficulty.

One purpose of my article—which I would have thought would be clear to any discerning reader—is precisely to challenge the artificial separation between history and politics, the academic and the activist. A good deal has been written in recent times to demonstrate the direct complicity between power and knowledge. In fact, few serious historians today would argue that it is possible to maintain a strict separation between history and politics.

Many, including myself, have gone further and suggested that such a separation—or rather the pretence of a separation—is not even desirable. Unlike Mr. D., therefore, I have nothing a priori against historians who write political pamphlets (although Mr. D.'s derisory comments seem to be reserved for those who write pamphlets opposed to the Hindu viewpoint: presumably, pamphleteering on behalf of the Bharatiya Janata Party and Vishwa Hindu Parishad is, in his view, quite professional).

I have myself written at some length about the politics of the current Ayodhya controversy and the simplistic demand, made by the Babari Masjid Action Committee, the Vishwa Hindu Parishad, the Government, and others, for proof of the earlier existence or nonexistence of a temple at the disputed site.[1] Lest this be misconstrued too, let me clarify my position. The appropriate question, in my view, is not whether there is such archaeological or historical proof. It is not even whether the god Ram was actually born at this site—though I continue to believe that it is a considerable diminishing of the concept of godhead to claim any such proposition as a literal truth. There are more important questions to be asked. For example, can something described as a "medieval wrong" be righted by another wrong perpetrated in our times? Can the religious feelings and aspirations of the Hindus be satisfied only by the destruction of an old, disused mosque and the construction of a grand temple to Ram at precisely that location and nowhere else in Ayodhya? What are the implications of such an action, in such a highly charged and disturbed time, in terms of the fears it generates among religious minorities and the meaning it has for the plurality of communities and cultures called India?

In any event, my argument rests on the proposition that we are all implicated in politics, whether we admit this or (like Mr. D.) strongly deny it. Indeed, political intervention on the part of ivory-towered intellectuals (historians and others) may well be a sign of sensitivity and concern in a society riven by strife, oppression, and inequality. Political debate and discussion is of vital importance in this society, and I agree with Mr. D. that dialogue has been somewhat lacking in both political and academic circles in India. But Mr. D. does nothing to advance his case for dialogue, or to substantiate his views, simply by labeling those with whom he disagrees politically "secessionist" and "antinational" elements. Let me turn now to this charge.

The first question that comes to mind here is what is legitimate and what is unacceptable in journalistic reporting. Notwithstanding the sensationalism of the yellow press and the need of any paper or journal to catch the eye of the reader, it is necessary to ask why a piece dealing with an article on historiography should be published under the title, "India in Fragments: Emotional Balkanization Is Tearing the Nation Apart," with photographs of Khalistani militants and anti-Indian Kashmiri demonstrators in the middle?

I use the term *fragment* in my article in two different ways. The first, and more important, is to indicate certain kinds of historical sources: I include among these fragments often neglected by orthodox historians, a weaver's diary, a book of poems on riots written by a little known local poet, women's writings, and for that matter, all those literatures of India so derided by Macaulay and his latter-day Indian counterparts. I also use *fragment* to refer to those different groups in Indian society that are branded minorities by the ruling class: "the smaller religious and caste communities, tribal sections, industrial workers, activist women's groups" are examples I give in my article.

Even if we forget my first usage, I would like to know how this defense of fragments becomes a "defense of the fragmentation of India"? How can support for the interests and demands of such minorities—working-class actions in search of better working conditions, women's groups' protests against Deorala,[2] a tribal or untouchable community's demand for an end to caste Hindu oppression, as well as the right of Muslims to live in peace in Ayodhya, for instance—be called secessionist?

The implication is that any challenge to the established structure of class and caste power in India, any call for a more equitable distribution of political, economic, and cultural resources, is automatically a call for the breakup of India. Some distinction ought to be maintained, however, between India and the India of the prosperous middle class's dream—which is what Mr. D. seeks to uphold. Out of simple curiosity, I would also be interested to know how the women of India, the working classes, lower-caste groups, or indeed any of our religious minorities (taken as a unity), could secede from this country.

Mr. D. asserts that "when Pandey rails against an alleged imposition of a Brahmanical culture, he is not underlining the absurdities and dangers of cultural regimentation in a country like India." This is more than the position of the magistrate pronouncing judgment on the nationalism or antinationalism of the ordinary mortals in the dock; it is the position of God, who knows better than any ordinary mortal what that ordinary mortal means. My article states, in almost so many words, that a minority viewpoint and culture (that of a get-rich-quick, consumerist, Brahmanical ruling class) is being foisted on the rest of the country as the viewpoint and culture of the country as a whole. This is being done, I argue, in the interests of profit and power, as much as because of a self-delusion about what is truly Indian, by a minority that refuses, of course, to recognize its minority status. If this is not pointing to a danger of cultural regimentation, I would like to know what is.

Much of what I and other concerned social scientists and historians have written over the last few years deals with the arduous and self-contradictory process of nation-building in the nineteenth and twentieth centuries, not only in India but everywhere in the world. We differ from the likes of Mr. D., who apparently believe that the character and boundaries of nation-states are foreordained, that nations—like God—are natural and eternal (and, in India, Hindu), and that the problems of nation-building are created only by those who do not accept this axiomatic wisdom.

In my article, and in a 1990 book on communalism (*The Construc-*

tion of Communalism in Colonial North India), I made the obvious histori-cal point that communities and nations, cultures and histories are con-structed. They are constructed through struggles involving large numbers of people of many different classes, out of collective endeavors based on shared as well as contested experiences; and they are, in some sense, always under construction—through continuing contests and changing visions. The same applies to those popular emotions and feelings that Mr. D. so generously compliments me on "almost" recognizing as being germane to sectarian strife.

The forces of the Hindu Right, which include journalists like Mr. D., have a particular vision of history and the future that they would like to sell to the country as natural. This vision has much to do with the gen-eration of those Hindu feelings of "perceived humiliation, bondage and pride," which Mr. D. commends to us as lying behind the controversy in Ayodhya. The complexity and power of this vision needs to be clearly rec-ognized, precisely so that it may be better combated. Hopes of peace, jus-tice, and a better life have been part of the dreams of most people in this country—as in every other; we may ask whether it is the forces of the Hindu Right that most directly threaten those dreams, or other forces? Do they threaten the breakup of democratic India or do we?

The Nation and Its Past

The remoteness of Delhi, of liberty and justice, of nation and state, which I discussed in the last chapter, has a great deal to do with centralization and the way Delhi and the nation are constructed. It will help to consider more closely this matter of the construction of the normalized political community. The process is wide-ranging, involved, and ambiguous, but something of its workings may be seen fairly clearly in the writing of the national history. What is at stake in the setting up of a national archive? How are histories categorized as mainstream or minority? How are the mainstream and the marginal, majorities and minorities, naturalized?

In the critique of historiography, as in that of politics, one may begin with a question about perspective: whose standpoint does the historian adopt, whom does s/he speak for? However, it is possible, and perhaps necessary, to ask a more fundamental question too. Whose voice *can* we recover (or represent)? Whose language do we write in? What are the rules of historical, or political, discourse that we are bound by?

At one level, the choice in recent historical writing has been between two very different kinds of knowledge claims. On the one hand is the claim of a dominant, unambiguous voice setting out to establish dominant, unambiguous Truths. On the other, a search for historical and political positions that acknowledge the incompleteness and imperfection, not to say messiness, of human achievement, including the achievement of written history. The paradigmatic example of the first is the voice of the state. The far less commonly noticed example of the second is the subaltern stutter. This chapter continues the investigation of these different types of articulation in the context of recent debates on the construction of the Indian past.

Scientific History

For the scientific historian since the nineteenth century, history has been a one-directional, interconnected story of progress (or, at least, movement) in a unified field—although the interconnections and unity are established in complex ways that are not always fathomed by the individual historian. The overarching categories, the larger problems for investigation, the big why questions of this history are given. In the received view, they are fundamental and unalterable. They have had to do, in the writing of modern history, with Progress and Enlightenment, the spread of science, rationality and liberalism, and (in relation to activities much more readily categorized as political) the ascendancy of concepts like nations and nationalism, development and modernization, equality and justice. The sophisticated Indian historiography of Indian nationalism exemplifies the position very well indeed.

There is by now a widespread consensus among historians in India, as elsewhere, that nations are not given from seed, but are constituted in self-contradictory struggles that are prolonged and in some senses ongoing. The Indian nation, it is conceded, even argued, was constituted in this way. However, even as this point is made, the notion of the natural unit or community that is the subject of Indian history persists in the actual writing of colonial and postcolonial history.

Let me illustrate this by reference to the historical writing on the Partition of 1947, which I have already mentioned in Chapter 2. The scholarship on Partition has worked largely with an unquestioned vision of the natural and the proper: that which was, and was not, meant to be. Perhaps the most obvious sign of the Partition of British India in 1947 was the massive violence that (as we are told) "surrounded," "accompanied" or (as we might put it) constituted it. I have cited the common estimates of half a million to one million people killed and twelve to fourteen million refugees produced by Partition. In addition, an uncounted number of women and girls were raped and abducted. A few months after coming to power, the governments of the two new dominions entered into an inter-dominion agreement to rescue and rehabilitate abducted persons left on the wrong side of the new international border. This program of compulsory recovery and repatriation, which entailed considerable coercion and physical violence, was continued officially for the better part of a decade.

How are we to write the history of this moment? Is it possible to suggest, as some of us have done,[1] that the history of Partition is the history of rape and abduction and killing, and of the subsequent state-sponsored drive to evict aliens and recover nationals (especially abducted women and children), irrespective of their personal wishes? The meaning of Partition is disturbingly captured in these acts. Or must we always face the objection, as we embark on these studies, that talk of rape and abduction and murder is all very well but it misses the main point—which, we are glibly told, is that the cause of all this was Partition. The *real* historical task, we are reminded, is to investigate the causes of Partition. It is to ask the question: what led to this tragedy, this departure from the normal, assigned course of Indian history?

There is, in India, only one big why question regarding Partition. What went wrong? What were the causes of this deviation? Who was responsible? In Pakistan, of whose intellectual climate and debates I know less, the question may, to some extent, be reversed. The year 1947 is Independence, not Partition. It is nationalism, not communalism. What, the Pakistani historian might ask, were the struggles and sacrifices that were needed to realize this natural course of history?[2]

What we tend to get, in both cases, is a refurbished narrative of Indian or Pakistani nationalism, in which the historian's chief contribution is a detailing of the economic, social, and cultural preconditions and the political moves or miscalculations that allowed for this noble victory or tragic loss. The loss or victory, Partition or Partition/Independence, and thence the normalization of particular communities and particular histories: all this remains largely unproblematized.

François Furet's important critique of the parallel procedures in the historiography of the French Revolution may be recalled here. Drawing attention to the "unvarying internal organisation" of the historical writing on this subject, he notes that "analysis is restricted to the problem of 'origins' or causes. . . . Narrative begins with the 'events,' in 1787 or 1789, and runs through to the end of the 'story' . . . as if, once the causes are set out, the play went on by itself, propelled by the initial upheaval." A phenomenon like the French Revolution, Furet goes on to say (and the point applies with equal force to Partition), "cannot be reduced to a simple cause-and-effect schema. . . . Let us assume for a moment that these causes are better understood than they actually are, or that some day it will be possible to list them in a more functional order; the fact remains that the revolutionary event, from *the very outset*, totally transformed the existing situation and created a new mode of historical action that was not intrinsically a part of that situation."[3]

The difficulties such an analysis points to, not least on the question of what constitutes the appropriate subject of history, have not seriously impinged upon nationalist historical writing in India, especially at the level of school and college textbooks. The naturalness of the Indian nation and the unnaturalness of something like Partition have strong roots in the history of Indian historiography. As is well known, the writing of history in a recognizably modern scientific mode began in India with colonialist writers who drew up a picture of the subcontinent as inhabited by discrete religious fraternities—Hindu, Muslim, Sikh, and so on—as well as a host of ethnic and linguistic communities. The argument that there could never be anything like stable unity in this multitude of separate communities, races, and nations was, ultimately, the raison d'être of British power in India, and it was the instrument of their rule.

As the English saw it, they had inherited the empire from the Muslims. It was the Muslims, therefore, who were liable to be least reconciled to British rule, the Muslims therefore who needed the closest surveillance and control. The proof was the great mutiny-uprising of 1857, described by colonial writers as a Muslim conspiracy.[4] Within a few decades of that event, the colonial ruling class had radically changed its position, and a decision was made to woo the Muslims (among others) as a counterweight to the rising force of Hindu nationalism—that is to say, a movement in which the majority of leaders happened to be Hindu.

The underlying perspective remained unaltered, however. Indian society was religious and bigoted—as opposed to being modern and scientific, which were the implicit hallmarks of Western society. It was a society made up of Hindus and Muslims (and sundry other communities), always at odds with one another because of the fundamental opposition of their worldviews and the history of Muslim conquest and rapine. Hence, precisely, the subcontinent's history of fierce communal riots, which, as administrator after administrator put it in the nineteenth century, broke out "from time to time"—especially before the establishment of British rule.[5]

Nationalist historiography arose as a direct answer to the colonialist analysis. Colonialist historiography had among its pioneers a host of practicing scholar-officials; nationalist historiography counted among its earliest practitioners a number of activist politician-intellectuals. For them it was Indians who had lost their independence, and so much more besides—through deindustrialization and the drain of wealth, for example.[6] The events of 1857 were therefore not a Mutiny but the First Indian War of Independence. Hindus and Muslims and all other Indians were, actually or potentially, united against the continuation of British rule in India.

As this historiography developed, it emphasized the history of coexistence and tolerance among India's many communities and religions: "Unity in Diversity." Nationalist historians pointed with pride to the emergence of a composite (Hindu-Muslim) culture in the courts of Mughal India and its successor states. Among the common people, they noted, Hindus and Muslims shared a great deal at the level of social life, even to the extent of participating actively in one another's religious festivals. Communal riots were rare in precolonial India, the nationalists argued. It was British policy that had made them a feature of the subcontinent's political life, and it was a motivated colonialist historiography that dug out and exaggerated the isolated examples of religious intolerance and conflict in earlier times.

Thus, a distinct and powerful Indian historiography, of the modern, scientific kind, emerged out of the struggle against colonial rule and the British denial of Indian nationhood and the possibility of self-government. Debates and writings in Indian history still carry the marks of that birth. Of the many results of this struggle and of Partition, one of the most significant has been a division of Indian historians into nationalist (and therefore, it is often implied, modernist, progressive, and secular) and antinational(ist) camps. On the one side are said to be those who empathize with—are at one with—the "trend of world history." On the other are those who are not. The former seek to write the history of the Indian nation and of the struggles to carry it forward. The latter end up—through their attention to the particular, the local, the oppositional, and the contradictory—on the side of those who support the nation's fragmentation.[7] One of the more troubling examples of the second kind of history writing, in the view of the more orthodox historians, has been the historiographical intervention named subaltern studies.

The Critique of Nationalist Historiography

The issues involved in the nationalist/antinationalist controversy are set out clearly in a wide-ranging review published in 1994. In this, a well-known left-wing historian K. N. Panikkar engaged with what he called "neo-colonial" historiography, which he managed to equate with "post-modernism" and with "micro-history," condemning all of these as they have come to be practiced in India. He charged the new "micro-historians" of "fracturing . . . [the] overarching categories" of Indian history, and protested against what he described as progressive shifts away from the appropriate locus of its study: "The province instead of nation, locality instead of province, and family instead of locality."

Panikkar quoted Eric Hobsbawm's defense of established historical procedures, published in 1980—"There is nothing new in choosing to see the world via a microscope rather than a telescope, so long as we accept that we are studying that same cosmos"—and went on to say:

Implying an integral connection between the micro[cosm] and the macro[cosm], Hobsbawm suggested that the former is not an end in itself but a means for illuminating wider questions, which goes far beyond a particular event, story or character. It is the pursuit of this connection which in a way enabled the "big *why* questions." In contrast, the tendency of neo-colonial history is to isolate the micro from the macro and to imbue the former with independence both from its origin and context.[8]

Before I take up the propositions contained in this passage, let me juxtapose with it another surprising statement, from an even more influential historian, doyen of early modern Indian (especially Mughal) history and an important commentator on the colonial and postcolonial experience in India, Irfan Habib. In several statements on *Subaltern Studies*, Habib has reiterated the argument presented in the last two paragraphs. I cite the concluding lines of one of his lectures:

The "Subaltern" historians . . . seldom touch upon the aggregates in statistics, e.g., those of national income and exports, the drain of wealth, taxation (indicating the exploitation of the Indian peasantry by indirect taxation), etc. . . . But if we want to know what was happening to India, we must keep the national level statistics in mind. Let us see what the Indian people in their majority were passing through and then find out what colonialism meant and what the Indian national movement was about.

All that I have said above about continuing assumptions regarding the naturalness of the nation is amply illustrated here. However, there are a number of other matters at stake as well. By way of explicating his position, Habib raises the question:

Are we going to have a modern nation, a nation with social equity, for which the national movement fought? Or are we going to have a divided country, living in a manufactured, imagined past of the most parochial kind and, therefore, leading ourselves towards disaster. I am sure that duty calls to all of us whether [as] historians or as citizens, who want to defend the Indian nation to close ranks in the battle of ideas that is now taking place.[9]

One response would be to point out that the battle of ideas can never be won, or for that matter much advanced, through closed ranks alone: what is required, at least as much, is open minds and persistent inquiry and questioning. Another question—closing ranks around what?—cannot easily be set aside today, when the unified revolutionary subject is so much less self-evident than it seemed a century and more ago. There is surely a need to investigate how a specific closing of ranks occurred in the first place, how the national movement was consolidated, how the idea of a nation arose, was modified and contested—and not just at some presumed originary moment. It is for this reason that the search for dissonant voices and fragmentary resistance, for elements that question the self-evidence of received totalities, becomes imperative. It is precisely to meet this need that projects like feminism, minority histories, the history of borders (and the grey areas and cultures that constitute frontier regions), and subaltern studies arise.

The *Subaltern Studies* intervention in the historiographical debate began with a critique of the sophisticated body of orthodox nationalist and Marxist historical writing in India. The obsolescent colonialist historiography, which was critiqued by earlier nationalist and Marxist writers as well as contributors to the new series, need not detain us here. What was perhaps new in the "subalternist" position was the challenge to the assumed unity and sanctity—the touch-me-notism—of Indian nationalism.

Early writings in the series posited the existence of two domains of politics—the elite and the subaltern. It was argued that the Indian national movement could not be portrayed as some straightforward, united, and undifferentiated struggle against the British for the achievement of a goal that was already fixed in all its dimensions by the 1870s or thereabouts and gradually realized over the next seventy or eighty years. Nationalism did not arise fully formed and elaborated, as it were, in the heads of some enlightened leaders, to then spread out and transform the consciousness of the people. Rather, the consciousness, deliberations, and actions of diverse groups of people, in different regions and in different economic, social, and cultural circumstances, conditioned and shaped the meaning of an Indian nationalism.

In other words, the seventy or eighty years from the 1870s onward, on which orthodox nationalist history writing had so heavily concentrated, was a period not simply of *realizing* but also of *thinking* the nation. Caste, class, region, gender, age, education, political and cultural heritage—all had a hand to play in this contested envisioning of the future society, and there were many hesitant, competing, and changing visions of what that nation might be. The subalternists went on to say that it made little sense to work with some facile distinction between nationalism on the one hand and social or economic protest on the other, the national movement on the one hand and the peasant (or labor or women's) movement on the other, or even—although this was (and is) much harder for secular Indian scholars to take on board—nationalism on the one hand and what in India is called communalism on the other. The score of Indian nationalism was made up of these diverse strains, their imbrication and pulling apart—and, as was evident, the contests were far from finished in 1947.

A second aspect of the *Subaltern Studies* critique of existing historiography—one that was elaborated only as the project developed—was to challenge the somewhat unthinking application to the Indian experience of European models of historical development and a European understanding of class struggle. Although Marx began to rethink this proposition toward the end of his life, his view that nineteenth-century England showed the rest of the world the face of its future had been widely accepted. From this kind of thinking developed the idea that the history of the rest of the world could only be a later, and usually poorer, copy of the history of Europe.[10] In such a reading, the categories of modern history—classes, nationalism, secularism, modernity—were all already known from the start, as of course was the ultimate, private place of religion. Even—or should we say, especially—in countries like India, religion was supposed to have (and therefore had!) little place in a history of modernity and development.

As it happens, even the spread of global capitalism has not produced the same kind of modern economy and economic relations in every country: compare Japan with Malaysia, or India with South Africa, or Brazil with Canada. And that's a small sample. The notion that classes would be the same everywhere, that agrarian (or industrial) differentiation and hierarchies would evolve in the same way, that the relation between town and country, or between the economic, cultural, and political moments of twentieth-century social formations, would be identical is plainly unhistorical. An abstract economic impulse has hardly proved to be an adequate explanation for the development of different kinds of political struggle, nations, and state forms in different parts of the world. In colonial India, as in E. P. Thompson's eighteenth- and nineteenth-century England,[11] to take two widely differing cases, caste, religion, region, gender, and generation had much to do with the evolution of new kinds of society, politics, and political communities.

It was in thinking about this diversity of cultural and historical conditions, and the many-sided and prolonged struggles that went into the forging of new (and often fragile) unities, that subalternist historians found Italian Marxist Antonio Gramsci's "Notes on Italian History"—his emphasis on an autonomous history of the subaltern classes, and his notion of hegemony (itself always contested and unstable)—especially useful. It was, again, to give fuller play to this diversity of conditions that this group of scholars opted for the relatively open terms of *elite* and *subaltern* rather than the better known categories of working class and capitalist, landlord and serf. The latter terms had become inflexible and rigid in many ways, since they were taken to be already known and universally valid. This step back from a fixed notion of class allowed a renewed investigation—very much in line with the original Marxist agenda—of concrete, and changing, relationships of power. It allowed investigators to think of structures of domination and subordination in which cultural and political factors played as much a part as the economic, and of social formations in which dominant and subordinate groups would be identified differently in different contexts.

Once the concrete, and complex, conditions of dominance and subordination were opened up for detailed investigation, the moment of resistance, which has everywhere been part of the life and activity of subaltern groups and classes, could also be more carefully elaborated. Thus, in their effort to rectify the elitist bias in the writing of the history of Indian nationalism, the contributors to *Subaltern Studies* sought to recover the agency of the different actors involved in the making of national consciousness or regional identity, caste movements, and sectarian or peasant protests, as well as by focusing on what they saw as the fragmentary, self-contradictory, and often religious idiom of the politics of subordinated and marginalized groups.

What this meant was a recognition of the subjectivity of the subaltern classes and groups—the lower peasantry and working people more generally, women, untouchables, tribal cultivators and the urban poor—who had been marginalized in academic accounts of the national movement and assigned to a realm of prepolitical, preconscious historical action. Hence the historian's insistence on the specifically *political* aspect of the consciousness of the peasants, the *politics* of peasant insurgency, and the deliberation and planning that went into every act of peasant (or other subaltern) defiance: the peasant could scarcely revolt in a fit of absent-mindedness, as Ranajit Guha points out, for s/he had too much to lose.[12]

However, the attempt to write about "the people on their own," or of peasant consciousness or the voices of women, led historians to new quandaries and questions. The participants in the *Subaltern Studies* initiative were not the first to discover this. Feminists and other critical intellectuals and radical philosophers had arrived at much the same finding, in other contexts. The recovery of subaltern subjectivity or consciousness was no simple task, and it required tools and methods of analysis not already available to the researcher. Subaltern classes and disadvantaged and marginal groups do not leave behind accounts of their endeavors. They appear in the institutional archive only as traces, fragments, the suggestion of a voice—an echo.

How were these voices and agencies to be recovered from the records except as accounts of forces and positions denied, and analyses of the conditions of such exclusion?[13]

The Question of Historical Evidence

We begin with an apparent paradox here. What the historian trades in, we are told, is facts. S/he inherits and collects and explores narratives.[14] Facts or, more broadly, evidence comes to the historian in the form of narratives and narrative fragments: the narratives, one might say with only a little exaggeration, of the ruling classes and the fragments of the subordinated.

Gramsci put the point well:

The history of subaltern groups is necessarily fragmented and episodic. Every trace of independent initiative on the part of subaltern groups should therefore be of incalculable value for the integral historian. . . . [T]his kind of history can only be dealt with monographically and each monograph requires an immense quantity of material which is often hard to collect.[15]

What the historian of subaltern groups has to work with, then, are precisely fragments, traces (in Gramsci's phrase) that appear in surviving narratives to tell of other, possible narratives and points of view, now suppressed.

The narratives that are preserved by the state in archives and other public institutions and that appear in the wider public discourse originate for the most part with the ruling classes, and owe their existence largely to a ruling class's need for security and control. Lodged in the records found in these institutions, however, are fragments (traces) of many lost (and usually irrecoverable) perspectives, prized out by a predatory official or observer from earlier (often unknown) contexts and situated in new ones. The statement of a "mute" subject under trial; rumors heard in the bazaar; slogans shouted by rebels or rioters; the Ashokan pillars in Ferozeshah Kotla (Delhi), and on the ridge near Delhi University; and the Lodi tombs in Lady Willingdon Park in New Delhi (which continues to be known by the more appropriate name of Lodi Gardens): elements that testify not only to the power of particular regimes and their appropriation of the richness of history, but also to the continued appearance of other shadows— the shadows of other presences and other pasts.

There are fragments of a similar kind found in nonofficial records. Such, for instance, is the evidence of two Muslim women being transported to Pakistan in the course of the abducted persons' recovery program after Partition, who told an Indian social worker when they were "recaptured" after running away from a transit camp en route, that all they had wanted was "to see, for one last time the respective [Hindu or Sikh, Indian] fathers of the children they were carrying [in their wombs] before being taken away forever."[16]

Or, to take some examples from interviews I conducted with people who lived through the Partition and Independence of India and Pakistan, consider the testimony of a middle-class Hindu woman writer, a male Sikh mechanic, and a poor male *dhobi* (washerman). Their accounts of 1947 are constructed in the course of conversations I had with them, but their answers still appear as fragments on a tape when I ask the question, "What were you doing on 15 August 1947?" "My son was unwell, I could do nothing but sit with him the whole day," responded the writer. "What were we doing? What do you think?" asked the Sikh mechanic somewhat angrily. A member of a refugee family from West Pakistan who had lived in Delhi since 1947, he went on to explain: "We didn't know where we'd be from one day to the next. . . . Would we be able to stay on, even here? . . . Worrying about this, that's what we were doing." And the old washerman looked at me with some surprise as he said: "What would I be doing? I was doing my work [washing clothes]."

There were other occasions when I was met with suspicion: although I was myself not always aware of this, my bona fides and the real reason for my unexpected visit were in doubt. Mistaken for an intelligence agent of some kind in one instance, I was invited back several days later by a highly articulate homoeopathic medical practitioner with whom I had had a long (and, as it seemed to me, remarkably open) interview. He told me that he had mistaken my purpose at first, and presented me with an interestingly different rendering of the story that I had been told earlier—with the same basic chronological sequence of events, but different nuances, subtle enough to challenge the official nationalist version of the history of those times in various ways without contradicting the doctor's previous nationalist account. I was also presented with a bundle of political propagandist pamphlets and leaflets of right-wing (communalist) inclination.

A businessman in his forties expressed anger that his eighty-year-old mother was being repeatedly interviewed. "Why do you all come here? What will you do with this?" he asked. "What will we get out of it? Others have come and interviewed her before, and made big promises about writing up this history. I don't believe any of you will publish our story."

Let me give, as one final example, the response of a person whom I had been asked to meet by several people from his village because of an unusual twist in his personal history. He had once been a Muslim, had converted to Sikhism in the "dreadful" days of 1946–47 (as he himself described them), but had—unlike many others in the village—stayed with the new religious affiliation even when circumstances improved. Now the owner of a fleet of taxis, a local Congress leader, and a municipal corporator in a town not far from this village, he never so much as mentioned his conversion. In the course of our interview I scribbled in my notepad: "This is just like [the documentation of] rape." How does the rapist, or the raped, talk about the experience of rape? How does the interviewer ask about it?

These are fragments that come to the historian as parts of alien, aggrandizing narratives—court records, newspaper accounts, civil servants' letters and reports, a social worker's memoirs, a researcher's interviews. Clearly, these are not the only sites they might inhabit, and they constitute, as I have already said, at least potentially a disturbance, a fracture in the narrative, which might enable us to prize it open and read it differently from the judge, the journalist, the bureaucrat, the social worker, and the nationalist historian. But those who seek to take fuller account of such fissures or cracks in the record are unlikely, in my judgment, to be able to write histories of a traditional sort.[17]

The Struggle to Recover Subaltern Speech

In regard to the issue of writing subaltern histories, the question is often asked why the historian does not look for and use an alternative, popular archive. In addition to the narratives of state officials and newspaper editors, and those found in institutional collections of private papers, historians also have available to them the narratives of storytellers and balladeers, not to mention individual and collective memories available in oral accounts (which are, in many cases, taped or written as well). There is the whole corpus of religious and social life, beliefs and practices, rituals and prayers.[18] And so much more.

Contrary to a common assumption, however, neither folksongs nor truncated statements of the kind I cited above can give us any simple, direct access to the authentic voice and history of subordinated and marginalized groups. The language of the dominant and the privileged—classical Hinduism and Islam, the Great Tradition, the pronouncements of the upper classes—mingle with folk forms and lower-class articulations. Guha makes the point very well in his comment on the tribal rites, usages, and myths that D. D. Kosambi used and enjoined us to use: "The pull of 'parallel traditions' and the pressure of upper-caste, especially Brahmanical, culture tend to assimilate and thereby transform them [these rites, myths, and usages] to such an extent that they show up as little more than archaic traces within an established Hindu idiom."[19]

Subaltern statements are even more inconsistent and fragmentary in instances when they are made for the benefit of the privileged or the powerful. The great African-American writer W.E.B. Du Bois has something to say on this fragile and uncertain quality of voice and identity. In his reflections on the condition of blacks in early twentieth-century America, Du Bois wrote of the question he was repeatedly *not* asked, that is to say, a question that was on the lips of many people he met but rarely enunciated: "How does it feel to be a problem?"[20] The African-American in the United States was a problem by definition. (Untouchables in India are a problem. So is the girl-child in large parts of the society. So were the raped and abducted women of Partition. It is almost unnecessary to point out that upper- and middle-class Hindu boys and men in India, usually belonging to the upper castes, like white Anglo-Saxon Protestant males in the United States, are never thought of as a problem in this generalized way.)

One consequence of living life as a problem, Du Bois suggested, was that one lived with a "double consciousness": "two souls in one dark body."[21] This is a profound insight, which has a great deal to tell us about all kinds of suppressed classes and marginalized groups—Partition sufferers, slaves, untouchables, laboring women. Their punitive, not to say violated, circumstances go a long way toward explaining the plucked-out, truncated, fragmentary, and often self-contradictory character of the subaltern account. Theirs are, inevitably it seems, fitfully told stories, sometimes stories that cannot be told, of coping with minimal resources in impossible conditions, of surviving—and trying to keep life alive—through the inhabiting of different subject-positions, all of which are scarcely scripted by themselves.

"Why did God make me an outcast and a stranger in mine own house?"[22] Du Bois asks the question on behalf of African-Americans. It is a question that numerous abducted and recovered women in India (and Pakistan) might have asked in the years after Partition. It is also a question that many women in Indian society, and not only in Indian society, are perhaps forced to ask even in what are construed as normal times.[23] For many who are forced to live in the shadows, it is sometimes a choice between "living life somehow, anyhow" and "dying in accordance with the rules of honour laid out by male society," as Veena Das puts it in a remark about the "truth of womanhood" in Partition and post-Partition India.[24] It is a choice between dying and accepting the living death of *bhek* that was the lot of innumerable widows in nineteenth-century Bengal, as Ranajit Guha points out in "Chandra's Death."[25] The question for us is how we might begin to write critical histories incorporating choices of this kind.

The Challenge of New Histories

It is sometimes said of examples of critical, oppositional history—whether written from a subalternist, feminist, or minority position—that "this is not history." What in fact does such an assertion mean? The enterprise of writing History in the singular, with a singular collective subject, arose in tandem with the need to give nations (or, more broadly, modern states) a past. The denial of this exclusive subject position to the already constituted nation or political community amounts to a denial of this singular History. That seems to me to be the crux of the issue regarding nonstatist constructions of the past and the common ground of the proposition that these are "not history." The insistence on staying with long-established overarching categories and wider questions of history follows from this.

Irfan Habib and K. N. Panikkar, whom I quoted earlier in this chapter, and other nationalist historians of India, are not alone in their objection to the fragmentation of the object of historical investigation. It was Lawrence Stone who coined the phrase the "big why questions," and restated the need for continued attention to them in an essay entitled "The Revival of Narrative: Reflections on a New Old History."[26] In his comment on this essay, the noted Marxist historian Eric Hobsbawm scarcely understated the call to investigate the larger questions, although he disagreed with much else that Stone had to say on the subject of recent historical writings.[27] In *The Past Is a Foreign Country* (1985), David Lowenthal made the same kind of argument against recent trends in history writing, citing Stone with approval in a footnote. He noted how the "once-popular broad sweep over entire cultures or nations" was now "condemned as egregiously simplistic," and that many historians went on to "scrutinize particular institutions and arenas circumscribed in time and space." Unfortunately, he added, "The focus is sometimes so narrow that 'case studies' seem eccentric rather than characteristic; failing to relate the lives and events they treat to larger trends, they further fragment knowledge of the past."[28]

More than the fear of the break-up of recognized nation-states, or societies, or cultures, motivates this criticism (not to say denunciation) of new kinds of investigation on the part of so many established historians. There is also a fear of fracturing the certainty of knowledge as it has been produced and accepted for a long time now. Joan Scott made the point a decade ago that history departments in the United States "regularly" refused to consider for positions in American history "scholars who write on women or African Americans (or homosexuals, or other particular groups), arguing that they are not generalists, unlike those who are no less specialists but have written about national elections or politicians' lives—subjects that are taken to stand for what the whole discipline is about."[29]

I suggest that the same kind of assumptions regarding "what the whole discipline is about" lie behind the objections of Habib, Panikkar, Stone, and others. What inspires their defense of old history is the comforting familiarity of fixed objects of investigation, established methods of research and writing, and known courses of history, all underwritten by the liberal assumption of inexorable linear progress toward nationhood and modernity. By contrast with this condensed, or elaborated, study of the already constituted object of inquiry, through a microscope or a telescope, what one needs is an investigation that sets out to uncover the cracks in the historical narratives presented to us and thereby recover the contested terrain of history, the uncertainty of other presents—now our past.

In an essay entitled "The Small Voice of History," Ranajit Guha draws attention to, inter alia, the "small voices" of the sick in nineteenth-century rural Bengal—stutters (in my phrase) that historians have consistently failed to hear, although they are present even in the official records so widely used by the profession. Guha quotes from various petitions submitted to those in positions of authority by the poor and sick to make the point that, to them, "absolution was . . . as important as cure." Abhoy Mandal of Momrejpur, deemed "polluted" by the asthmatic attacks suffered by his mother-in-law, submitted himself for expiation to the local council of priests: "I am utterly destitute; would the revered gentlemen be kind enough to issue a prescription that is commensurate to my misery?" Panchanan Manna, suffering from anal cancer, pleaded before the parallel authority in his home village of Chhotobainan: "I am very poor; I shall submit myself to the purificatory rites of course; please prescribe something suitable for a pauper."[30]

"Are we to allow these plaintive voices to be drowned in the din of a statist historiography?" the author inquires. "What kind of a history of our people would that make" which turns a deaf ear to these cries for absolution, and concentrates—as historians' history has usually done in such instances—solely on the fact of educational or economic deprivation? Who is it who nominates an event or a deed, or statements that speak of these events or deeds, as historical in the first place? Guha asks in the same paper. "It should be obvious," he says, "that in most cases the nominating authority is none other than an ideology for which the life of the state is all there is to history."[31]

"The right to speak," Veena Das writes in another context, "has been appropriated by the state." This has not been accomplished by coercive police action alone, but also by the state's exercise of a paternalist, benevolent function.[32] The privileged discourse of modern times has been the discourse of the expert—the social worker, the judge, the medical scientist, the historian. Their authority and the province of their expertise has expanded over the last two centuries, at the cost of other voices and other truths that might once have been heard.

Changes have occurred even in the practice of the experts. Contemporary historians have come to use their sources in two very different ways: as repositories of the truth (reality), or as sites of contending histories and politics aimed at establishing the ascendancy of particular social and ideological positions.[33] The early writings in *Subaltern Studies* shared both these tendencies, for they retained a belief in some kind of ultimate truth, which the historian could uncover by peeling back the layers of elitist historiography and interpretation and delving deep into the historical records. More recent studies in this vein have been a great deal more reflexive, recognizing at once the extraordinary difficulty of recovering and representing the authentic subaltern voice.

That alternative, nonofficial, popular sources need to be tapped, that oral historians have rewritten the history of modern Africa and many other parts of the world, that the critical historian, like the ethnographer, is responsible to a large extent for creating her or his own archive goes without saying. Yet, this is the beginning rather than the end of the matter. The question is how these alternative sources, or fragments, as I have called them—and the fragments to be found in better known and well-exploited official sources—are to stand up to the authority of the proclamations of the state. And, again, whether they can be tamed and made part of a consistent, coherent narrative—and if so, how.

I have already made the point that the fragment in this usage is not just a bit, the dictionary's "piece broken off" from a preconstituted whole. Rather, it is a disturbing element, a disturbance, a rupture, shall we say, in the self-representation of particular totalities and those who uncritically uphold them. The mark of the fragment is that it resists the whole (the narrative). It cannot be assimilated into the narrative and its claims to wholeness. It speaks to us of what *cannot* be written of the whole (and indeed of the fragment), and in that sense becomes symptomatic of a particular claim to wholeness or completeness.

The appeal to the fragment is thus a call to interrogate the historical construction of the totalities we work with, the contradictions that survive within them, the possibilities they appear to fulfill, and the possibilities they suppress at the same time: in a word, the fragility and instability of the subjects (and the overarching categories) of history.

As modern individuals and scientific historians, we are uncomfortable with the truncated narratives and undisciplined fragments of subaltern history. We seek to appropriate and unify them in fully connected, neatly fashioned historical accounts, without any jagged edges if possible. In the monopolizing authority we claim for these accounts, however, we only perpetuate the standpoint and privilege of those in power.

I could have called this chapter "Writing in the Margins." Perhaps, at some points, that is the best we can do. Writing *from* the margins becomes a possibility, it seems to me, only when the margins can lay claim to the (or *a*) center. As critical historians, and concerned citizens, what we might wish to learn from the history of the subaltern, the unprivileged and the marginalized, is that the hope of science lies in responding to our inadequacies—or, as Gramsci would say, in the struggle itself—and not in the production of infallible truths.

4

Monumental History

The last two decades have seen the emergence of a powerful right-wing Hindu movement in India, built around an insistence on the *truth* of a national culture and a national monument. The culture in question is that of a Hindu India, the monument a disused sixteenth-century mosque in Ayodhya, a small town in the north Indian province of Uttar Pradesh. Between 1986 and 1992, when the mosque was torn down by a huge gathering of Hindu militants yelling victory to their gods and their nation, the Babari Masjid in Ayodhya (Babar's mosque, allegedly built at the instance of the first Mughal king in 1528) was the symbolic center of a movement to liberate India by reclaiming the alleged birthplace of the popular deity Ram, which was said to be at the precise spot occupied by the mosque.

The battle over the site has become quieter since then, but it is hardly finished. The issue continues to fester; it comes to the fore periodically, threatening to set off (or actually, as in Gujarat in early 2002, becoming the occasion for) new rounds of open violence against Muslims. The tension increases whenever the date approaches for a crucial hearing or pronouncement in the extended court cases regarding the disputed site, and before critical elections. Looming over all this is the question of what constitutes the national culture, how this is to be defined, and by whom.

The conflict over the Babari Masjid in Ayodhya is part of a larger Hindu drive to reclaim the national culture from its enemies—Muslims, but also secularists and westernizers. This war over culture has been waged at numerous sites in recent years—in the cinema, where nudity and lesbianism (and other professedly non-Indian practices) are banned; in modern art, where a renowned Muslim painter has been targeted for his semiclad representations of Saraswati, the goddess of learning (although Hindu goddesses have been represented nude or semi-nude in temple sculpture and cave paintings for a millennium);[1] in educational institutions, on public buses, and on the streets, where women have on occasion been attacked for dressing in jeans and skirts or comporting themselves in other Western (that is to say, untraditional) ways; in history textbooks, the writers of which are asked to underline the great achievements of the Hindu past, and to recognize "the indigenous origins of the Aryans" (i.e., that the Hindus, unlike Muslims, Christians, and other so-called migrants, always belonged to this land); and so on.

This renewed attempt by the Hindu Right to reclaim the cultural and political center of India was provoked by changes in the electoral situation, which led different parties to redefine the nation in an attempt to forge a new alliance capable of delivering victory at the polls. With the collapse of the old Brahman/Dalit/Muslim (upper-caste/untouchable/minority) coalition that had brought the Congress back to power for a long period, social democratic parties of leftist inclination sought to build a rainbow coalition of lower castes and minorities (who, together with the Dalits, or ex-untouchables, constitute an overwhelming majority of the population) around an increasingly prosperous and politically assertive group of rich peasant castes.

The more conservative and upper-caste right wing turned instead to rebuilding the nation in a more pronounced Hindu mold. This was represented by the leading Hindu political party, the Bharatiya Janata Party (BJP), and associated cultural and political organizations, such as the Rashtriya Svayam Sevak Sangh (or RSS), the Vishwa Hindu Parishad (or World Hindu Council, VHP), and the Bombay-based Shiv Sena. Many of these organizations had well-organized militias or storm troopers, which played a leading part in the assault on the Babari Masjid and on other antinational cultural symbols. This Hindu movement benefited from the open or tacit support of elements of the old Congress Party, including several Congress governments in the 1980s and 1990s, in part motivated by the same kind of electoral calculations.

Much of the struggle over new political constituencies and the definition of the *real* India has taken the form of a struggle over history. The resurgent Hindu movement of the last twenty years has actively advanced what it sees as a new, alternative history of India, one that is said to be in tune with the unique character and traditions of the people. Its historians have warned against "distorted" and "un-Indian" interpretations of the past served up by "pseudo-secularist" historians. A leading Hindu spokesperson and newspaper editor argued, for example, that "the Indian elite"— including professional archaeologists and historians, but curiously excluding himself—"has a special fondness for abstract principles divorced from social, economic and political realities." By contrast, he declared, Hindu historiography chooses to emphasize "concrete" historical circumstances and "ground realities."[2] This is the kind of assertion commonly made by right-wing movements claiming to represent the "sons of the soil," and it requires closer scrutiny.

The extremist Hindu argument is very well illustrated in the new Hindu history of Ayodhya. Indeed, this history may serve as a shorthand for the renewed political and cultural assertiveness of Hindu propagandists. It is a history that seeks to establish a new historiographical orthodoxy in India, a new chronology of Hindu-Muslim military contests in the subcontinent, and underlying this, a renewed belief in the inevitability of such contests, given the character of the people on the two sides. An outline of some of the main points of dispute in the controversy regarding the real history of Ayodhya is provided in an appendix to this chapter. What I want to do here is to analyze the procedures of this brand of history writing, in order to unravel something of its organizing principles, the subject positions it affirms, and the notions of time that it works with. Through this exercise, it may be possible to arrive at a somewhat better appreciation of the relation of this history to the modern, statist histories that it so vociferously condemns, and to say something about its efficacy too.[3]

The Hindu History of Ayodhya

Pamphlets containing a condensed version of the Hindu history of Ayodhya have been published in large numbers since the mid-1980s. Perhaps the first thing that would strike the academic investigator about this history is its pulp quality. Sold (or distributed) by Hindu right-wing enthusiasts and sympathizers in Ayodhya and elsewhere, along with audio-cassettes, badges, posters, images of gods and goddesses, other memorabilia, moral tales, and books of common prayer or devotional songs, the pamphlets—produced in very cheap and short-lived editions, crudely written, and poorly printed on rough paper—seem scarcely worthy of notice. Only the power of the political movement with which they are associated and which they project and reinforce has drawn social analysts' attention to them.

The next observation that one might make, if one has bothered to collect and examine a number of these histories over the years, is that they are remarkably repetitive: so much so that they are hard to read with the best will in the world. Having looked at one or two, one is persuaded (perhaps rightly) that there is no need to look at any more. Their repetitiveness is marked. Later publications are often no more than quick copies of earlier productions with minor variations; individual articles follow the same pattern. The uniformity and the repetitiveness start with the very titles of these productions. Here are five titles:

Shri Ram Janmabhumi: Sachitra, Pramanik Itihasa (An Illustrated and Authoritative History of Shri Ram Janmabhumi), Ayodhya 1986. The booklet itself provides the translation "An Illustrated and Authentic History," and the authenticity is underlined by the announcement that the author has an M.A. and Ph.D. in archaeology and history.

Shri Ram Janmabhumi ka Pramanik Itihasa (The Authoritative/Authentic History of Shri Ram Janmabhumi), date and place of publication not given.

Shri Ram Janmabhumi ka tala kaise khula: Shri Ram Janmabhumi ka Romanchkari Itihasa (How the Locks [placed on the gates of the Babari Masjid/Ram Janmabhumi complex in 1949] Were Opened: The Horripilating History of Shri Ram Janmabhumi), Ayodhya, n.d.

Shri Ram Janmabhumi ka Rakt Ranjit Itihasa: Tala kaise khula? (The Blood-Stained History of Shri Ram Janmabhumi: How the Gates Were Unlocked), Ayodhya, n.d.

Mukti Yagya: Shri Ram Janmabhumi ka Sampurna Itihasa (Sacrifice for Liberation: The Entire History of Shri Ram Janmabhumi), Ayodhya, 1991.

The sequence of events (or chronology) that provides the core of these works is also noteworthy for its marked repetitiveness. This chronology is as follows, with only slight variations of dates and numbers in different accounts:

1. 900,000 years ago—Birth of Ram and hence of Ram Janmabhumi (RJB).

2. 150 years B.C.E. (Greek and Kushana times)—Battle to liberate RJB.

3. 100 years B.C.E.—Vikramaditya's rediscovery of RJB, and construction of grand RJB temple.

4. Salar Mas'ud's time—two battles to liberate RJB.

5. Babar's reign—Destruction of temple, construction of mosque; four battles to liberate RJB.

6. Humayun's reign—ten battles to liberate RJB.

7. Akbar's reign—twenty battles to liberate RJB.

8. Aurangzeb's reign—thirty battles to liberate RJB.

9. Sa'adat Ali of Avadh's reign—five battles to liberate RJB.

10. Nasiruddin Haidar's reign—three battles to liberate RJB.

11. Wajid Ali Shah's reign—two battles to liberate RJB.

12. 1857—Attempted compromise between Hindus and Muslims over RJB (thwarted by British machinations).

13. British rule (1912 and 1934)—two battles to liberate RJB.

14. December 1949—Appearance of Ram (in the form of the infant Ramlala), and installation of images of Ramlala inside the mosque. Building locked by administrative order to maintain the peace.

15. 1986—Opening of locks on Babari Masjid/RJB temple.[4]

Note that this chronology, based on one of the earliest in the new series of Hindu histories of Ayodhya, a text explicitly acknowledged as the source of some of the later accounts, gives a total of seventy-nine battles fought by the Hindus for the liberation of the Ram Janmabhumi. The magic number was, however, subsequently fixed at seventy-six, which is the number of battles supposedly fought since the time of the Mughals, with whom the history of Muslims in India is readily equated. The battle for the liberation of the RJB that was launched in the mid-1980s was, therefore, always referred to as the seventy-seventh.

The purpose of this history is to enumerate the many occasions when the Hindus are supposed to have risen in defense of the Janmabhumi, and to catalogue their enormous sacrifices. The opening pages of another early publication in this series, *Ham Mandir Vahin Banayenge*, make the point explicitly.[5] The first chapter begins with the heading "*Lakhon shish chadhe jis thaon: Shri Ram Janmabhumi ka itihasa—Amar balidan gatha*" (Where *Lakhs* of Lives Were Offered Up: The History of Shri Ram Janmabhumi— A Saga of Eternal Sacrifice).[6] Above the title on the title page is a note that seventy-seven battles have been waged and three hundred thousand lives sacrificed by the Hindus for the protection and liberation of the Ram Janmabhumi *temple*.

The initial paragraphs of the volume set the tone of the narrative that follows. After a statement on the antiquity of the town of Ayodhya, the text continues:

Foreign aggressions on Ayodhya also have a very ancient history. The first aggressor was the . . . notorious King of Lanka, Ravana, who destroyed Ayodhya during the time of the ancestors of Shri Ram. Ravana's death, along with his entire family, at the hands of Shri Ram is a story known all over the world.[7]

In history, the second external attack upon Ayodhya was by the Greek king Milind or Mihirgupta (Menander), who was the first aggressor to have destroyed the Shri Ram Janmabhumi temple. But Indian pride arose to punish this irreligious foreigner for his evil deed [*dus-sahasa*; lit., "misguided or foolish bravery"], and within three months Raja Dyumatsena of the Sunga dynasty had killed Milind in a fierce war and again liberated Ayodhya.

The third aggressor to attack Ayodhya was Salar Masud, a nephew of the notorious Muslim plunderer, Mahmud Ghaznavi. Destroying temples as he went along, Masud reached [the environs of] Ayodhya and destroyed temples in the vicinity. But the united strength of the Rajas of Ayodhya and the surrounding areas and the attacks of the *sadhus* of the Digambari *akhada* prevented his conquering army from entering Ayodhya. He then moved to the north, but in 1033 A.D., 17 local Rajas led by Raja Suhail Dev surrounded that beastly irreligious tyrannical plunderer . . . in Bahraich, and sent the entire invading army to their graves. After this, all of Mahmud and Masud's successors were also beaten and driven from the country.

The next plunderer who attacked Ayodhya with the object of destroying the Shri Ram Janmabhumi temple was Babar. . . . This ungrateful plunderer [who had been given refuge, food, and shelter by people in various parts of India] responded to India's native tolerance and hospitality by ordering his Commander-in-Chief, Mir Baqi, to destroy the huge, palatial Shri Ram Janmabhumi temple that had stood in Ayodhya since Vikramaditya's time, in order to simply please two evil Muslim *faqirs*. But, the people [the country] rose in fierce opposition to this vile attack on their national honour. The historian Cunningham writes,[8] "At the time of the destruction of the Janmabhumi temple the Hindus sacrificed every thing and it was only after 1 *lakh*, 74 thousand Hindu lives had been lost that Mir Baqi succeeded in bringing down the temple with his cannons."[9]

Through the many recensions of the Hindu history of Ayodhya, this story of foreign aggression and native valor, of eternal Hindu activism and sacrifice is endlessly repeated. Context—the very heart of the historian's discipline, one might argue—counts for nothing. I will return to this point; for the moment, let me draw attention to two other evident features of this Hindu history.

One is the importance of numbers. Numbers are crucial here, and not only for their suggestion of statistical accuracy and historical precision: seventy-six (or seventy-seven or seventy-nine, as the case may be) battles fought for the liberation of the RJB; the seven hundred soldiers of Babar's army that Devi Din Pandey accounted for with his sword alone and in the face of a constant rain of bullets in just three hours (which, according to the Hindu account, Babar himself confirms); and, finally, in describing Devi Din's inevitable offering of his own life in this process: "On 9 June 1528 A.D., at 2:00 P.M., Pandit Devi Din Pandey breathed his last." The precision of these numbers, dates, and times, for an age in which the surviving historical records give us precious little information of this kind, represents the excess that characterizes all nationalist narratives. In the same vein, we have the 174,000 Hindu lives sacrificed before Mir Baqi was able to bring down the temple; the hundreds of monkeys who attacked the Mughal camp one day during the same period, engaged the soldiers in battle for several hours, and silenced their guns and cannons; the ten thousand tong-wielding (*chimta-dhari*) *sadhus* who defeated Aurangzeb's army "with their tongs alone"; or, to combine a nonnumerical example with a numerical one, the "indescribably beautiful" Rani Jairaj Kumari, who formed a band of several hundred (or several thousand) female guerrillas to attack the Ram Janmabhumi on numerous occasions during the reigns of Babar, Humayan, and Akbar.

Numbers are important, too, in fixing the boundaries of the (unchanging) community (or nation)—of us and them. A pamphlet entitled *Angry Hindu? Yes, Why Not?* puts it as follows: "I [the Hindus personified] form eighty-five percent of this land: why should I be denied my rights?" The Hindu is these hundreds of millions of people—of one opinion and one vision. As *Ham Mandir Vahin Banayenge* has it, in a note that appears at the top of the title page, that title itself ("We shall build the temple *there*") is the pledge, determination, and vision (*sankalp*) of "the 700 million Hindus of the entire world."

A final feature of Hindu histories that deserves notice is their straddling of the worlds of religious and historical discourse. As I have mentioned, these histories are sold (or distributed) at pilgrim sites, along with images of deities, religious calendars, prayer books, and the like, and are bought perhaps as often for the decoration of a household shrine or prayer room as for reading individually or in groups. They are prefaced or headed frequently by an Om, a *mantra*, or a longer prayer to Shri Ram. They begin in the age of Ram, over nine hundred thousand years ago, and they are marked by an easy (and, in a sense, unceasing) intervention of the divine or, to put it in other terms, a realization of the ineffable that lies behind the illusions of this fleeting world.

Thus, to begin with the most recent examples, Hindu history tells us of the miraculous appearance of the infant Ramlala inside the Babari Masjid on a cold December night in 1949, attested to (in the Hindu account) by the Muslim policeman who was there on guard duty. We also have Ram, "unable to bear the suffering of his *bhaktas* (devotees) any longer," intervening through a local lawyer and a local magistrate in Faizabad to have the locks on the mosque/temple opened in 1986. There is supposed to be evidence of divine intervention again in November 1990, when a number of *kar sevaks* "miraculously" scaled the Babari Masjid and attained the tops of the domes in a matter of moments (a feat, we are told, that took the trained commandos at the site, with all their equipment, over half an hour to accomplish). There is talk also of a large monkey that sat for a long time on top of the central dome with the *bhagwa dhwaj* (saffron flag, emblem of the Hindu movement) in "his" hands: veritably, it is claimed, this was the monkey god, the greatest *Rambhakta* (devotee) of all, Hanuman himself.

The sequence of divine intervention began, of course, a long, long time ago. In historical times, its first startling manifestation occurs at the time of Emperor Vikramaditya, who rediscovered Ram Janmabhumi. As this Hindu account has it, a tired Vikramaditya, accidentally separated from his companions, was resting by the river Saryu to catch his breath when he saw a handsome black prince, dressed in black from head to toe and mounted on a black horse, enter the river. When the horse and rider came out again a few moments later, an amazing transformation had taken place: the prince's mount, his clothes, his face were all now shining white.

Overwhelmed, Vikramaditya approached the strange prince and asked him to explain the meaning of this vision. The prince explained: "I am Tirtharaj Prayag [the pilgrimage center, Prayag or Allahabad, personified]. Every year [at a prescribed time] I come with the countless sins I have taken onto myself from the millions of pilgrims who come to cleanse their sins at Prayag, and these are washed away by the Saryu." In this tale, therefore, the Saryu river in Ayodhya becomes even more efficacious than the confluence of the Ganga and the Jamuna at Allahabad as a site of pilgrimage, a place for cleansing one's sins, and a step to salvation. Asked for further advice and guidance, Tirtharaj Prayag tells Vikramaditya to reestablish the Ram Janmabhumi. Aided by signs and measurements given to him by Tirtharaj, Vikramaditya rediscovers Ayodhya, establishes the exact site of the Janmabhumi by setting free a cow newly delivered of a calf (milk begins to flow from her udders as soon as she reaches the sacred spot), and builds there a grand temple on eighty-four pillars of black touchstone.

The subsequent history of the Ram Janmabhumi is in line with this half-human half-divine, "neither-this-nor-that" scenario—as indeed it has to be at the earthly birthplace of God. The point is illustrated dramatically by the difficulties allegedly experienced by Babar in converting the temple into a mosque. After Babar had overcome the Hindus in a long and furious battle, in which the Mughal forces were beaten back time and again, he left Ayodhya, instructing his lieutenant, Mir Baqi Khan of Tashkent, to build a mosque on the site of the temple using the materials of the temple. However, this proved to be no easy task. "The walls that were built during the day came down [as if by miracle] at night," and this continued to happen day after day, until Mir Baqi in despair urged Babar to return and see things for himself.

Babar returned and, seeing his people utterly frustrated, resorted to a consultation with the local *sadhus* (Hindu ascetics or holy men). He was then forced to accept a compromise that the *sadhus* offered as a way out of the situation. The *sadhus* said that Hanuman opposed the construction of the mosque, and no building could occur until he was won over. In the end, as (according to our Hindu historians) Babar himself has written in his memoirs, the Hindus laid down five conditions: "The *masjid* was to be called 'Sita Pak' [Sita's *rasoi*, or kitchen]. A space had to be preserved for circumambulation around the central structure [*parikrama*]. A wooden door was to be erected at the main entrance. The turrets/spires were to be brought down. And Hindu *mahatmas* [religious leaders] were to be allowed to conduct their prayers and recitations [from the Hindu scriptures]." Every one of these conditions negated the concept of a mosque, according to the Hindu account. Thus, it was not the Hindus but Babar who ultimately surrendered. Even in the form of a mosque, the RJB remained a temple. Even in defeat the Hindus were (as, implicitly, they always will be) victorious.

The Subject and Object of Hindu History

I have suggested that a sense of eternal (and united) Hindu activism and sacrifice, of numbers (which testify again to Hindu strength), and of a divine play or order (once again revealing the power of the Hindu) actuates this right-wing reconstruction of the past. Its extraordinary emphasis on hard facts—what one might call materiality or palpability—should also be noticed.

The Hindu history of Ayodhya, in all its recent versions, is not about the region, much less the people, of Ayodhya. It is not even about a spot now claimed as the Ram Janmabhumi; it is about a building on that spot. This entire history is focused on a monument: the grand temple built (and rebuilt) on the site of Shri Ram's birth. Consider the opening paragraph of Ramgopal Pandey Sharad's *Shri Ram Janmabhumi ka Romanchkari Itihasa* (The Thrilling History of Shri Ram Janmabhumi):

[Nine hundred thousand] years ago, the supreme ideal of manhood, Lord Shri Ramchandraji, took on his earthly incarnation in precisely this hallowed land/area. He rolled in the pure dust of this sacred spot . . . and, along with Bharat, Lakshman and Shatrughanji, thus enacted his rare and divine childhood. The Hindu rulers who graced the throne of India [Bharat] many centuries before Christ defended it all along. [Note this unheralded first reference to the site of Ram's birth, the Ram Janmabhumi, as a monument.] They repaired it from time to time, but at the time of the Kiratas and the Huna invasions, they turned their attention away from the site. As a result, the ancient temple [the first mention of this] was destroyed and no trace of it remained. In the end, a century or so before Christ, the shining light of the Hindu family, Emperor Vikramaditya, rediscovered the site after great effort and constructed a grand temple at the sacred spot.[10]

There is much to be said about the ease with which this paragraph moves from the alleged birth of Ram, nine hundred thousand years ago in the Treta Yuga, to the Hindu kings who graced "the throne of India" in the centuries before Christ, to the destruction of what may well be described as an eternal, not just an ancient, temple (for its construction is nowhere talked about), to the rediscovery of the site and the construction of another grand temple by Vikramaditya, a king who has still to be satisfactorily identified. But the point I wish to underscore is the centrality of the temple even when it is mentioned, as it were, in passing.

The Hindu history of Ayodhya revolves around this monument. The narrative begins with the destruction of the monument, and returns to this issue again and again. Two paragraphs, which appear as a preface in one edition of *Shri Ram Janmabhumi ka Romanchkari Itihasa* and a postscript in another, illustrate the point very well. The first paragraph, headed "The Hindu Signs at the Janmabhumi," begins: "Several Hindu features remained when the temple was demolished and given the form of a mosque: these are features that Babar was forced to retain because the walls [of the proposed mosque] kept falling down on their own."

The second, headed "The Pillars of Black Touch-Stone," reads as follows:

The ancient Shri Ram temple was built on 84 black touch-stone pillars. These had been constructed by King Aranya of the . . . Surya dynasty. Ravana defeated Aranya in battle and carried the pillars away [to Lanka], from where they were brought back to Ayodhya by Shri Ram after his victory over Ravana. . . . The [Babari] *masjid* was built upon these very pillars, upon which the aforesaid images [of Hindu gods and goddesses] can still be seen, along with inscriptions of Maharaja Aranya, Ravana and Lord Shri Ram on some pillars. Of the 84 black touch-stone pillars, 11 are in the Babari Masjid, 2 at the entrance to the *mandir* [i.e., the same *masjid*] and [another two?] at the [nearby] grave of Kajal Abbas [one of the Muslim fakirs said to have incited Babar to demolish the Ram Janmabhumi temple], and some are added to the glories of the museums in Lucknow, Faizabad and London.

What follows in all the accounts published in the 1980s and 1990s is a longer or shorter description of one battle after another fought by the Hindus to liberate the site, remove the mosque, and rebuild the grand temple: seventy-six battles before the current one, which is the seventy-seventh. The monument, one might say, is the history.

This marks a significant change from earlier histories of the Ram Janmabhumi, the Krishna Janmabhumi, and so on, examples of which may still be found in Mathura.[11] Here, at the site of the claimed Krishna Janmabhumi (the birthplace of the Lord Krishna), the pulp histories on sale concentrate on the life of Shri Krishna, and stories of his exploits as a child and an adult are presented alongside a bland account of the several temples built at nearby sites, the destruction by the Mughal emperor Aurangzeb of the last grand temple, and the establishment of organizations to promote the worship of Krishna in Mathura and improve facilities for pilgrims, Indian and foreign.

Traces of a somewhat more open and tentative history of Ayodhya may also be found in some of the earlier publications associated with the latest round of Hindu agitation for the liberation of the Ram Janmabhumi. Some of these begin with descriptions of the grandeur of the "ancient city," as presented in Valmiki's *Ramayana*, for example, and acknowledge the gaps in our knowledge of this history: the difficulty of establishing who the Vikramaditya of tradition was and how he rediscovered Ayodhya; the fact that Ayodhya was built many times and many times fell into ruin; and the long periods when the city had little habitation or activity (even down to the so-called Muslim period).

No such tentativeness or uncertainty is to be found in the mature Hindu history contained in works like the *Romanchkari, Rakt-ranjit,* or *Sampurna Itihasa* mentioned above. The eighty-four black stone pillars, straddling the world from the age of Ram (and even earlier) to the age of colonial and postcolonial museums, capture the spirit of this history as it is evoked by the recent Hindu historians of Ayodhya: its antiquity, its beauty and solidity, its destruction, and its continued existence.

It goes without saying that the eighty-four pillars stand for much more than a town called Ayodhya: they stand for the Ram Janmabhumi, Hinduism, the Hindu spirit and culture, the Hindu people, and the Indian nation. Ayodhya—or should we say, the black stone pillars—are a symbol (*pratik*) of the eternal, undefeated (*Ayodhya* literally means "that which cannot be defeated") Hindu nation. The new Hindu history refers constantly to the religious and national spirit of the Hindus of Ayodhya, ever engaged in battle against the "irreligious, foreign invader"; the "Hindu kings who graced the throne of India [Bharat] in the centuries [even millennia] before Christ"; the united struggle of kings, *sadhus,* and the common people (Hindus) against any insult to the national honor—referring almost always to the Ram Janmabhumi.

Remarkably, however, this history of Ayodhya, which I suggest also stands for the history of India, is not about the *construction* of the Ram Janmabhumi temple. It is about its *destruction.* To that extent, it is a history not of the temple but of the mosque built upon its ruins, not of the greatness of the Hindu but of the wickedness of the Muslim.

It is notable that the construction of the most ancient of the series of temples that is supposed to have occupied the site of the Ram Janmabhumi is not mentioned. Its existence is already given at the beginning of these histories (however many millennia ago). Nor is the construction of Vikramaditya's later but equally grand temple ever detailed; only his rediscovery of the site is. What is spelled out in detail is the act of destruction: how long it took, at whose hands it occurred, the subterfuge and sweat that were necessary for the destruction, and the features of the temple that were, nevertheless, left standing.

Even more significantly, the number of battles fought for the liberation of the Janmabhumi is fixed at seventy-six: the number of battles allegedly fought for the liberation of the site since the time of Babar. The battles fought before Babar's time and listed by some early Hindu historians, including the two battles supposedly waged to fend off the invasion of Salar Mas'ud Ghazi, do not count, for this is in fact a *history of the mosque* and attempts to obliterate it. It is no accident, then, that so many of these histories begin their account of the history of Ayodhya with a statement of the Hindu signs still to be found in the mosque (before its destruction), or that the volume entitled *Shri Ram Janmabhumi ka Sampurna Itihasa* (The Entire History of the Shri Ram Janmabhumi) should add on its inside cover "from 1528 A.D. [that is, the date when the Babari Masjid is supposed to have been constructed] to today."

If the monument constitutes the history of Ayodhya/India, and the monument was in fact a mosque, it follows that the Hindu account is very close indeed to the colonial account of the Indian past. As in the colonial account, Hindu and Muslim here are fully constituted from the start, and all of Indian history for centuries prior to the coming of the British becomes a history of perennial Hindu-Muslim conflict. The differences are minor, but noteworthy. What were "riots," "convulsions," or "symptoms of a disease" for colonialist writers are "wars" for the Hindu historian (though it must be noted that many colonialists too were happy enough to describe Hindu-Muslim conflicts as religious or national wars). Wars have their heroes and villains, and Hindu history quickly runs up a long list of Hindu heroes and Muslim villains (joined only occasionally by Hindu villains), whereas for colonialist historiography, Hindus and Muslims were commonly villains (or at any rate simpletons) with rare exceptions.

Another difference follows from the preconstituted character of the Muslims as congenitally evil and the Hindus as tolerant, hospitable, liberal, and—in an extension of colonial stereotypes that would have been unacceptable to the colonialist—part of the divine. Curiously, given the all-embracing character of Hindu philosophy, this modest status of being a small part of infinity is not accorded to the Muslim. Rather, the Muslim, "foreigner," "invader," and "irreligious being," who may be seen as scheming, greedy, lustful, and bigoted, is fully to be blamed for his actions (women figure, on both Hindu and Muslim sides, merely as property; extraordinary cases, like that of Rani Jairaj Kumari, are after all extraordinary). The Hindus, on the other hand—kings, landlords, *sadhus*, and even ordinary villagers—since they are all part of the divine, only serve a divine purpose and are, in that sense, not responsible for their actions. It is in that sense, too, I suggest, that they can never be defeated, according to the canons of Hindu history.

The remarkably different subject positions occupied by Hindu and Muslim point to the vexed interpenetration of different orders of time, indeed different domains of history, that take place in the Hindu account. The construction of the original Ram Janmabhumi temple and its destruction represent the quintessence of these different orders and different histories, the divine and the mundane.

From the time of Shri Ram (and even earlier), which can scarcely be described, which is beyond human time, to the ossified exhibits of colonial and postcolonial museums, divine time runs into historical (and archaeological) time. Hindu history is quite untroubled by this colossal chronological span, or by the huge gaps in it—for example, between (1) and (2) in the chronological table set out in the early part of this chapter; or, on an altered, modern historical time scale, between (3) and (4); or, in the greatly accelerated chronological arrangements of contemporary history, between (13) and (14).

There is a timeless, epic quality to this history in its proposition of beginnings that are not beginnings, destruction that is not destruction; in the circular character of the narrative, which returns to the same point again and again, and in which nothing changes; and in its suggestion that those participating in the liberation war against Babar (or against pseudosecularists today) are one with those who joined the war against Ravana, the demon-king of the ancient epic of Ram. The account atemporalizes events. Even the enumeration of battles fails to change this aspect of the narration. While enumeration usually implies linearity, the enumeration here has no such logic attached to it. It might be random or entirely self-contained, and it does not necessarily grow. The seventy-six battles do not build up to different ends, not even somewhat different ends, but are in the end all the same.

The curious mixture of cyclical time and instrumentality found in these accounts has the structure of a rudimentary fable, where all events ultimately point one way. The collision of times is striking. Remote, golden, happy; overturned by a mythic cycle of bloodletting, savagery, and valor; disrupted into linearity once again by the possibility of an end today. Mythic time schemes appear to leak into positive, historical, realist time. Marked by what Koseleck has called "the self-accelerating temporality of the modern,"[12] epic time seems to turn back upon itself in the demand for a final resolution *now*.

The Muslim invasion (equated frequently in both Hindu and colonialist historiography with the rule of the Great Mughals, and here dated to 1528, for Babar's attack on the Ram Janmabhumi is the central motif) and Indian independence (the appearance of Ramlala in 1949 is taken as a sign of this) are the two precisely dated historical events around which the discourse of the Hindu history of Ayodhya and the accompanying political campaign turns. At one pole is Babar, the foreigner and invader, and with him all Indian Muslims, the progeny of that invader (*Babar ki aulad*) and a blot on India's history (not unlike the Babari Masjid). At the other end, this history is animated by the "continued slavery" of India (and especially of India's Westernized ruling class) even forty years after formal independence, which does not allow us (the Hindus—that is, the nation) to build a temple at this, our most sacred site, in our own country—the "only Hindu country in the world" (Nepal, of course, becomes part of the larger, natural India here). Eternal, epic conflict between the gods and the demons there has long been at the Ram Janmabhumi, but final victory, it appears, is now at hand. Seven hundred million Hindus have awakened, and they will build the temple at precisely that spot, with their own hands, today.

In the end, then, this account belies its pretensions to epic status. If the epic tradition is distinguished by the absence of beginnings, middles, and ends, and of unidirectionality, by the refusal to privilege a single point of view, by the problematizing of the good and the bad, then Hindu history departs radically from it. In many senses, it is closer to the worst kind of realist melodrama, where Good is Good and Evil is Evil, a thief is a thief, and that's all there is to that.

Hindu history seems to be very far removed, too, from the kind of antistatist history that it claims to be, giving voice to society and community. Let me make the point by quick reference to a local nineteenth-century history of a weaving center in northern India, in which, as in the Hindu history of Ayodhya, the community is the subject of history and community honor the object of analysis.[13] The differences between the two accounts are very striking indeed. In the case of the weaving *qasba*, although the local community is valorized, it has no firmly fixed boundaries. Rather, the notion of the community attaches itself to different collectivities and has several different meanings, depending on context. In Hindu history, by contrast, the subject and object of analysis is a clearly enumerated community (as emphatically in the case of the Hindu as in that of the Muslim), with boundaries that appear fixed from the beginning of time. In that sense, it has no history. This Hindu community can realize itself in only one way: through a return to power at the center. That has of course been the point of recent Hindu history and politics.

The Power of Assertion

Insistently, over the last two decades, Hindu propagandists have appealed to what they call the truth of the past in order to establish the truth of Hindu claims in the present. They have proffered evidence of the historical wrongs allegedly perpetrated by an undifferentiated and unchanging body called the Muslims on an equally undifferentiated and unchanging body called the Hindus. A notable result of all this has been the demonizing of religious/cultural modes and practices that depart in any way from those of the groups in power, the putative mainstream: in other words, the stigmatization of those marks of difference that allegedly constitute a threat to the nation and its culture—usually by no more than the simple fact of being different.

The immediate pretext for the Shri Ram Janmabhumi Liberation Movement (or movement for the liberation of the birthplace of the god, Shri Ram) in Ayodhya was the alleged partisanship of the secularism professed by the Indian state and by the national and provincial governments from Independence in 1947 until at least the 1980s—what Hindu propagandists now call a pseudosecularist pacification of the Muslims and other minorities. This policy of pacification of an intolerant minority was itself said to be the consequence of a much advertised Hindu tolerance that has, in the view of the new Hindu militants, been too long mistaken for cowardice and submissiveness. What followed was the call to Hindus to awake and take back their country.

There is an irony in that this call to take back the country is initiated by those who are already in power, the majority of the nation as they claim themselves to be: the Hindus. Yet this kind of "majority backlash" is hardly unique: examples of it are to be found, in one form or another, in many parts of Europe and in the United States, as well as in the economically less advanced parts of the world. We have observed that the relationship between nations and histories is closer than historians have generally been willing to acknowledge. The contest over history and the rights of nations rages on—in the advanced, capitalist North as well as in the developing or backward South—even as the death of nationhood and history is announced periodically. It is renewed time and again by a question that, far from going away, seems to be asked as insistently as ever by a growing body of right-wing opinion all over the world: "What is the real culture of this land?" which may be translated as, "Whose country is this anyway?" In response to this question, new claims are made, or (more often) old claims are refurbished and put forward in a new package.

Identity and politics in an increasingly mixed world have in many places tended to become more stridently pure. Paradoxically, the claim of purity is associated with being ancient and modern at the same time. Purity has to do with the preservation of ancient, or at any rate long-established, cultures and traditions. But it is also part of what it means to be modern. For modernizers are, in their self-image, also purifiers, by contrast with premodern peoples who lived, it is said, with a jumble of confusing and confused beliefs and practices. The modern, which is the ground that the nation (and, in India, the Hindus) occupy, appears as a place of reason, freedom, reasoned debate, and change. The premodern, which is where the Indian Muslims allegedly live, is marked by unchanging darkness and confusion.[14]

Predictably, then, the larger theoretical ground of the right-wing Hindu charge against the Muslims is linked with the question of change in crucial ways. A standard method of demonizing the other in our times is by attributing to them an inability to change, reform, or modernize and thereby assimilate to the mainstream of modernity. This is how Hindu propagandists have presented the history and culture of the Muslims of India: an unchanging, not to say primitive, community that is a drag on the country's progress. And at the same time they assert the changelessness (the eternal strength and resilience) of the national (Hindu) culture.

This history functions, and persuades many of those whom it persuades, by simple assertion. Hard facts and stunning statistics. "The heart of the matter," declares one Hindu historian, "is why the site in question [the disputed Babari Masjid site] has been known as Janmasthan as far back as we go into its history."[15] Fortunately for this historian, he does not go back very far. Otherwise he would have learned that it was nineteenth-century colonial officials who asserted that the Babari Masjid had been built on the site of a *janmasthan* temple. Into the present century, as the successors of those same officials testified, more than one old temple staked a claim to being the real *janmasthan* temple.[16] Indeed, had this historian bothered to take the trouble and travel the distance, he would have discovered that there is in Ayodhya to this day a separate *janmasthan* (spot of birth) temple, located at some distance from the site claimed as the *janmabhoomi* (land of birth), where the Hindu right wing proposes to build anew the original temple to Ram.

Assertion on the one hand, an all-too-practiced sleight of hand on the other. Let me illustrate the latter by reference to the same propagandist's comments on the recent history of Indian Islam.[17] "Indian Islam," we are informed, "underwent . . . radical change in 1965 and 1971 when the myth of superior Muslim valour was laid to rest." This must rank as an outstanding example of vacuous speculation, dependent as it is on collapsing several different levels of analysis. Yet it comes from a camp that accuses more rigorous (but "secular" and "Westernized") historians of inattention to "historical specificity" and "ground reality."

In this statement, it is not the beliefs of Indian Muslims (or, as one might more cautiously say, some Indian Muslims) that are said to have changed, not, let us say, the cockiness of an arrogant minority, but Indian Islam itself—which is, of course, taken to be but an expression of Islam in its more general form. The corrective to the Muslim psyche, which is also invoked in the analysis, is implicitly said to flow from the Hindu (not Indian) victories in the wars of 1965 and 1971. (It would be naïve to expect the Hindu historian to notice how many Muslims fought on the Indian side, not only as regular members of the Indian Army but also in the innumerable popular militias of the Bangladeshi liberation movement.)

Indian Islam had changed at an earlier juncture too, the writer proceeds. This was in 1947, when those who regarded themselves as the legatees of the Mughal empire migrated to Pakistan. Who are these legatees? Everyone from Syed Ahmad Khan to Mohammad Ali Jinnah—that is, everyone who migrated to Pakistan or "would have" had they been alive. Although, the historian concedes, Jinnah, the acknowledged leader of the Pakistan movement, came "from a very different background."

This is, of course, not only tautological, but also highly pernicious as an account. Considering backgrounds alone, we might recall just a few examples of Muslims who never accepted this change in Indian Islam by migrating to Pakistan: Maulana Abul Kalam Azad, the president of the Indian National Congress in 1947 and the first education minister of independent India; Dr. Zakir Husain, a leading educationist and later president of the country; and many Muslim theologians, including prominent members of the renowned Deoband seminary in northern India, as well as thousands of others who traced their ancestry to Arabia and were therefore no doubt legatees of the (Turko-Mongol, Iranian, Afghani) Mughal Empire. And we might remember artists like Josh Malihabadi, Ustad Bade Ghulam Ali Khan, Sajjad Zaheer, Sahir Ludhianvi, and Qurratulain-Haider, who migrated only to return, so uncertain were the meanings of home, roots, and cultural heritage in 1947. Not to mention the Muslim colleagues and friends so many of us live with, parts of whose families were forced to migrate (in consternation, distress, incomprehension), bits of whom were torn from them.[18]

However, it would do violence to the new Hindu self-image of confidence, militancy, and absolute knowledge to allow the smallest element of doubt or ambiguity to creep into the historical narrative. Historical truths that are established by assertion must be absolute truths. Such a history can appear in nothing but stark shades of white and black.

The Appeal of Hindu History

It is easy enough to mock this history for the obvious inconsistencies of time, place, and circumstance contained in it, the fallacious logic, fraudulent use of sources, and fabrication of many historical events.[19] But this is of little help in seeking to understand the extensive hold of the Hindu account. Its influence has been explained in various ways. That a powerful political movement, with massive financial and organizational resources, has been able successfully to disseminate its version of historical truth is hardly surprising, it is said. From the 1990s, right-wing Hindu parties have furthered this agenda through their control of or participation in government at the central and state levels. The argument is also made that economic misfortunes and the availability of a ready explanation—a scapegoat—for these have contributed to the popularity of this kind of history.

Although these arguments are suggestive, they are plainly inadequate. They do not begin to tell us why other powerful political movements (for example, of the Left) and other available explanations (such as the argument about rampant and growing corruption) have not aroused the same kind of emotion. They also do not seem to recognize that widespread acceptance of the Hindu version of the history of Muslims in India has contributed greatly to the new right-wing Hindu ascendancy, and not just the other way around. What are some of the factors *internal* to the practice of writing and reading history that might explain the influence of the Hindu construction?

I have outlined in the previous chapter the circumstances in which a modern nationalist historiography emerged in India, one that was broadly inclusive and self-consciously proud of the country's pluralist heritage. This historical work stressed the uniqueness of this plural society and the mutual enrichment that came from centuries of coexistence of Hindus and Muslims and Parsis and Christians and Sikhs—both unity in diversity, and syncretism.

Progressive scholars have suggested in recent years that both early nationalist and colonial historians accepted a communalist perspective in their very treatment of Hindus and Muslims as two separate communities, although one stressed rapprochement between them and the other irreconcilability.[20] Abandonment of these communal categories was therefore seen as a fundamental requirement of a new secularist outlook.' Hence many secular and Marxist historians went to considerable lengths to emphasize the primacy of the economic. In the 1960s, 1970s, and 1980s, argued one scholar in a review of the historiography of precolonial (medieval) India, there has been "a movement of the study of history of medieval India towards society's lower end, indeed towards its lowest end: a study of the actual labour processes. . . . The ecology of a region . . . the given technology . . . [the] social organization of labour utilization. . . . The very complexity of this study allows religion merely the share that is its due in social life."[21]

One may be permitted the liberty of expressing a doubt. The rigorous study of labor processes and political economy does nothing automatically to put religion in its place. It does, however, perpetuate an indifference to popular beliefs and popular consciousness. Thus the secular historian is driven by his opposition to sectarianism into an alarmingly narrow economism or (more broadly) a hard-headed rationalism. S/he calls for the study of production processes and constitutional developments in order to understand communalism. S/he brushes away religion as a false consciousness. And yet the thing lives.

In what might at first sight seem the direct opposite of this move, Hindu history poses as a history of this consciousness and of the *samaj* (society) in which it lives. It presents itself as a history of the local community, society, or nation, as against the state. It professes, in other words, to be a history that speaks in the language and voice of the people about their most deeply rooted beliefs and desires, which have (in this view) been too long suppressed. Further, and obviously in relation to this claim, it asserts its position as an authentic Indian history, as distinct from the slavish imitation of Western histories produced by deracinated scholars ensconced in privileged positions in the universities and research institutions of the subcontinent (and abroad).

One illustration of this, from the Hindu point of view, is provided by the secular discourse in India, and especially its academic form. The secular historians' inattention to the language of religion and faith is one area in which the right-wing Hindu claim often sticks. However, the charge against the secularist may be made, and is frequently made, in a more literal sense too. The more prominent secular social scientists in India do not commonly write in Hindi, Urdu, Bengali, Tamil, and other regional languages. In the main, they write in English for a small English-speaking, modern, secular, cosmopolitan audience living in India or overseas.

Some of the most important secular contributions to historiographical and political debates in Hindi, Bengali, Marathi, and Tamil, as they are conducted, say, in Delhi, Calcutta, Bombay, and Madras, appear in the form of translations. It is as if the regional language press has been handed over by an arrogant metropolitan intelligentsia to those with more parochial concerns—people who are not quite so secular, modern, or cosmopolitan.[22] All of this feeds into the notion of *two* Indias that populist politicians have promoted very actively since the mid-1980s, when the young, high-tech Rajiv Gandhi was prime minister of the country: India versus Bharat, the privileged versus the unprivileged, the English-speaking versus the sons (and daughters) of the soil, the antireligious, Westernized secularists versus religious, truly nationalist Indians.

The Hindu Right's use of Hindi, Marathi, Malayalam, and and other languages for their political propaganda is of course important. However, the use of local languages reflects, or perhaps produces, a wider sensitivity to language (and to linguistic/cultural sensibilities) that English-speaking secular academics and journalists in India could certainly learn from. The English-language press and social-scientific discourse in India have sometimes too readily accepted the Hindu right wing's chosen terms of self-description. This was illustrated all too well in the debates over the Babari Masjid. In the course of the debate that raged between the late 1980s and 1992 (the date of the mosque's destruction), it is notable that liberal and left-wing commentators began using the term *Ram Janmabhumi* in speaking of the disputed site. And they used this term to refer to the precise spot occupied by the small sixteenth-century mosque, rather than to the general area of Ayodhya, which is, in Hindu belief, the *bhumi* (land, zone, region) of Ram's birth.

Left and liberal analysts took to designating the right-wing Hindu forces leading the Ram Janmabhumi Liberation campaign as the forces of Hindutva, thus conceding the entire heritage of Hinduness (or Hindu tradition) to those who spuriously claimed it and surrendering the polemical charge of calling the right wing's reactionary politics by a more widely recognized and expressly political label. Worse, they wrote of *sadhus* and *sants* (even translated as saints in the English press) and of the *Sangh Parivar* (the family sprouted by the Rashtriya Swayamsevak Sangh), and described the motley crew of Hindu religious leaders assembled at Ayodhya—the self-proclaimed pontiffs and guardians of the Hindu religion—as the *Dharma Sansad* (religious parliament? parliament of religions? parliament of religious figures?).

There was no trace of irony in the secularists' use of these supposedly descriptive terms. By contrast, the terms used in journals like *Organizer* and *Paanchjanya* to describe the political opponents of the Hindu Right were supercilious and disdainful: "secular *giroh*" (gang of secularists), "pseudo-secularists" (and now the word *secularism*, having been associated so long with terms like *pseudo-* and *minorityism*, is often by itself enough of a condemnation), "slaves of the West," and so on.

Consider, again, the great importance attached by the so-called *Sangh Parivar* to the word used to describe the mosque at the center of the Ayodhya dispute. In 1990s India, the very name of the building on the site became a matter of political contention. It was a sign that one held a secular political position—or belonged to the minority Muslim community—to speak of the Babari Masjid. For activists and sympathizers of the Hindu Right, the building was not a *masjid* (mosque); it was the "so-called *masjid*." It was a *mandir* (Hindu temple) that had nevertheless to be destroyed, because it had for a while taken the shape of a mosque. It was a "victory monument," "a sign of [Hindu] slavery [to Muslims] [*ghulami ki nishani*]" or of betrayal (*haram ki nishani*); or it was, in more legalistic terms, the "disputed structure." The latter designation quickly passed into the vocabulary of mainstream political (and historical) discourse in India. So successfully that even Prime Minister Narasimha Rao, who was recognized as a good Hindu and a friend by the Hindu Right, was condemned the moment he used the name Babari Masjid.

Religion, Nation, History

Another set of factors that has clearly contributed to the widespread impact of Hindu history has to do with common assumptions about religion (that religion and religious belonging are, quite simply, natural and fundamental); about the particular qualities of the religion called Hinduism (that it is the most tolerant and accommodating religion in the world); and about the relationship between religion and nationalism.

The movement for the Ram Temple, it was argued, was more than a religious movement: it was a *national* movement. Hinduism is not a religion. It is the way of life, the manner of being of people living in this part of the world. (Everyone who lives in *Hindu-sthan*, literally "the land of the Hindus," is a Hindu.[23] Thus Bhai Parmanand could be asked in the United States in 1905 whether every Hindu was a Muslim, and Imam Bukhari, currently the head imam of the Jama Masjid of Delhi, on a visit to Mecca, whether he was a Hindu.) Ram is not only a Hindu deity: he is a great national hero. It is not necessary that every Indian, Hindu or non-Hindu, worship Ram. But to revere his memory as part of the great cultural heritage of India is a condition of Indian citizenship. This was not an argument about religion, it was claimed; it was an argument about culture.

In fact, of course, it was religious and cultural *and* political, all at the same time. Today in India, as in many other parts of the world, the *religious* is the *national*. At any rate, that is a commonly propagated and broadly accepted view. The political importance of the national is hardly negligible in a country where (as in all Third World countries and now, increasingly, in so many of the erstwhile Second World) the manifest difficulties of progress and development make the question of appropriate political arrangement far more contentious than in the more prosperous and stable capitalist societies of the West.

The Hindu view of history is bolstered by the way in which the history of India has been written and purveyed from James Mill's day until our own. It is reinforced by the history of strife between Hindus and Muslims, which took on an entirely new dimension in the later nineteenth century, became a central feature of Indian politics in the 1920s, reached an undreamed of climax in the period of Partition, and has recurred frequently since then. Propaganda and strife have fed one another and led to far more vicious and generalized constructions of self and other, and far more vicious and generalized forms of violence, than were known before.

In India, as in Pakistan, the history of all Muslim politics, and in a less obvious but in my view equally emphatic way, Hindu politics, is written up as the prehistory of Partition—or what amounts to the same thing: the struggle to avert it. Hindu propagandists and historians, in turn, describe separatism as an inevitable consequence of the Muslim character. The movement for Pakistan begins, in this view, with the very first Muslim efforts at reform and organization in the nineteenth century, if not with the arrival of Islam in India.[24] If such longevity and constancy is attributed to something called Muslim politics, it cannot logically be denied to Hindu politics either. The history of Hindu politics has, therefore, been treated in much the same way—as part of a very old tradition, as an expression of a natural unity, and as the natural course of political development in India.

Much of the above flows from a firm belief in the naturalness and unambiguity of religion, of religious belonging, of national belonging, and of the national frame for the writing of history. On the latter, there is not a very great difference between the secular, nationalist historiography and the communalist one. Secular, liberal, and left-wing historians in India—and I use the term broadly to include political figures, journalists, and others writing historical accounts—have worked consistently over the last hundred years and more to construct a unified, standardized, and (by extension) undifferentiated Indian history. Understandable as this effort was, it can plausibly be argued that this very homogenization constitutes the ground for the uniform, undifferentiated, and insistently unified Hindu histories that right-wing Hindu historians are propagating.

To put it in other words, the new Hindu history continues, in a vulgarized and more brutal form, a secular trajectory. Disciplinary history has insisted not only on the form or end of history writing (the facts, the narrative), but also on the protocols or means—protocols that insist on the separation of the divine and the mundane, for example, on verification, contextualization, and so on. The new Hindu history seems to have abandoned the protocols of the profession, while maintaining its ends—facts.

Perhaps this is part of the reason for the *excessive* nature of its facts: *precisely* at this time, on *precisely* this date, in *precisely* these numbers, with *precisely* these weapons.[25]

This history can go on to speak of *precisely* this land, which belongs to *precisely* this community, also called the common people of India, in the same sort of way: and here it shares the fact, or end, of the naturalized nation with the secular varieties of Indian history. Right-wing historians are able to adopt a successful populist persona because left-wing and liberal democratic counterparts inhabit the same populist space in their insistence on an unbroken, unchallenged, homogenous nation with a unified, homogenous history. In the next four chapters, we turn to the question of how citizenship comes to be marked (or unmarked) in the nation's handling of the issue of pluralism and difference. I begin this part of the analysis with an examination of the militant Hindu version of the nation and its people.

Appendix to Chapter 4:
Ayodhya and the State

The following comment was written in September 1989 and published in the Delhi monthly, Seminar, *in its issue of December 1989.[1] I reproduce it here in the form in which it was first written, both because it provides a succinct statement of the main steps in the development of the controversy over the Ram Janmabhumi/Babari Masjid at Ayodhya, and because it may help to convey a sense of the political and historiographical controversies that were occasioned by this dispute. By way of amendment, and to bring the statement up to date, I have added a few lines to take account of the attacks on the mosque in 1990 and 1992, to clarify the source of a particular tradition cited at one point in the argument, and to suggest that the state has not done very much to deal with this issue since that time. These additions are indicated by italics and square brackets.*

There are three simple points about the Ram Janmabhumi/Babari Masjid question that I wish to make, or rather reiterate—for all these things have been said before. The first is that it is humanly impossible to identify a particular site, anywhere, as the place where the Hindu god Ram was born. The second is that it is, from an orthodox Hindu point of view, not only unnecessary but even ludicrous to do so, for such historical and geographical placement of a divinity supposed to have assumed human form in the Treta yuga can only make a mockery of a profound religious tale. Geography, like history, functions here as a metaphor. Reducing geography to actual sites makes complete nonsense of it.

On this particular point, one needs perhaps only to cite Mohandas Karamchand Gandhi—surely one of the greatest and most devout Hindus of the twentieth century. Mahadev Desai once reported Gandhi's views on the irrelevance of the search for the original text of the *Bhagavad Gita*: "His attitude is that in the last analysis it is the message that abides, and he is sure that no textual discovery is going to affect by a jot the essence or universality of the message. The same thing may be said about questions of the historical Krishna and the genesis and history of the Krishna Vasudeva worship."

Gandhi himself wrote: "Even in 1888–89, when I first became acquainted with the *Gita*, I felt that it was not a historical work, but that, under the guise of physical warfare, it described the duel that perpetually went on in the hearts of mankind, and that physical warfare was brought in merely to make the description of the internal duel more alluring. This preliminary intuition became more confirmed on a closer study of religion and the *Gita*. A study of the *Mahabharata* gave it added confirmation. I do not regard the *Mahabharata* as a historical work in the accepted sense. The *Adiparva* contains powerful evidence in support of my opinion. By ascribing to the chief actors superhuman or subhuman origins, the great Vyasa made short work of the history of kings and their peoples. The persons therein described may be historical, but the author of the *Mahabharata* has used them merely to drive home his religious theme."

So much for the historicity of Ram and Krishna, their origins and their places of birth. Ram and Krishna are greater—by far—than any historical persons, and must be so for every Hindu. They represent a message, a religious theme—not a factual history. To deny this is to denigrate Hinduism.

The final point that I wish to raise relates to the state. Regarding an issue like the Ram Janmabhumi/Babari Masjid controversy, a modern state with secular claims cannot afford to act like Hindu or Muslim kings of olden times. Today, in India, it is dangerously close to doing so—and the consequences in terms of heightened tension between Hindus and Muslims, frequent rounds of violence, and repeated curfews, are plain for all to see. But to pursue this point, and with it the earlier one regarding the impossibility of identifying any particular site as the Ram Janmabhumi, it may help to set out in a brief chronology what little is known about the early history of present-day Ayodhya and some of the more recent events that have contributed to the current flare-up.

A Chronological Summary of the History of "Ayodhya"
from Ancient Times to Today

1. *The Ayodhya of Dashratha and Ram,* believed to have flourished in the Treta yuga of the Hindu calendar.

2. *The rediscovery of Ayodhya* in historical times by Vikramaditya (identified by many scholars as Skandagupta, who lived in the middle of the fifth century A.D.) when Buddhism had apparently begun to decline in the face of Brahmanical resurgence.

3. *The so-called Muslim conquest* and, around 1528 A.D., the destruction of a temple and construction of a mosque in its place by Babar's general, Mir Baqi.

4. *The eighteenth century*: Ayodhya becomes a major center of Hindu pilgrimage under the patronage and protection of the (Muslim) Nawabs of Awadh.

5. *Major riots in 1855,* beginning at the Hanumangarhi site in Ayodhya and leading to a major attack on the Babari Masjid/Ram Janmabhumi, occasioned (it is said) by the unsettled conditions that followed from the decline in the Nawabs' power and the growth of British influence. British troops intervened to stop further clashes.

   In 1856, after the British annexation of Awadh, a railing was erected around the actual masjid to protect the Muslim area of worship, and a platform was constructed outside the fence but within the compound of the building for Hindus to offer their own worship.

   (There were other major riots in Ayodhya-Faizabad in 1912, 1934, and possibly also in 1893, but as a historian of the city has pointed out, these were part of a more general scenario of deteriorating political relations between Hindus and Muslims in parts of northern India and not directly related to the Mandir-Masjid question.)[2]

6. *Night of 22 December 1949*: A handful of people enter the mosque and install idols there. The building is attached and put under padlocks by administrative order, on the grounds that there was danger of a breach of the peace if entry was permitted to either Muslims or Hindus.

7. *October 1984*: Vishwa Hindu Parishad intervenes to try and make the temple-mosque question a national issue through its 'Ram Janmabhumi Mukti Yajna'.

8. *February 1986*: Padlocks removed by order of a district judge stating that "it is unnecessary to keep the locks on the gates for the purpose of maintaining law and order or the safety of the idols."

9. *Build-up to the 1989 elections*: widely publicized proposal to demolish the mosque and build a Ramjanmabhumi temple complex over the disputed site, with bricks brought especially for the purpose from all over India and from foreign lands.

[*10. October 1990: Volunteers of the extreme Hindu right wing (described as "kar sevaks" in Hindi) attempt to storm the Babari Masjid in Ayodhya.*

11. December 1992: Demolition of the Babari Masjid by an assembled crowd of several hundred thousand.]

For recent times, it is possible to flesh out this chronological skeleton with a great deal more detail. But for the purposes of the present discussion, this minimal outline will suffice.

It is clear that there are large gaps in the early part of this chronology. Our knowledge of ancient sites is always somewhat speculative—perhaps more so in this country, where recorded history has earlier beginnings than in most other parts of the world but the records of courts and religious institutions are mostly not available to supplement the evidence of archaeology and popular memory. Ayodhya is no different from many other ancient Indian sites in this respect.

Much uncertainty still attaches to the early history of Ayodhya, to the question of whether today's Ayodhya and Ram's Ayodhya are one and the same city (if we take Ram as being a local north Indian king with a capital called Ayodhya), and to the question of whether any site can be definitely identified as the birthplace of this historical prince called Ram.

As for the other Ram, the incarnation of Vishnu in the Treta yuga, historians and geographers so inclined may try forever to locate the sacred sites associated with his life. There is surely little hope of success, for, even in their own terms, the rules of historical and geographical truth in the Kali yuga can scarcely apply to the symbolic truths of the Treta.

In any event, no historian, so far as I know, has claimed a continuity of existence for this fabled city of Ram's birth from the Treta yuga to the present. Hindu historians and popular tradition alike acknowledge that Ayodhya was established many times and ruined many times. Writers on Ayodhya also seem to agree that the place was in ruins—a "wilderness" (*van avadh*), as it has been called—when it was rediscovered by Vikramaditya.

A word about this rediscovery. Historians were long undecided about the identity of the Vikramaditya who, according to local tradition, rediscovered Ayodhya. On the strength of very limited evidence, Skandagupta now appears to have emerged as the chief candidate for the honor. It is clear that the Guptas at some stage shifted their capital from Pataliputra to Saketa, which was then renamed Ayodhya. It is also established that Skandagupta liked to compare himself with Ram and claimed that the Guptas were continuing the traditions of Ram's dynasty and had restored

Ram's capital to its ancient glory. But the fact that in Kalidasa's poetry, written at the time of Chandragupta II, two generations before Skandagupta, Saketa and Ayodhya are already used as names of the same town throws some doubt on Skandagupta's claims. We are also told that Chandragupta II was the last Gupta king to refer to Pataliputra, which again may suggest that the move to Saketa/Ayodhya took place during his time or immediately after.

Whoever it was who made the move (rediscovered Ayodhya), it is not at all clear that this rediscovery amounts to the revival of a physical site once actually inhabited by a Dashratha or a Ram. Consider the arguments of Radhey Shyam Shukul, a historian of Ayodhya who is concerned to demonstrate precisely such identity of sites. "That Saketa is indeed Ayodhya," he writes, "*who first recognized this and when, is not known*; but this much is certain that by the time of Mahakavi Kalidas, Saketa and Ayodhya were the names of the same town. In his great work, *Raghuvamsha*, Kalidas has used the names Saketa and Ayodhya interchangeably. To challenge this identification made by a scholar of the stature of Kalidas some 1500 years ago . . . is meaningless."[3] The author adds in a footnote that "for a long time there was disagreement among scholars as to whether Saketa was indeed Ayodhya or not, but there is no disagreement now!"

In fact, the evidence of the *Raghuvamsha* establishes no connection between Saketa and some older Ayodhya. All it tells us is that Saketa and Ayodhya were in Kalidas's time names of the same place, which indeed they were, since the Gupta rulers had (recently?) renamed Saketa Ayodhya. In that renaming, as in Skandagupta's claims to be like Ram and so on, it is more plausible to see not the rediscovery of a hallowed, ancient capital but the harnessing of a powerful local tradition, an existing north Indian legend of the incomparable rule of Ram, by a dynasty seeking to promote its own glory and longevity.[4]

Local accounts in Ayodhya in the nineteenth century recounted that Vikramaditya's main clue in locating the ancient city was the course of the holy river Saryu, and his next a shrine known as Nageshar-nath dedicated to Mahadeo.[5] Note that it is the course of the river and a temple dedicated to Shiva: nothing here about the worship of Vishnu, the traditions of Ram, or the sites associated with him. On this site, thus located, which became their new capital, the later Guptas, who proclaimed themselves to be devotees of Vishnu, raised hundreds of temples to Hindu deities, including Ram, Sita, Lakshman, and Hanuman.

Regarding one of these temples, Radhey Shyam Shukul writes, "According to an inscription inside the temple, Skandagupta had it constructed in honour of Sharangin Vishnu. Sharangin Vishnu—or Vishnu with a bow—can also be a synonym for Ram. It is possible that this was the Shri Ram Janmabhumi temple."[6] ("Can also be . . . " and "it is possible . . . ": these phrases are noteworthy. They are hardly a sign of infallible truth. But this was written in 1986, in the early days of [in] the Hindu Right's Ram Janmabhumi Liberation Movement.) I would like to propose another possibility, which seems to me to make rather more historical sense.

The construction of temples in the new Gupta capital at sites designated as being associated with great moments in the lives of Ram, Sita, Lakshman, and so on, is perhaps best seen as an act of translation, a mythical geography being recreated on the ground. We have living instances of such creation at hundreds of places in India even today. At the important annual celebration of the Ramlila at Ramnagar near Banaras, for example, a certain area is marked out as Lanka and the enactment of the crossing of the sea from Rameshwaram is performed over a small waterless tank. I should stress that the fact that this is a mythical geography, symbolically recreated, does not make it any the less sacred. But, to reiterate M.K. Gandhi's statement, its sanctity derives from the larger religious theme, not from the literal truth of particular associations—that, in Ramnagar or elsewhere, this little mound is the mountain that Hanuman carried back for the *sanjivani buti* or that little shade a spot where Ram and Sita rested.

To return to the point about a lack of historical continuity in Ayodhya, the place seems to have declined considerably in the centuries after the rule of the Guptas, *before* the arrival of any Muslim rulers in northern India. Shukul writes: "[The evidence] amounts to this that *the worship of Lord Ram began* at the time of Kumaragupta and Skandagupta. No less surprising is the fact that *after the Guptas the worship of Ram was again suspended* for three or four hundred years."[7]

It was locally affirmed in the nineteenth century that when Muslim rulers established their sway in the area, there were only three important Hindu shrines in Ayodhya "with but few devotees attached," and that the place was then little more than a wilderness.[8] There is a suggestion of some recovery under the early Muslim rulers, but the patchy evidence available indicates that the town was still fairly neglected when Babar came there, broke down a temple at or near what was later called the *Janmasthan*, and erected a mosque in its place. [*It needs to be stressed that no contemporary source refers to this event, but nineteenth-century oral history, recorded by the British, put it in this light.*]

About this act of destruction, which has become the central point in the present controversy from the Hindu point of view, it should be noted that the destruction of the cultural symbols of a king's enemies was an accepted part of the declaration of sovereignty in premodern times in India and abroad. At Ayodhya itself, there is some evidence that the Janmasthan temple allegedly destroyed in Babar's time had been erected (presumably by the Guptas) in place of an earlier Buddhist temple. Carnegy wrote in the 1860s of the well-preserved columns of the earlier structure that still adorned the Babari Masjid: "These are of strong close-grained, dark slate-colored or black stone, called by the natives Kasoti [literally touchstone] and carved with different devices. To my thinking these strongly resemble Buddhist pillars that I have seen at Benares and elsewhere."[9]

Or, to take a very different example, one may see at Machali in the Dangs district of Gujarat, the ruins of a Shiva temple that according to local belief, was destroyed by the Raja of Gadhvi, a leading Bhil Raja, who set out to efface the symbols of the "Gavali" or Yadav Raj (c. 1216–1312 A.D.) that had preceded Bhil rule.[10]

Peter van der Veer has noted that it would have been impossible for a Muslim ruler in medieval times to neglect the "call of religion," especially when (as the story goes in the case of Babar) he was repeatedly urged by religious advisors to bring down a temple and build a mosque as a sign of his religious devotion. But, as the same scholar observes, there is no evidence of a general suppression of Hinduism in Ayodhya at this time or later. Any such attempt would have been politically suicidal for Muslim rulers in northern India—and let us underscore the point that almost all rulers, past and present, have been centrally concerned with the establishment and perpetuation of their political power. It was plainly also against the inclinations of many Muslim rulers in this country, for different Muslim rulers responded very differently to the "call of religion" and the needs of the subject population—Hindu and Muslim.

Babar himself appears to have patronized both Hindu temples and Hindu religious men. In Ayodhya, at around the time of the construction of the Babari Masjid, he made a revenue-free grant of five hundred *bighas* (over three hundred acres) to Swami Shatrughan of the local Dantdhawan kund. This "consecrated" ground and the papers regarding the grant can still be seen in Ayodhya, according to the Hindu historian R.S. Shukul.[11]

Even Aurangzeb, that archvillain in the Hindu (and, I might add, British colonial) construction of the Indian past, took some pains to protect the Hindu inhabitants of his empire. Along with the evidence of his other policies, his oppressions and his acts of grace, is a *farman* issued in Hijri 1069 (1658–59 A.D.) which reads:

Let Abul Hasan . . . know that . . . in accordance with holy law we have decided that the ancient temples shall not be overthrown but that new ones shall not be built. . . . Information has reached our most noble and holy court that certain persons activated by rancour and spite have harassed the Hindu residents [the Hindi translation at the Bharat Kala Bhawan, Banaras Hindu University, has "some Brahmans"] in the town of Banaras and a few other places in that neighbourhood, and also certain Brahmans, keepers of the temples, in whose charge those ancient temples are, and that they further desire to remove these Brahmans from their ancient office, and this intention of theirs causes distress to the community. Therefore our Royal command is that after the arrival of [this *farman*] you should direct that in future no person shall in unlawful ways interfere with or disturb Brahmans and other Hindus resident in those places. So that they may peacefully carry on in their trades [occupations] and continue to offer their prayers and worship in our God-given Empire that is destined to last forever.[12]

This point about the range of responses to be found among Muslim rulers, and the political compulsions that lay behind these, is demonstrated again by the history of Ayodhya in the eighteenth and nineteenth centuries, when it gained the invaluable protection and patronage of the Nawabs of Awadh. The rule of the Awadh dynasty depended all too evidently on the collaboration of Hindus and Muslims. During this period, then, many Hindu groups attained to great social and political prominence—and Ayodhya prospered. Safdar Jang's *diwan,* the Kayasth Nawal Rai, built and restored several temples in the town; Safdar Jang himself granted land to Abhayramdas of the Nirwani *akhara* to build a temple on what was known as Hanuman's hill; Asaf-ud-daulah's *diwan,* the Kayasth Tikait Rai, supported the later building on this spot of the temple-fortress of Hanumangarhi, the initial site of the 1855 riots.[13]

The comparatively recent character of much that is presented to us as "eternal" needs to be carefully noted. Tulsidas composed that extraordinary and extraordinarily beautiful work, the *Ramcharitmanas,* in the later sixteenth century. This was the first time that the epic of Ram became available in the vernacular in such richness and detail, and it was after this that the cult of Ram became the most popular religious cult among the Hindus of northern India. It was in the eighteenth century under Nawabi rule—

as far as we can tell from the historical evidence—that Ayodhya developed into a Hindu pilgrimage center of primary importance. Again, the Ramanandi *sadhus* who dominate the temple scene in Ayodhya today came to occupy this privileged place in the course of the twentieth century "as the result of a long-term process in which they increasingly abandoned their peripatetic lifestyle for 'sedentary' life in places of pilgrimage."[14] The promoters of the argument about the everlasting centrality of Ayodhya (and of the Ram Janmmabhumi) should bear some of these facts in mind.

It is on the new uncertainties and anxieties let loose on this uncertain terrain by the inauguration, course, and end of British rule that recent communalist forces have largely fed. It was only five years ago, in 1984, that the Vishwa Hindu Parishad began concerted efforts to convert the Ram Janmabhumi–Babari Masjid controversy into a major national issue—and it did so, to some extent, against the wishes of Ayodhya's local Hindu leaders. How the secular Indian state has responded to this recent build-up of pressure and tension is the final question I wish to address. It makes for perhaps the murkiest chapter in this murky tale.

What the Indian state has done in response to the deteriorating situation of the past few years and months will be clear even from the incidents recorded in the brief chronological table presented earlier. Its guardians have set aside, for the sake of electoral advantage, many of the finest ideals for which an earlier generation of nationalists valiantly struggled. It may have seemed appropriate to Hindu rulers and Muslim rulers and those of other religious denominations, in the past, to assert their authority by promoting their religion and destroying the symbols of other religions and cultures; a state that claims to be modern and secular cannot afford to act in this manner. But what is the recent record in Ayodhya?

In 1949, the government acquiesced in the installation of idols inside the mosque by some "unknown persons" acting by stealth at dead of night. The police guard on duty either could do nothing or refused to do anything to prevent this illegal act. The district magistrate and his personal assistant (both Hindus) may have had a hand in this acquiescence; in any event, both were retired for their openly pro-Hindu stance during the riots that followed. The High Court has to this day not disposed of the cases that were then instituted, by local Hindus as well as Muslims, regarding the protection of their rights. By administrative order, padlocks were placed on the gates of the mosque/temple, stopping the entry of both Hindus and Muslims in order to prevent any further breach of the peace.

In February 1986, the local district and sessions judge decided that the gates should again be opened to allow the entry of worshippers, arguing that it was no longer necessary to lock them, either for the preservation of law and order or for "the protection of the idols."[15] Note that the idols were installed *illegally*, but now, in a judgment that took the state one step closer to the Hindu camp, the protection of this illegal encroachment was declared to be one of the primary responsibilities of the administration. In this instance, it seems clear from all the evidence that not only the local authorities but the provincial and national governments at the highest levels acquiesced in or, more accurately, orchestrated this new Hindu victory.

Doordarshan (the government-owned television service) cameras were, miraculously, present at the scene, and the sight of the temple gates being opened was flashed on the national news within hours of the judgment. It was the Hindu part of an electoral quid pro quo in which the Muslims had been rewarded with the infamous Muslim Women's Protection Act.[16] Few responsible elected governments, let alone secular regimes, have acted so irresponsibly, not to say disgracefully, for the sake of short-term political gain. The long-term costs in terms of human lives, destruction of property, and the growth of antagonism and fear among neighbors and fellow countrymen and women still remain to be seen.

Today, three and one-half years after these shameful events, the government of India still shows no signs of moving with any urgency to find a solution to this damaging conflict. It has done nothing, of course, to encourage a speedy disposal of the cases regarding the rights of Ayodhya's Hindus and Muslims, which have been pending with the High Court since 1949. It has taken no step to try and get agreement on the one obviously sensible proposal to have emerged from public discussions on this question: to declare the masjid a protected national monument under the control of the Archaeological Survey. The government (and the opposition, barring only the two Communist parties) has refused to do anything directly regarding the threatening proposal to construct a large temple at the disputed site. To support the proposal means the loss of Muslim votes. To oppose it means the shrinking of Hindu support. It is best to do nothing—as long as you can. Meanwhile, if India burns, let it.

[*Much of this last paragraph still holds good in 2004. Eighteen years after the opening of the locks on the disputed Babari Masjid, and twelve years after the demolition of the masjid itself, the numerous court cases around the issue have yet to be decided, and the question of compensation or justice for those who lost family members or livelihood or dwellings in Ayodhya and elsewhere in the widespread anti-Muslim violence of 1992–93 has hardly been taken up.*]

5

The Question of Belonging

Naturalness, one might suggest, is a claim especially made by ancient nations. The *national* community is a *natural* community. This may be seen in its boundaries, its linguistic or religious practices, its social structure and customs, and not least, in the unity that flows from these. Thus, it has been argued that India (Hindustan, Bharatvarsha, Aryavarta, Jambudwipa) has the most natural boundaries in the world. "There is no part of the world better marked out by Nature as a region by itself than India, exclusive of Burma."[1]

The Hindus are the obvious, the original, the natural inhabitants of this land, as the very names *Hindu* and *Hindustan* testify. The suggestion has been elaborated further. Given that there has never been any dispute over the proposition that the English, the French, and the Germans constitute the nation in England, France, and Germany, it is mystifying that there should be any confusion about the identity of the nation in Hindustan. "Hindu society living in this country since time immemorial is the national [and natural] society here. . . . The same Hindu people have built the life-values, ideals and culture of this country and, therefore, their nationhood is self-evident."[2]

"Undoubtedly . . . we—Hindus—have been in undisputed and undisturbed possession of this land for over eight or even ten thousand years before the land was invaded by any foreign race."[3] In this way, we are told, there came into being what is assuredly the most natural nation in the world. "Living in this country since pre-historic times . . . the Hindu Race

[is] united together by common traditions, by memories of common glory and disaster, by similar historical, political, social, religious and other experiences." "Historically, politically, ethnologically and culturally Hindusthan is one, whole and indivisible and so she shall remain." "If the Hindus do not possess a common history, then none in the world does"; indeed, as the same writer goes on to say, the Hindus are "about the only people" who are blessed with those "ideal conditions . . . under which a nation can attain perfect solidarity and cohesion."[4]

It is another feature of narratives of nationhood that they assert the superiority of their own particular community or nation. The Hindus are pronounced the most ancient and civilized nation in the world, unparalleled in their philosophical and spiritual achievements, accommodating, tolerant, united, luxuriant, even—in a fundamental way—unconquerable. "Great as the glories of the English world are, what on the whole has it to show to match the glories of the Hindu world?" "The very first page of history records our existence as a progressive and highly civilized nation."[5]

Loss and Retrieval

Right-wing Hindu discourse submits that a spirit of nationalist unity has guided the history of the Hindus from the beginnings of historical time. The goal of uniting all Hindus inspired the kings of ancient India, who were honored with the titles Chakravartin (unifier of all Hindus) and Vikramaditya (destroyer of all foreigners) if they were successful in their endeavors.[6] Later, the Hindus lost control over the land. A long millennium of resistance followed. For a thousand years, from the time Muslim rulers first established their sway over a part of northern India until 1947, the Hindus waged an incessant battle for liberation from alien rule. A whole hagiography has developed around the heroic deeds of the Rajputs, the Marathas, and the Sikhs, detailing the valiant actions and martyrdom of Maharana Pratap, Shivaji, Guru Gobind Singh, and others in their struggles against the Mughals.[7]

This resistance continued throughout the colonial period, we are told. The Hindu struggle is exemplified, according to Hindu spokespersons, by the great uprising of 1857 and the careers of Rammohan Roy, Dayanand Saraswati, Lokmanya Tilak, Swami Vivekananda, and legions more. Here is what the Rashtriya Swayamsevak Sangh (RSS) supremo, M. S. Golwalkar, has to say about the anti-British rising of 1857, which demonstrates once again, in his view, how the "living vision of Hindu Rashtra" inspired "all our valiant freedom fighters in the past and in modern times":

> The great leaders of that revolution, at the very first stroke, captured Delhi and . . . reinstated [Bahadur Shah Zafar, the last Mughal King, nominally emperor of India until he was dethroned and exiled by the British in 1858] . . . as the free Emperor and . . . the leader of the War of Independence. . . . But this step made the Hindu masses suspect that the atrocious Moghul rule, which was smashed by the heroic efforts and sacrifices of Guru Govind Singh, Chhatrasal, Shivaji, and such others would once again be revived and foisted on them. . . . Historians say that this was one of the decisive factors which ultimately led to the collapse of that revolution [of 1857].[8]

Indeed, we sometimes have the remarkable proposition that all social and political activities of the nineteenth and twentieth centuries in which Hindus took part were geared to the task of reestablishing the Hindu nation in its superior and glorious splendor. Any political leader and reformer of the period who happens to have been a Hindu may be appropriated to the history of Hindu nationalism, including at times (albeit with some bitterness) Mohandas Karamchand Gandhi and even Jawaharlal Nehru.

> The whole race of [revolutionary terrorist] martyrs in Bengal, in the Punjab, U.P., Maharashtra, Madras, throughout the length and breadth of the country, who have been grimly fighting for their mother—the Hindu Race and Nation. . . . And with other weapons, the staunch fighters Lok[manya] Tilak, Lala Lajpat Rai, Bipin Chandra Pal and a host of others; and the day's notaries—M. Gandhi and others, *all Hindu workers*, rightly conceiving the national future or not, but all sincerely and sternly fighting the foe. Surely the Hindu Nation is not conquered.[9]

It is worthwhile pausing to note how the Hindu nation is constructed in this argument, and how its deep commitment to the cause of independence is demonstrated. The underlying proposition is that of a mystical unity and a primary, unquestioned (and unquestionable?) commitment to its preservation. This is based on an eliding of historical data, even as history is paraded as witness.

There is not the slightest indication in Golwalkar's statement on 1857, for example, that Muslims played a large part in the revolt. Yet in nationalist folklore, Maulvis Ahmadullah Shah and Inayat Ali stand alongside the Rani of Jhansi, Nana Saheb, and Kunwar Singh as the heroes of the event, and for long after 1857 the British rulers of India were apprehensive of another uprising led by the fanatical Muslims.

Golwalkar portrays it as a mere tactical mistake on the part of what are obviously meant to be the Hindu leaders of the revolt that they invited Bahadur Shah Zafar to resume his throne and lead the struggle. To put this claim in perspective, let us recall the findings of all recent research: that a reluctant emperor was practically dragged out of retirement and coerced into accepting the leadership of the rebellion, not by any of its famous leaders—Hindu or Muslim—but by the soldiers who had marched from Meerut to Delhi for the express purpose of laying siege to the Red Fort and proclaiming the end of *firangi* (foreign, British) rule.

The tactical mistake of the leaders is matched in Golwalkar's account by the unanimous determination of the Hindu masses to ensure that they not be subjected to Muslim rule again. Faced with the prospect of once more being returned to that "atrocious" condition, they prefer the rule of another set of foreigners. Hence, the passage implies, the Hindu masses, as a body, withdrew their support from the popular struggle of 1857. "Historians say"—the scientificity of the statement is noteworthy, although not a single historical work or historian's name is cited—"that this [withdrawal of Hindu support] was one of the decisive factors which ultimately led to the collapse of that revolution."

In the end, the claim is this: that every Hindu reformer, thinker, and political activist who fought for local rights, self-respect, or increased opportunity, anywhere at any time, was part of one and the same struggle: the struggle for a Hindu Rashtra. It is striking, for instance, that the Sikhs are included unproblematically in this category of fighters for Hindu freedom, in spite of the long and successful Sikh struggle from the last decades of the nineteenth century onward, through the very period when this Hindu discourse was acquiring its modern, militant form, to establish a Sikh identity distinct from that of Hindus.[10]

If Hindus, or people who were nominally Hindu, or those who should have acknowledged their Hinduhood, are known to have risen in protest against someone or something, that is enough to establish the Hindu purpose of their crusade. It is appropriate, therefore, to ask when goals like that of a Hindu Rashtra were first articulated, and indeed when the word Hindu acquired its present signification.

Mobilizing the Hindu

It would appear that the notion of a Hindu Rashtra—India as a nation and a Hindu nation, the land of the Hindus—was first advanced in the 1920s,[11] and the first steps toward the mobilization of Hindus *as a nation* were taken at this time. This is well illustrated in the argument about the need for Hindu *sangathan* (organization) put forward by the Arya Samaj leader, social reformer, and militant nationalist, Swami Shraddhanand, in the pamphlet *Hindu Sangathan: Saviour of the Dying Race*, published in 1924.

"In the following pages," this religious *sadhu* turned reformer and propagandist wrote in the preface to his pamphlet, "an attempt has been made to describe the history of the Hindu decline. . . . As a corollary an attempt has been made to show the way to the nation's emancipation." Shraddhanand advocated, as a first step toward organizing the Hindus, the building of a Hindu Rashtra Mandir, or Hindu National Temple, in every city and important town of India. Each *mandir* was to have a compound capable of holding an audience of 25,000 and a large hall for recitations from the holy texts and epics. "Let some living cows be there to represent plenty," Shraddhanand wrote,

Let "Savitri" [*gayatri mantram*] be inscribed over the gate of the hall to remind every Hindu of his duty to expel all ignorance and let a life-like map of Mother-Bharat be constructed in a prominent place, giving all its characteristics in vivid colours so that every child of the Matri-Bhumi may daily bow before the Mother and renew *his* pledge to restore her to the ancient pinnacle of glory from which she has fallen![12]

Unlike other Hindu temples, which are associated with a particular tradition or sect and dominated by their particular deities, these Hindu Rashtra Mandirs were to be dedicated to the worship of "the three mother-spirits"—the cow; Saraswati, the goddess of learning; and Bhumi-mata (mother earth, the goddess of plenty and the provider of food). To make absolutely clear the connection between the nation and the mother-provider, Shraddhanand asked for a lifelike map of Mother India to be put up in a prominent place "so that every child of the *Matri-Bhumi* may daily bow before the Mother and renew his pledge to restore her to the ancient pinnacle of glory." It was as part of this nationalist proposition that he called for the integration of untouchables, prevention of child marriage, the sanctioning of marriage for widows, and protection of the cow. In addition, he urged the introduction of a uniform script (Devanagari) and national language (Hindi) as "absolutely necessary" for the advancement of the nation.

The Swami's intervention came in the context of increasing strife between Hindus and Muslims in urban centers throughout northern India, and growing demands for *shuddhi* (purification) and *sangathan* (organization) on the Hindu side, with matching calls for *tabligh* (propagation of the faith) and *tanzim* (organization) on the side of the Muslims. For many Hindu publicists and politicians, the Khilafat movement and the Mappila revolt had raised the specter of a thoroughly united, well-organized, and militant Muslim populace, all set to wipe out the Hindus and their culture. The relative increase in Muslim numbers that the decennial censuses had apparently established, and the question of the place of untouchables and tribal groups that were only loosely attached to Hindu society, now acquired a new importance.

Shraddhanand's pamphlet made these concerns very clear.[13] Educated Hindus were reluctant to mix with each other, he noted: the reason was that "they have no common meeting place." Even their bigger temples seated barely a hundred or two hundred people. By contrast, in Delhi alone, "besides the Juma and Fatehpuri mosques which can accommodate big audiences consisting of 25 to 30 thousands of Muhammadans, there are several old mosques which can serve as meeting places for thousands" (p. 139). It was to rectify this imbalance that the author suggested building Hindu Rashtra Mandirs capable of holding 25,000 people in every town and city.

An appeal for organization, discipline, and training accompanied the call to build these temples. The large compounds were also to provide space for *akharas* where wrestling and gymnastics would be practiced and would also serve as venues for dramatic performances. All these activities, and the temples themselves, were to be run by the local Hindu Sabhas (p. 140). "Protection of the cow is a powerful factor not only in giving the Hindu community a common plane for joint action," wrote Shraddhanand,

but in contributing to the physical development and strength of its several members. But if the drain upon the depressed classes [untouchables and other low castes] continues and they go on leaving their ancestral religion on account of the social tyranny of their co-religionists, and the onrush of Hindu widows towards prostitution and Muhammadanism, on account of the brutal treatment of [by] their relations, is not stopped by allowing them to remarry in their own community, the number of beef-eaters will increase. (p. 138)

Thus, the questions of reform in the position of untouchables and widows, of conversion to other religions, of the physical development and strength of the Hindus—in a word, of organizing and unifying the Hindu Nation—acquired a new urgency in the 1920s. The context for this was provided by the emergence of countrywide mass political organizations and agitations; what was perceived as a quite new and threatening level of Muslim organization, preparedness, and militancy; a powerful Sikh campaign for the reform of their *gurdwaras* and the establishment of community control over these institutions; and much else that historians of nationalism and popular protest have written about. The position in the nineteenth century had been very different.

For a start, many of the nineteenth-century leaders who are now claimed as the (modern) founders of the movement for Hindu nationhood were active before the idea had gained the fixity of a popular prejudice that nations and nation-states are the only appropriate and natural form of the political existence of peoples. If the colonial writers and commentators of the time were persuaded that India had no nation, that Hindus and Muslims had always been separate and antagonistic races, and that it would be a very long time before notions of self-government had any meaning in such climes, Indian thinkers and publicists were also deeply ambivalent about the political prospects and possibilities.[14] The evidence suggests that it was only in the first decades of the twentieth century that the pronounced loyalism of most Hindu and Muslim spokespersons, and even of organizations like the Indian National Congress, waned and a demand for *swaraj* (or self-rule) was articulated; even then, there were many questions about how the "we" of a possible Indian nationhood might be constituted.[15]

In the twentieth century, there was considerable experimentation regarding names for the "we" of a putative Indian nation. Muhammad Iqbal wrote in his famous "Song of India" (*Tarana-i-Hind*): "*Hindi hain hum, vatan hai Hindostan hamara*" (We [the people] are Hindi, our homeland is Hindustan). And if Iqbal is taken to be an exception, we have more prosaic examples of similar terminological usage. V.D. Savarkar, an acknowledged founder of the modern Hindu political movement, provides an excellent example. In his book, *Hindutva,* written in prison during the years of the First World War and first published in 1923, Savarkar submitted that *Bharatiya* and *Hindi* are synonymous with "an Indian" and that either term may be used for "a countryman and a fellow citizen."[16]

The term *Hindu* was also used at times, throughout this period, to designate the collectivity of people of India—Hindu, Muslim, Parsee, and so on. In a famous lecture delivered in Ballia (Uttar Pradesh), apparently in 1884, Bharatendu Harishchandra declared: "Whoever lives in Hindustan, whatever his colour or caste, is a Hindu." He went on to elaborate his meaning with the proposition that "Bengalis, Marathas, Panjabis, Madrasis [*sic*], Vaidiks, Jains, Brahmos, Musalmans" were all Hindus involved in a common historical project.

It has been argued that the propositions "Hindustan is ours because we are Hindus" and "He who inhabits Hindustan is a Hindu" were two ways of arriving at the same conclusion—that India and Hindu were synonymous.[17] There is force in this argument: this is the kind of pragmatic approach that has certainly been adopted by many Hindu propagandists from the later nineteenth century on. At the end of the nineteenth century, however, there was still considerable uncertainty about the appropriate designations for emerging solidarities and new goals and movements, and the meanings and uses of many terms remained fairly fluid. It is interesting to note, for example, that Sir Syed Ahmad Khan (1817–1898) used the term *Hindu* in exactly the same way as Bharatendu, to mean "the inhabitants of Hindustan," in a lecture given in Lahore in the same year, 1884.[18]

A couple of decades later, this usage had become very much less common or even permissible. "It is only in America," wrote Bhai Parmanand of his experience there in the early 1900s, "that the word 'Hindu' is correctly used to denote the inhabitants of Hindustan, be they Hindu, Sikh or Musalman by religion." Hence, he observed, the question that an American acquaintance had once asked him: "Are all Hindus Musalmans?"[19]

Hindu as the designation for people belonging to a particular religious tradition, or set of traditions, was of course already the most common meaning of the term in India, even in the later nineteenth century. Thus, in the same Ballia lecture in which he included among the Hindus all the inhabitants of Hindustan, Bharatendu Harishchandra also had passages addressed to different sections of the collective Indian community—sections he called "Hindus" and "Muslims" (or, more specifically, "Hindu Brothers" and "Muslim Brothers"). But even where people spoke of Hindus, Muslims, Sikhs, and so on, referring to religious groups, it was not always apparent who was included in the category.

In 1911, for example, E. A. Gait, India's census commissioner, directed regional census supervisors to gather locally used criteria to establish who was considered a Hindu. The result was telling. "A quarter of the persons classed as Hindus deny the supremacy of Brahmans, a quarter do not worship the great Hindu gods, . . . a half do not regard cremation as obligatory, and two-fifths eat beef."[20] Yet, if the Hindu was a puzzle for the colonial official, it was in many ways a problematic category for the Hindu propagandist too.

At the turn of the twentieth century, there was still much uncertainty about the collectivity called the Hindu community, and many different meanings still attached to the term *Hindu.* One question had by then been posed sharply: whether Buddhists and Jains, Sikhs, members of different *bhakti* sects such as the Kabirpanthis and Vallabhacharyas, and above all the untouchable and tribal groups and castes who literally lived on the physical fringes of settled Hindu society—outcastes, as they were often called, the *pancham* (or fifth estate) outside the four-*varna* classification—were to be included among the Hindus or not.

There is a great deal of evidence to show that in day-to-day reckoning the untouchables were often not thought of as Hindus by upper-caste Hindus. Officials in Chhattisgarh (eastern Madhya Pradesh) observed early in the twentieth century, to take only one example, that whereas "over most of India" the term *Hindu* was contrasted to *Muslim,* "in Chhattisgarh to call a man a Hindu conveys primarily that he is not a Chamar, or Chamara according to the contemptuous abbreviation in common use."[21]

"Over most of India" is a misleading phrase, of course, based almost certainly on nothing but a general impression. Does this include all of the northeastern states of present-day India, and the bulk of the South Indian peninsula—in other words, a very large part of the land and people of India? In Tamil Nadu, and I would guess in other parts of southern India and indeed in many parts of northern India, the term *Hindu* is used to this day specifically to differentiate upper-caste Hindus from untouchables, or Harijans (which is what the Gandhians called them), or Dalits (which is the designation that Dalit activists prefer).

It was precisely this question of who was a Hindu that V. D. Savarkar set out to resolve, once and for all as he would have it, in his *Hindutva.*[22] The problem came into being, he suggested, because of the loose and eclectic usage of the terms *Hindu, Hinduism,* and *Hindutva,* especially in the recent past. The question was important because new challenges had arisen, old categories were being redefined and "unified" in new ways, and the religious and cultural tradition(s) now designated as "Hindu" (or "Hinduism") was also in the process of rearticulation.

Savarkar begins his book with a long discourse on the importance of a name:

As the association of the [name] with the thing it signifies grows stronger and lasts long, so does the channel which connects the two states of consciousness tend to allow an easy flow of thoughts from one to the other, till at last it seems almost impossible to separate them. And when in addition to this a number of secondary thoughts or feelings that are generally roused by the thing get mystically entwined with the word that signifies it, the name seems to matter as much as the thing itself. (pp. 1–2)

The idea of a mystical unity of word and thing, derived perhaps from Sufi tradition and certain traditions of devotional Hinduism or *bhakti*, here has a political application. Savarkar considers at some length the relative merits of different names that have been applied to India: Aryavarta, Brahmavarta, Dakshinapath, Bharatvarsha, Hindustan. He opts for Hindustan, which is, in his reading, the original, authentic, and most sacred name of this sacred land.

The commonly accepted argument, then as now, was that the terms *Hindu* and *Hindustan* were derived at some time in the distant past from *Sindhu*, the name given by immigrant Aryans to the river Indus and, later, to all rivers in the subcontinent and also to the seas. Savarkar, while accepting this view, contests the originality of the Aryan word *Sindhu*. "It is quite probable," he writes, "that the great Indus was known as Hindu to the original inhabitants of our land and owing to the vocal peculiarity of the Aryans [the easy conversion of the sound *h* to *s*, and vice versa] it got changed into Sindhu." "Thus," he goes on,

Hindu would be the name that this land and the people that inhabited it bore from time so immemorial that even the Vedic name Sindhu is but a later and secondary form of it. If the epithet Sindhu dates its antiquity in the glimmering twilight of history then the word Hindu dates its antiquity from a period so remoter [*sic*] than the first that even mythology fails to penetrate—to trace it to its source. (p. 10)

The earliest is regularly adjudged in this nationalist discourse to be the best. Or if the best requires a leaven of the modern, of reform, of adjustment to capitalist and industrial times, the earliest is nevertheless the purest, the roots of a nation's glory, an infinite source of strength. As time passed and the Hindus consolidated their sway all over this land, new names arose, Savarkar writes. But they never wiped out that first "cradle name of our nation in India." "Down to this day the whole world knows us as 'Hindus' and our land as 'Hindusthan' as if in fulfilment of the wishes of our Vedic fathers who were the first to make that choice."

Hindu, Hindustan, Hindutva, then, are not mere words but a civilization and a history, which can and should be precisely defined. "*Hindutva*," declares the author, "is not a word but a history. Not only the spiritual or religious history of our people as at times it is mistaken to be . . . but a history in full. Hinduism is only a derivative, a fraction, a part of Hindutva. Unless it is made clear what is meant by the latter the first remains unintelligible and vague."

"*A Hindu*," he says further, "means a person who regards this land of Bharatvarsha, from the Indus to the seas as his Fatherland as well as his Holyland, that is the cradle land of his religion":

Aasindhusindhu paryanta yasya bharat bhumika;
Pitrabhu punyabhushchaiva sa vai hinduriti smritah.²³

"*Hinduism* means the 'ism' of the Hindu; and as the word Hindu has been derived from the word Sindhu, . . . meaning primarily all the people who reside in the land that extends from Sindhu to Sindhu [the Indus to the seas], Hinduism must necessarily mean the religion or the religions that are peculiar and native to this land and these people" (p. 104). The term *Hinduism* has been wrongly used for Vaidik or Sanatan Dharma alone (p. 109). "Properly speaking [it] should be applied to all the religious beliefs that the different communities of the Hindu people hold" (p. 105).

The importance of Savarkar's exercise of establishing a precise definition for *Hindu, Hindutva,* and *Hinduism* is well illustrated by the reactions to his book. The publisher's preface to the fourth edition of the book, published in 1949, observed that "the definition [of Hindutva] acted as does some scientific discovery of a new truth in re-shaping and re-co-ordinating all current Thought and Action. . . . At its touch arose an organic order where a chaos of castes and creeds ruled. The definition provided a broad basic foundation on which a consolidated and mighty Hindu Nation could take a secure stand" (p. vi). Swami Shraddhanand had responded in similar terms to the first publication of the book: "It must have been one of those Vaidik dawns indeed which inspired our Seers with new truths, that revealed to the author of 'Hindutva' this Mantra . . . this definition of Hindutva!!" (p. vi).

One may discount the hyperbole in these reactions and yet recognize that for the champions of Hindutva and Hinduism an adequate, acceptable, workable definition of the terms was still being sought in the 1920s. Hence, the propagandist's statement appeared in the form of a "scientific discovery." It was like a "revelation." It brought order out of growing chaos and gave the advocates of Hindu organization and Hindu politics a clearer foundation from which to work.

Which of Us Are Hindus?

Community identities are built upon identifications and exclusions by differentiating between us and them, the self and the other. Savarkar had established to his own satisfaction and that of many other advocates of Hindu assertion who was and who was not to be included in the Hindu community. His comments on the Sikhs sum up his position. "Along with us [they] bewail the fall of Prithviraj,[24] share the fate of a conquered people and suffer together as Hindus."

There is much that could be questioned in this tendentious historical reconstruction—its assertion of a subcontinentwide sympathy for Prithviraj Chauhan and its collapsing of the suffering of the Sikhs and all other Hindus into one—but let that pass. The author of *Hindutva* finds further evidence of the Sikhs' Hinduness in what he calls their "adoration" of Sanskrit as a sacred language and the language of their ancestors.

The land spread from the river, Sindhu, to the seas is not only the fatherland but also the holyland [of] the Sikhs. Guru Nanak and Guru Govind, Shri Banda and Ramsing [*sic*] were born and bred in Hindusthan; the lakes of Hindusthan are the lakes of nectar (Amritsar[25]) and of freedom (Muktasar). . . . Really if any community in India is Hindu beyond cavil or criticism it is our Sikh brotherhood in the Punjab, being almost the autochthonous dwellers of the Saptsindhu land and the direct descendants of the Sindhu or Hindu people. (pp. 123–24)

The Hindu ideologue goes on to clarify that the Sikhs are not Hindus in a religious sense, and that the Sikh protest against their classification as Hindus arose only because the Sanatanists had appropriated the word *Hindu* for themselves.

Sikhs are Hindus in the sense of our definition of Hindutva and not in any religious sense whatever. Religiously they are Sikhs as Jains are Jains, Lingayats are Lingayats, Vaishnavas are Vaishnavas; but all of us racially and nationally and culturally are a polity and a people. . . . Bharatiya indicates an Indian and expresses a larger generalization but cannot express [the] racial unity of us Hindus. We are Sikhs, and Hindus and Bharatiyas. We are all three put together and none exclusively. (p. 125)

This sense of *Bharatiya* or *Hindi* ("Indian") enabled Savarkar to accommodate in his polity those Indians—predominantly Muslims and Christians—who were not, in his view, Hindu. The vast majority of them, he acknowledged, were local converts and had "Hindu blood" flowing in their veins. But even if India, Bharatvarsha, Hindustan, was in this sense their Fatherland, they no longer recognized it as their Holyland. They did not, moreover, look upon Sanskrit, the language of the Vedas and other ancient Hindu texts, as a sacred language. What followed from this?

An American may become a citizen of India. He would certainly be entitled, if *bona fide*, to be treated as . . . Bharatiya or Hindi a countryman and a fellow citizen of ours. But as long as in addition to our country, he has not adopted our culture and our history, inherited our blood and . . . come to look upon our land not only as the land of his love but even of his worship, he cannot get himself incorporated into the Hindu fold. (p. 84)

For Savarkar and other Hindu nationalists of the 1920s and 1930s, the Muslims and Christians who lived in India, and had lived there in most cases as long as the Hindus, had a place in the country—as citizens (Bharatiya or Indians), but not as part of the cultural mainstream or core of the nation. The emerging and contending visions of the future nation-state had no room as yet for the notion of separate territories for any of these communities. Later Hindu propagandists have been rather more inflexible in their formulation of the meaning of Hindu nationhood, precisely because the notion of a separate territory gained ground first as an idea and then as a political reality—in Pakistan. For many of these propagandists, the Indian nation has come to be coterminous with the Hindu community. Explicitly or implicitly, Pakistan (and, since 1971, Bangladesh) has become the place where Indian Muslims belong.[26]

The inclusions and exclusions that go to make up community and nation in the Hindu discourse are, in fact, far more restrictive than Savarkar or any other Hindu writer openly suggests. The Hindu is far from being a transparent category, even today. Indeed, it can be shown that only a section of Hindus appear as truly Hindu and truly national in this Hindu discourse. M.S. Golwalkar's speeches and writings, collected in his *Bunch of Thoughts* published in the mid-1960s, provide a very good illustration of the point.[27]

"The Hindu . . . has ever been devoted to Bharat and ready to strive for its progress and uphold its honour. The national life values of Bharat are indeed derived from the life of Hindus. As such he [*sic*] is the 'national' here" (p. 218). By definition, therefore, Golwalkar's Hindus are the nation. There are, however, several groups in the country who are not only ambiguous in terms of nationality, but even antinational. The RSS head's *Bunch of Thoughts* makes this abundantly clear. In the section of the book entitled "The Nation and Its Problems," by far the longest chapter is entitled "Internal Threats." The three subheadings for the chapter are: "The Muslims," "The Christians," and "The Communists."

Listing Muslims and Christians is predictable, and the reason for it not far to seek: both are foreigners in this discourse, people who have allowed themselves to be sold to a foreign ideology and who no longer acknowledge, or are at best ambivalent about, their national religion, culture, and traditions. The inclusion of communists, however, requires some comment.

A war over international boundaries had been fought between India and China in 1962, in which the Indian armed forces had been worsted. Jawaharlal Nehru, prime minister of India until his death in 1964, and his defense minister, V. K. Krishna Menon, had come in for much criticism for what was called their policy of appeasement toward China and for the country's lack of military preparedness. This, and the India-Pakistan War of 1965, in which India's armed forces fared rather better, provide the immediate context for what Golwalkar has to say in this book about the communists, international relations, and the need for military strength. Before we discuss this, however, it is well to recall that modern nationalism in general has tended to emphasize the importance of a modern army in a modern nation.

"Non-violence is of no use under the present circumstances in India," Major-General K. M. Cariappa, deputy chief of the Indian Army Staff, declared in 1947, two months after Partition and Independence; only a strong army could make India "one of the greatest nations in the world."[28] Durga Das, a young correspondent of the pro-Congress *Hindustan Times*, went further and demanded that a strong state be built by liquidating "enemy pockets," and a strong army organized on the Nazi model.[29] Nathuram Godse, Gandhi's assassin, put it no less plainly a couple of years later in explaining his opposition to Gandhi: India needed to become a "modern" nation, "practical, able to retaliate, and . . . powerful with armed forces."[30]

Golwalkar shared these views. But the India-China War and his own extremist chauvinism provide the setting for his specific articulation. His discussion of the "nature of [the] yellow peril," in a chapter entitled "Fight to Win" written "in the wake of [the] Chinese invasion in October 1962," will suffice to indicate the character of the argument:

China has always been expansionist. It is in its blood. Over 150 years ago Napoleon had fore-warned not to rouse that yellow giant lest he should prove a grave peril to humanity. 70 years ago Swami Vivekanand had specifically warned that China would invade Bharat soon after the Britishers quit. . . . Now, added to the expansionist blood of China is the intoxicant of Communism which is an intensely aggressive, expansionist and imperialistic ideology. Thus in Communist China we have the explosive combination of two aggressive impulses. It is a case of—*api cha kapi, kapishayan madmattah* (Already a monkey, moreover drunk with wine). (p. 381)

A selective xenophobia, an upper-caste racism that has marked a good deal of Hindu political and social commentary at least since the later nineteenth century, and a narrow nationalism that is readily reduced to the question of territorial integrity and little else besides, runs through this and other Hindu propagandist statements of the period. The racist character of Golwalkar's attack upon the Chinese ("intoxicated monkeys") is striking,[31] as is the touching faith in the foreknowledge of Europeans (Napoleon's warning). The RSS ideologue goes on to make the comparison in so many words: "The Englishmen [who ruled India] were a civilized people who generally followed the rule of law. The Chinese are a different proposition" (p. 382).

It will be evident that the Hindu attack on the Chinese, and communists more generally, has other nationalist aspects to it. Here and elsewhere, the charge is made that communism is a foreign ideology and therefore has no place in India.[32] As a foreign ideology, communism and, by extension, any communist in India becomes antinational, almost by definition. However, there are also two additional grounds for the rejection of communist ideology by Hindu ideologues. One is that it is against religion—further evidence of its demoniacal character and its alienness to Indian (Hindu? spiritual?) traditions; the other that it is antidemocratic.

Hindu propagandists concede at times that the Bolshevik overthrow of tsarism in Russia was a blow against oppression and inequality. But oppression and inequality remain entirely abstract concepts in this discourse. The end of landlordism, largely accomplished in Russia and China and threatened in India in the 1950s, is of another order.[33] It strikes at the heart of bourgeois freedoms, that is, the right to property. Communism threatens other bourgeois freedoms too: freedom of speech, a free press, the right to association, the already mentioned freedom of religion, and so on. Much of this was evident, after all, in the practices of communist regimes in many parts of the world. But it is the right to property that is the crucial right. To deny this is to deny all social distinctions and hence the very basis of good nationhood; as Golwalkar put it in 1939, a good country or nation should have "all four classes of society as conceived by Hindu Religion."[34]

In Golwalkar's account of the national interest, the Hindu (i.e., the truly national) is presented as emphatically non-Muslim, non-Christian, and noncommunist. However, the construction of the category is not completed by these exclusions alone. The Hindu is also *male, upper-caste,* and, though I will not press this point too far, probably *north Indian* as well. Let us turn first to the question of caste (and class), which is sharply focused in the debate on the place of untouchables in Hindu society.

Untouchables: The Fallen Hindus

As already noted, census redefinition, and the exceptional importance attached to numbers in the political and administrative calculations of the Raj, contributed directly to the Hindu fear of losing the untouchables. Historians have commented on the impact of the so-called Gait Circular, which directed that separate tables be drawn up in the 1911 census for groups—like the untouchables and many tribal communities—who were not unambiguously Hindu. The circular "proved a good tonic for the apathy of orthodox Kashi," the reformist (Arya Samaj) leader Lala Lajpat Rai wrote:

One fine morning the learned pandits . . . rose to learn that their orthodoxy stood the chance of losing the allegiance of 6 crores of human beings who, the Government and its advisers were told, were not Hindus, in so far as other Hindus would not acknowledge them as such, and would not even touch them. . . . The possibility of losing the untouchables has shaken the intellectual section of the Hindu community to its very depths.[35]

As the assertion of community identity gathered steam at many levels—Hindu, Muslim, Sikh, Nadar, Patidar, Namasudra, Bihari, Oriya, Telugu—and economic and political competition between (and among) these groups acquired a new edge, militant Hindu leaders and organizations initiated a variety of moves to consolidate the Hindu community. Among these was the *shuddhi* (purification) campaign, which had gained significant support among reformist Hindus by the early decades of the twentieth century.

Shuddhi was a direct rejoinder to Christian missionary attacks on Hinduism and their efforts at converting low- and, to a lesser extent, high-caste Hindus in the nineteenth century. In response, the Arya Samaj cast itself, against the grain of orthodox Hindu practice, in the mold of a proselytizing Christian sect. As Lajpat Rai put it, "The Arya Samaj, being a Vedic *church*, and as such a Hindu organization, engages itself in reclaiming the *wandering sheep who have strayed from the Hindu fold*, and converts anyone prepared to accept its religious teachings."[36]

In the 1920s, Arya Samajis (joined by a few even of the more orthodox Hindus) "rediscovered" the *Devalasmriti*, said to have been written in the century or so after the first Arab raids on Sindh, which prescribed lengthy rules for readmission into Hinduism of Hindus who had been forcibly converted, and in the 1930s, the *vratyastoma* rites (supposedly laid down in the *Atharvaveda* and the *Brahmanas*) for readmission of those who were earlier judged to have fallen out of Aryan society.[37] *Shuddhi* now came to have a much broader significance than its original sense of purification would have suggested. It was now applied not only to:

reclamation, that is, raising the status of the *antyaj* (depressed) classes and making them full Hindus; but also to

re-conversion of those who had at some stage in the recent or distant past taken to a "foreign" religion; and to

conversion to Hinduism of people belonging to "foreign" religions.[38]

Over the same period, from the late nineteenth century on, many Hindu reformers spoke out against "perverse" Hindu religious notions and practices, "silly" antinational distinctions of caste, restrictions on inter-dining and travel overseas that were until that time fairly strictly observed, as well as ideas of pollution and the consequent difficulty of reconversion, which ensured that "millions of forcibly converted Hindus have remained Muslims even to this day."[39] Yet the matter was not easily settled, for Hindu beliefs and practices are heavily dependent on notions of purity and pollution and the accompanying structure of caste. The point is well illustrated by some of the compromise solutions reached during the debate on untouchables in the 1920s.

A special session of the Hindu Mahasabha, held at Allahabad in February 1924, discussed a resolution urging that untouchables be given access to schools, temples, and public wells. The resolution went on to say, however, that it was "against the scriptures and the tradition" to give the untouchables the "sacred thread" (*yagyopavit*), to teach them the Vedas, or to inter-dine with them. The Mahasabha hoped, therefore, that "in the interest of unity" Hindu workers would not insist upon these items of social reform. Several of the Arya Samaji delegates present at the meeting strongly opposed any such compromise, so this clause had to be amended. However, the final statement that came out of the deliberations still tried to have it both ways. "As the giving of 'Yagyopavit' to untouchables, inter-dining with them and teaching them Veda was opposed to the Scriptures according to a very large body of Hindus, i.e. the Sanatanists, these activities should not be carried on in the name of the Mahasabha."[40]

The question of *shuddhi* also proved contentious. Despite serious divisions, the Mahasabha ultimately (and unanimously) adopted the pronouncement of seventy-five pandits of Banaras whose opinion it had sought. The pandits had declared: "Any non-Hindu was welcome to enter the fold of Hinduism, though he could not be taken into any caste!"[41] A remarkable decision, given that the attribute of caste has long been a central feature of the identification of a Hindu.

The great difficulty of defining what would be appropriate "Hindu tradition and practice" in relation to the untouchables and other converts meant that many, non-Hindus especially, would continue to ask whether untouchables and tribals were, in fact, Hindus. Veer Bharat Talwar has argued that acceptance of *varnashrama dharma* (recognition of caste and the four stages of life an individual is supposed to go through)—which includes recognition of the supremacy of the Brahmin, worship of the cow, and burning of the dead—marks the beliefs and practices of all Hindus.[42] On the question of veneration for the cow and the manner of disposal of the dead, even those Hindu reformers who oppose caste would almost certainly agree. Yet, on those grounds alone, much of the tribal population of India must be reckoned as being outside the Hindu fold even today, for many among them eat beef and bury their dead.[43] A similar question could be asked about several other sections of the depressed classes (or untouchable communities), even if they live in closer geographical proximity to mainstream Hindu society.

"The depressed classes are Hindus," Lajpat Rai asserted; "they worship Hindu gods, observe Hindu customs, and follow the Hindu law." But even he could not claim that all of them worshipped the cow. "A great many of them worship the cow and obey their Brahmin priests."[44] Savarkar put the argument even more strongly in his analysis of the boundaries of Hindutva. Regarding the "Santals, Kolis, Bhils, Panchamas, Namashudras and all other such [depressed] tribes and classes," he wrote,

This Sindhusthan is as emphatically, the land of their forefathers as of those of the so-called Aryans; they inherit the Hindu blood and the Hindu culture; and even those of them who have not as yet come fully under the influence of any orthodox Hindu sect, *do still worship deities and saints and follow a religion however primitive,* are still purely attached to this land, which therefore to them is not only a Father-land but a Holyland.[45]

It is important to note the special pleading that goes into these statements. The depressed classes are untouchables but still indubitably Hindu: They "do . . . worship deities and saints," and some of them even worship the cow—even if they are, on the whole, rather "primitive." Many of the tribal and untouchable communities are fallen Hindus, it is said—Hindus who do not know (or have forgotten) that they are Hindus, and need to be reeducated in this truth. In the interests of unity and the continued privileges of Brahmins and others among the elite of Hindu society, however, these marginal Hindus were to be assigned an entirely subordinate place in Hindu society.

In the nineteenth-century reassertion of Hinduism, the argument had been made that the Aryans of Aryadesh were the original, and the most civilized, inhabitants of the world. In the Hindu propaganda of the time, this Aryadesh, or Hindustan, frequently appeared to be co-extensive with northern India. Even Dayanand Saraswati, the founder of the Arya Samaj, drew the southern boundary of Aryavarta at the Vindhya mountains: it was only in his last years that he seems to have developed an awareness that India south of the Vindhyas must also be drawn into the Arya movement.[46]

Physical boundaries, however, were only one part of the problem. The physical boundaries of Aryavarta, Hindustan, could be drawn by the Sindhu (from "Sindhu to Sindhu," the river to the seas) or more expansively from the northwest frontier of British India, the gateway to Central Asia, to the Bay of Bengal (from "Attock to Cuttack," as Hindu propagandists had it). Beyond this lay *mlecchasthan*, the land of the *mlecchas* (the unclean people). The physical bounds therefore connoted spiritual bounds as well. These spiritual bounds were of course to be found *within* the territory of India too—separating the Muslims, Christians, and others who were, by definition, primitive, dirty, and uncivilized. It is at this point that the uncertainty of the untouchables' position surfaces again.

Let me cite the writings of Swami Shraddhanand once more. Here was a strong advocate of the abolition of untouchability who in the 1920s expressed his anger at the ambivalence of the Hindu Mahasabha on this question. Inter-dining "alone can solve the problem of untouchability and exclusiveness among the Hindus," he wrote. Therefore "inter-dining among all the castes should be commenced at once." Nevertheless, care had to be exercised. The inter-dining was not to be "promiscuous eating out of the same cup and dish like Muhammadans." Instead, it was to be the "partaking of food in separate cups and dishes, cooked and served by decent Shudras."[47] "Decent"—that is to say, "clean"—Shudras were cultivating and artisanal communities who had aspired to and in places obtained a higher economic, political, and cultural status within the local community. Even such equality—the equality of being allowed to cook for and serve the higher castes—could not be conceded to the lowest classes, the menial laborers, the truly unclean, whether Shudra or untouchable.

In a statement cited above, Savarkar states that the depressed classes are "as emphatically" Hindu as the so-called Aryans,[48] even though they practice a rather primitive religion. Later propagandists have been wary of any such proposition, which concedes that some of these castes and tribes have been living in India from before the coming of the Aryans.

A special number of the RSS journal, *Panchjanya*, devoted to the tribal peoples of India and published in March 1982, is significantly entitled "*Veer Vanvasi ank.*" The use of the term *vanvasi* (forest or jungle dwellers) in place of the designation *adivasi*, which is the more commonly used term among social scientists and political activists talking about tribal groups in India, is not an accident. *Adivasi* means "original inhabitants," a status that the Hindu spokespersons of today are loathe to accord to the tribal population of India. *Vanvasi*, on the other hand, points directly to the primitive—the character that is being imputed to these "brave" (*veer*) but backward, not to say uncivilized, sections of society that have still to be fully reclaimed for Hinduism.[49]

What we have in the Hindu discourse, then, is an urge to Hindu unity and militancy overdetermined by a concern to preserve natural order.

The right-wing Hindu opposition to communism, noted above, is in this account based in no small part on the threat that communism poses to landlordism (*zamindari*) and to class distinctions in general. "A good country . . . [or] Nation," as Golwalkar said, "should have all four classes of society as conceived by Hindu Religion."[50] I have shifted here quite deliberately from a Marxist sense of class to the Hindu notion of caste, for the two reinforce each other in Hindu discourse. But the primary moment is probably that of the *varna vyavastha*, with its underlying notions of a hierarchical order based on caste or birth, with differing duties, rights, and privileges according to one's place in that order.

Mlecchas, Golwalkar goes on to say immediately after the statement just quoted, are "those who do not subscribe to the social laws dictated by the Hindu Religion and Culture."[51] It needs to be stressed that the *mlecchas* of this vision often include not only Muslims, Christians, and communists, but also insufficiently reclaimed untouchables and tribals, Kabirpanthis and Satnamis. On occasion, the term also seems to apply to women, South Indians, the people of the northeastern states of India, and indeed any other group or sect that challenges the social laws of the Hindus as defined by the men of the upper castes and classes of Hindu society. In Golwalkar's statement, as in most other so-called Hindu pronouncements, "Hindu Religion and Culture" stands for Brahman and Kshatriya dharma and for the dharma of other classes as defined by Brahman and Kshatriya men. This is a point that may be further illustrated by a consideration of the profoundly masculinist character of right-wing Hindu discourse.

Feminine Hindus/Masculine Hindus

The figure of Woman plays a crucial part in this discourse, as it does in nationalist discourse generally, in India and elsewhere. Shraddhanand was hardly unique when he wrote of his wish that "every child of the Matri-Bhumi [motherland] may daily bow before the Mother and renew *his* pledge to restore *her* to the ancient pinnacle of glory from which she has fallen!"[52] "Every child" that mattered was of course male. The community was a community of men—sometimes, indeed, only Brahman and Kshatriya men. "May spiritualized Brahmins take birth in our State, may bold champions of Truth and chastizers of enemies of Dharma, [i.e.] Kshatriyas, may milch cows and strong bulls, fleet horses and cultured ladies, together with youthful sin-conquering members of State be born in our midst."[53]

"The Hindu People . . . is the Virat Purusha, the Almighty manifesting Himself."[54] Yet the symbol of the community in its modern, national form is female: the Motherland, Mother Bharat. Golwalkar explains this as follows:

As human life evolves, the concept of mother also takes a wider and more sublime form. . . . [Man] sees the rivers which give him food and water. He calls them mother. Once he outgrows the use of his mother's milk, he sees the cow which feeds him with her milk throughout his life. He calls it mother-cow. And then he reaches the state of understanding that it is the mother soil which nourishes him, protects him and takes him in her bosom even after he breathes his last. He becomes conscious that she is his great mother. Thus to look upon one's land of birth as mother is a sign of a high state of human evolution.[55]

The decision to so look upon it was, however, always that of men: the Mother was inevitably born of a Father. Witness Savarkar's advocacy of the name *Hindusthan* in accordance with the wishes of "our Vedic fathers."

Woman appears in right-wing Hindu discourse as Mother and Nurturer, Preserver of Tradition, and Property. Her appearance as Mother Earth, Mother India, or the Nation represents not only a borrowing and an emulation of European nationalist movements: the French Republic (Marianne), Britannia, and so on; it is also an amplification and extension of the role of the individual woman as articulated in Indian nationalist discourse: provider and nurturer, luxuriant, beautiful, and generous by nature, a being capable of infinite sacrifice.

Woman's place as Mother and Nurturer, begetter of glorious sons of Aryavarta, has been underlined and analyzed by several scholars in recent times. Woman appears in Indian (and Hindu) nationalist discourse as Container or Vehicle, the repository of Indian (Hindu) tradition, the essence, the inner side, the spirituality and greatness of Hindu civilization. Here again, Matri-Bhumi, Bharat Mata, Woman is constructed in the image of individual upper-caste (middle class?) Hindu women: traditionally dressed, traditional in taste, ever serving, self-sacrificing, gentle, tolerant, passive.[56]

Finally, and perhaps most obviously, Woman appears in this discourse as Property. "The *Hindu* is being worsted everywhere—in *his* own country and in foreign lands. *His women* are being raped." "The *Hindus* have been completely wiped out. . . . *Their property* has been looted. *Their women* have been raped."[57] The association of women and property, ladies and cattle, is striking. The prayer invoked by Shraddhanand speaks of "milch cows and strong bulls, fleet horses and cultured ladies." And his advice to Hindus as regards the best way of avoiding conflict with Muslims is "to take care of your own women and children."[58]

That last injunction points to another aspect of Woman's being—her sexuality, which has long appeared deeply threatening to men. Woman is pure as a symbol of the nation, repository of its traditions, its spiritual side and inner strength. She is impure and even dangerous as a sexual being capable of independent thought and action.

Woman's impurity is physically evident at regular intervals: during the monthly period, pregnancy, and childbirth, when the Hindu woman, herself polluted, can pollute those who come in contact with her. But impurity, or its potential, is present in a more continuous sense as well. The sexual desire of women, combined with their alleged innocence and lack of rationality (their primitive instincts), leads them to turn from their benign role as mothers, wives, and widows and become temptresses and loose women, threatening order, morality, and the appropriate division between men's and women's spheres. Ignorant and weak, women may easily be misled and sullied.

As property and as sacred symbol, Woman and the Cow occupy parallel positions in the Hindu discourse. However, the Cow, in no way threatening to the community and the dominance of men, can never be made impure. It may be killed but never diminished. Not so with women. Compare the following sanctions contained in the circular letters, or *patias*, that formed a part of the Hindu call to arms for action against Muslims in the Shahabad (Bihar) strife of 1917. "Whatever Hindu, on seeing this *patia*, will not come, shall incur the guilt of killing 5 [or 7, or 12] cows." As against this are the sanctions involving women: if you do not circulate the *patias*, and follow their injunctions for specified actions against local Muslims, then "you do mount on your daughter, drink your wife's piss, and mount on your sister's daughter. It would be better indeed to marry your mother to a Musalman."[59]

There were other times when the sacrifice of women passed from metaphor to grim reality. Some of the most disturbing episodes in the undeclared war of 1947 arose out of the readiness of Hindu men (though not of men alone) to sacrifice women who had been—or were supposed to be in danger of being—polluted, that is to say, abducted or raped. Several recent studies have provided details of instances in which women were forced into acts of collective suicide or killed by male relatives fighting to preserve community honor. Women who were actually raped and abducted sometimes proved to be an even greater burden to their families and kin, who were loathe to acknowledge that the family or community had suffered any such dishonor and frequently refused to take back such unfortunately "fallen" women.[60]

The point that emerges from right-wing Hindu discourse is that Woman—saint and potential sinner at one and the same time—is to be not only protected but also segregated and controlled. The emphasis on modesty, on the place of woman in the kitchen and inside the home, the promotion of carefully structured, limited, and separate education for girls, and Dayanand Saraswati's prescription of *niyoga* (strictly regulated sexual relationships for the purpose of procreation) in order to prevent widows from straying into "immorality,"[61] were all part of this drive to protect, discipline, and maintain control in an era when the needs and organization of the wider community had clearly changed in important ways. With all that, however, the main task of the (male) community was seen as being that of regaining its strength, in other words its manliness, and thereby protecting its women, its property, and its dharma.

A number of historians have written about the great emphasis placed on *baahubal* (physical strength) and on traditions of military glory and valor in the nationalist, and Hindu, discourse of the late nineteenth century. Behind this was a perception Hindu publicists and thinkers had imbibed from nineteenth-century colonial writings that the Hindus were singularly lacking in manliness and military vigor. For the colonialists, this was part of the long, unchanging history of Hindustan, a consequence of its climatic conditions. For Hindu leaders, there was need for a different kind of explanation, and for hard training and effort in the present to make up for this lack. Hence the proposition that the great, ancient Hindu nation went into decline with the coming of the Muslims. Hence the discovery of the heroic struggles of the Sikhs, the Marathas, and the Rajputs, and the portrayal of the latter as the common ancestors of all Hindus, be they Bengali, Gujarati, or Tamil. Hence Bankimchandra Chattopadhyaya's construction of Krishna as a perfect, controlled, rational man of action, untouched by any element of playfulness or eroticism; and hence Vivekananda's prescription of beef and football as ready means for the regeneration of the Hindus.[62]

The emphasis on military valor and training has not diminished. Indeed, the establishment of an Indian nation-state has accentuated it further; witness the opinion of General Cariappa and others cited in a previous section, and the widespread political support for the Indian government's initiation of a nuclear weapons program in 1998—the ultimate in national masculinization. It was in accordance with this line of thinking that militant Hindu organizations decided to support the British war effort in India and seek military training for Hindus during the Second World War, and that Savarkar, the president of the All-India Hindu Mahasabha at this time, advanced the inelegant slogan, "Hinduize all Politics and Militarize Hindudom!"

The assessment made by M. S. Golwalkar in 1966 would, I suspect, have been widely shared by Hindu and other nationalist propagandists:

No nation can hope to survive with its young men given over to sensuality and effeminacy. . . . In the First World War, the Generalissimo of the "Allied Forces" was Marshall Foch, a Frenchman. Such was the heroic state of that nation at that time that they fought the Germans with grim resolve and won the war ultimately. They even pocketed a sizeable portion of Germany. But after the victory, Frenchmen succumbed to sensuality and enjoyment. They lost themselves in drinking, singing and dancing with the result that in spite of their huge military machine and their formidable "Maginot line," France collapsed within fifteen days of the German onslaught during the Second World War. The sudden and total collapse of France was due to *effeminacy which had sapped the energy of the heroic manhood of France.*[63]

The world understands nothing but the language of strength, this Hindu leader of the extreme right continued. The true Dharm is the Kshatriya dharma—the warrior's philosophy of victory. The Hindus, grown weak, must become strong again if they are to protect their women, their property, and their rights. "*Bhay binu hoy na preet*" (Without Fear, there can be no Love).[64] Hindus must therefore instill fear in the non-Hindus who live with them before true love can emerge. This is a faith that Hindu propagandists and Hindu crowds have adopted with evident glee in the violent attacks on Muslims and other religious minorities that have occurred in India with alarming frequency, and on a frightening scale, from the 1980s on.

At the same time, the message of nonviolence has been increasingly reviled. Gautama Buddha and Mohandas Gandhi are held to be equally responsible for the decline and emasculation of the Hindus through their "mealy-mouthed formulas of Ahimsa and spiritual brotherhood."[65] The founders of Buddhism and Jainism are at times treated with some sympathy on the ground that they advocated "relative Ahimsa" in an age when this philosophy had some meaning. Not so Gandhi, who is said to have espoused a creed of "absolute non-violence."[66] On account of this creed, we are informed, the "glorious struggle for national freedom" which had lasted for a thousand years was shamelessly surrendered in the thirty years of Gandhi's leadership of the national movement, and the Hindus were forced to accept the "unchallenged domination of the aggressor over huge portions of our land": this is a reference to the establishment of Pakistan (now Pakistan and Bangladesh) in the northwest and the northeast of the territories that made up British India.

Virtues like nonviolence and tolerance are all very well—and, as it happens, Savarkar writes, every Hindu imbibes the lesson of tolerance along with his mother's milk.[67] Nevertheless, historical context and political circumstances must determine the extent to which these virtues are to be upheld. In respect to intolerant foreign religions, "the very extremely enraged intolerance, which seeks to retaliate their atrocities with *super-atrocious reprisals,* itself becomes a virtue."[68]

It is in this context that the RSS, Hindu Mahasabha, and other extreme right-wing Hindu organizations have asked, periodically from the 1940s on, how Mahatma Gandhi with his feminine *charkha* (spinning wheel) can possibly be considered the Father of the Nation? In recent years, they have even celebrated the actions of Gandhi's assassin, Nathuram Godse, as the harbinger of another Hindu tradition and the symbol of another nation—one wedded not to femininity and nonviolence but to masculinity and violence, not to Truth but to Victory.[69] Thus is the modern, national Hindu to be mobilized.

6

Marked and Unmarked Citizens

In the present chapter, I continue the examination of the process of construction of the unmarked national, the real, obvious, axiomatically natural citizen—Indian, Nigerian, Australian, American, British, whatever. I investigate the simultaneous construction of the hyphenated (or marked) citizen—Indian Muslims, Indian Christians, Indian Jews, or African Americans, Mexican Americans, Native Americans, and so on. The latter have often lived in the nineteenth and twentieth centuries—the centuries of nationalism—under the sign of a question mark. What, I want to ask, are the enabling conditions for such question marks?

Two tasks confront the advocates of a natural national identity. The first is to establish the oneness of the people claimed as a nation. The second is to find the appropriate political arrangement to make room for those who do not naturally fit into the unified, undifferentiated nation—and we scarcely need to remind ourselves that such groups exist to a greater or lesser extent in all modern political communities. The challenge is perhaps greater in a country like India, where millennia of settled existence and layer upon layer of migrants moving into the land from the earliest stage of the country's recorded history have made for a very mixed and hierarchically differentiated population.

The previous chapter showed how the most fervent promoters of natural nationhood in India sought to create the unmarked national by denying or effacing marks of internal division and domination. In this chapter, I turn to the question of how the nation-state handles historically recognized religious and cultural difference by constructing majorities and minorities. I also explore the demand that arises at the same time for loyalty—proof of genuine belonging—from those who do not inhabit the nationalist core: the minorities and marginal groups who might almost be allowed to be part of the nation but never quite.

It goes without saying that majorities and minorities, like nation-states, are means of organizing and distributing political power. All of these are established by defining boundaries. However, boundaries are not generally—or perhaps ever—easily defined. In negotiating this difficulty, nations and nationalisms have commonly moved along the path of identifying the core (or mainstream) of the nation. Alongside have emerged notions of minorities, marginal communities or groups, the fuzzy edges and gray areas around which the question of boundaries—geographical, social, and cultural—is negotiated or fought over.[1]

I seek to track this negotiation through an examination of the assertions of citizenship and demands for proof of loyalty that were made in India at the time of the transfer of power and the partition of the subcontinent in 1947.

Terms of Nationalist Discourse

Two terms that have been central to the discourse on the Muslim question, as it is called in India, will serve as a useful starting point for this part of my discussion. Though both date to before 1947, they acquired a new urgency, even a new meaning, with Partition and Independence. The first is the figure of the Nationalist Muslim, the second the official Indian understanding of *minority* and *majority*.

Perhaps the first point to be made about the Nationalist Muslim is that there is no equivalent category for Hindus, or for that matter any of the other religious groupings in India. Interestingly, in speaking of the politics of Hindus, the term is frequently reversed to read Hindu nationalists. The reversal is of course not coincidental. What does the term *Hindu nationalists* signify? It does not refer simply to nationalists who happen to be Hindus. It is, rather, an indication of their brand of nationalism, in which the Hindu moment has considerable weight. It is a nationalism in which Hindu culture, Hindu traditions, and the Hindu community are given pride of place.

Alongside the rise of Hindu nationalism, and much more emphatically over time, a more inclusive kind of nationalism had developed, which emphasized the composite character of India society and refused to give the same sort of primacy to the Hindu element in India's history and self-consciousness. This would later come to be called secular nationalism, real or Indian nationalism, "something quite apart from . . . [the] religious and communal varieties of nationalism and strictly speaking . . . the only form which can he called nationalism in the modern sense of the word," as Jawaharlal Nehru put it.[2] This was the Indian nationalism of the Indian constitution—"nationalism" pure and simple, in Nehru's phrase. Because of the coexistence of these two brands of nationalism from the late nineteenth century onward, politically conscious Hindus have been divided into Hindu nationalists and secular (or Indian) nationalists.

There were of course signs of a growing Muslim nationalism in the same period. Like Hindu nationalism, this Muslim variant developed side by side with the broader Indian nationalist movement, in which large numbers of Muslims were also involved (from Badruddin Tyabji and Maulana Mohamed Ali to Mohammad Ali Jinnah and Fazl-ul-Haq, not to mention Mukhtar Ahmad Ansari, Abul Kalam Azad, Zakir Husain, Sheikh Abdullah, and Khan Abdul Ghaffar Khan). However, politically active Muslims were not divided into Muslim nationalists and secular nationalists; they were divided instead into Nationalist Muslims and Muslims—and here the proposition extended of course to more than just those who were politically involved.

The Hindus—or the majority of politically conscious Hindus, for there were in this view many who formed part of a large inert mass and at least a few loyalists—were, in other words, nationalists first and foremost. Whether they were Hindu nationalists or secular nationalists was a subsidiary question. All Muslims were, however, *Muslims*. Their political inactivity or inertia made little difference in this instance. Some Muslims were advocates of Indian nationalism, and hence were Nationalist Muslims. The remainder of that community—in town and country, north and south, handloom workshop or building site, modest hut or railway quarters—were not seen as being likely supporters of Indian nationalism, on account of their being Muslim. The peculiar history of Hindu-Muslim political differences from the late nineteenth century onward, and British efforts to keep the Muslims on their side against the rising tide of what they saw as *babu*, Hindu nationalism, had contributed to the development of this view. But the years immediately preceding Partition and Independence,

Partition itself, and the fact of agitation for separate Muslim rights clearly had more than a little to do with its wide acceptance as an axiomatic truth.

Two other terms that require some attention in their contemporary political usage, not only in India but in much of the rest of the world, are *minority* and *majority*. When used in conjunction with religion or ethnicity or culture, these terms result in a curious ambiguity, as Talal Asad has reminded us. For whereas *majority* and *minority* belong primarily to a vocabulary of electoral and parliamentary politics and the shifting terrain upon which these politics are supposed to be carried out, culture (like religion, race, and so on) is "virtually coterminous with the social life of particular populations, including habits and beliefs conveyed across generations." To speak of cultural, ethnic, or religious minorities is therefore to posit what Asad calls "ideological hybrids." It is "to make the implicit claim that members of some cultures truly belong to a particular politically defined place, but those of others (minority cultures) do not—either because of recency (immigrants) or of archaicness (aborigines)."[3] Or, one might add, simply because of unspecified but (as it is asserted) fundamental difference—as in the case of the Indian Muslims.

Partition and Independence fixed these terms in a national, countrywide sense for Indian society and politics. The Muslims were now a minority, as of course were Sikhs, Anglo-Indians, Indian Christians, Parsis, and Jains, although these latter did not seem to matter as much in 1947–48, for a variety of reasons that I will shortly discuss. The Muslims were now the minority even in districts, cities, or towns where they happened to be a numerical majority; the latter term applied only in a descriptive sense. They were the minority that had fought for, or wanted, Pakistan, and they now had not only to choose where they belonged but also to demonstrate the sincerity of their choice: they had to prove that they were loyal to India and, hence, worthy of Indian citizenship.

The Hindus were the majority, even if substantial numbers of those designated or claimed as Hindus had little to gain from the appellation, were denied access to sacred Hindu sites and texts, or (as in the case of the Dalits, whom we will discuss in the next chapter) themselves tended to discard the denomination Hindu altogether. In the tumult of Partition and Independence, however, the Hindus (often encompassing both Hindus and Sikhs) were spoken of as a unity, which was ranged for the most part against the Muslims. The search was on for the genuine, unambiguously loyal citizen. The Hindus, it was said, had no other country (save Nepal, which was seen in this perspective as something of an adjunct to India). Their attachment to the Indian nation was beyond doubt. Hindu or Indian was an irrelevant distinction; the terms were interchangeable. The question boiled down, instead, to an inquiry into the appropriate status of the minorities in the new nation-state.

Before I turn to the details of this nationalist inquiry and its implications, there is one other point that needs to be made about nationalism. Although this is especially applicable to the anticolonial nationalisms of the late nineteenth and twentieth centuries, which struggled to form a unity of the people in the effort to stake claim to independent statehood, it seems to me to have wider resonance. Everywhere, I would argue, the nation/ people has historically come into being through struggles to define and advance a national interest. Everywhere, however, there is a simultaneous and, as it seems, almost necessary desire to present the nation as given, an already formed totality, even a spirit or essence.

Once the nation has a state of its own or (in nationalist parlance) is realized in the nation-state, this essence, this totality, becomes concretized in the state and its territory. The national interest is equated with the integrity of the state and its boundaries, and the preservation of the state is described as the first duty of the nation. Loyalty to the nation, the widely touted test of true, unquestioned citizenship, becomes loyalty to an already existing state and the interests of that state (all that it stands for and even, literally, where it stands!). There is usually a catch in all this: the test of loyalty is in fact required only of those who are not real, natural citizens.

All over the world, there has been a tendency for the equation "the nation = the people" to be mapped onto the equation "the nation = the state." The categories *majority* and *minority* appear with their full political force when these two equations are collapsed into one. As categories, one might say, majority and minority hold these equations together.

Nationhood in the Subcontinent

Partition and Independence, on 15 August 1947, was the moment of establishment of the two new nation-states, India and Pakistan. But it was also—and here the date becomes less clear-cut—the moment of the congealing of new identities, relations, and histories, or of their being thrown into question once again. The particular circumstances attending this birth scarcely require restatement. Practically the entire minority population of certain areas was driven out: Hindus and Sikhs from the West Pakistan territories and Muslims from East Punjab and several neighboring tracts in India, as well as Muslims and Hindus from the two halves of Bengal (although this happened on a lesser scale and somewhat more gradually). Incalculable numbers were uprooted, murdered, maimed, looted, raped, and abducted—I have mentioned the common estimates of half a million or more people killed and twelve to fourteen million driven out and transformed into refugees.[4] All of erstwhile northern India (including both the eastern and western wings of Pakistan), and many of the central and southern states (among them Hyderabad in southern India) were more or less seriously affected.

What made the moment of independence particularly bitter was that neither of the two new states turned out to be quite what its proponents had hoped for. Pakistan has perhaps had the more anguished history in this respect. It had been proposed as a Muslim homeland, the country of the Muslim nation of the subcontinent. There was never any question, however, that the ninety million Muslims of undivided India—spread out all over that territory, with Muslim-majority regions in northwestern and northeastern India and pockets (towns and subdistricts) elsewhere—would all be accommodated or even wish to migrate to the areas that became Pakistan.

To complicate matters further, the political leaders who founded the state of Pakistan seemed, at the moment of its foundation, to turn away from the proposition of an Islamic nation-state to the conception of a secular, multireligious Pakistan. This is what Mohammad Ali Jinnah had to say in his famous speech at the opening session of the Constituent Assembly of Pakistan, on 11 August 1947: "You may belong to any religion or caste or creed—that has nothing to do with the business of the state. . . . We are all citizens and equal citizens of one state. . . . You will find that in the course of time Hindus would cease to be Hindus and Muslims would cease to be Muslims, not in the religious sense, because that is the personal faith of each individual but in the political sense as citizens of the state."[5]

This new tone produced considerable bewilderment among followers of the Muslim League and a heated counterattack. "How could Muslims cease to be Muslims and Hindus cease to be Hindus in the political sense when the religions . . . were, in Jinnah's passionately held belief, so utterly different from one another? Was Jinnah giving up the two-nation theory?" one Pakistani commentator subsequently asked.[6] In a letter to the *Civil and Military Gazette* of 21 October 1947, Muhammad Sa'adat Ali of Lahore protested a Pakistan minister's statement that Pakistan was "a secular, democratic and not a theocratic state." Such a statement "has absolutely no support of the Muslims," he wrote. "Ever since Mr. Jinnah undertook to fight our case, he has, on occasions without number, proclaimed emphatically that Muslims were determined to set up a state organized and run in accordance with the irresistible dictates of the Islamic Shariat. . . . If secularization were our sole aim, India need not have been partitioned. . . . We raised this storm for partition because we wanted to live as free Muslims and organize a state on Islamic principles."[7]

On the Indian side too, this confusion and the ongoing transfer of populations in the midst of unprecedented violence and bloodshed provoked angry questions. The Muslims had fairly widely supported the movement for Pakistan—though, as was already becoming evident, few had clear ideas about what that goal meant. Be that as it may, opponents of the Pakistan scheme now declared that the Muslims had after all got a state of their own, as they wanted. Large numbers of Muslims had migrated to the new state. Others were fleeing. Those that remained harbored sympathies for Pakistan, it was widely rumored, and many of them were gathering and storing arms. It was asked over and over: Was this just for self-defense? Were they entitled to take such defense into their own hands instead of putting their faith in the governmental authorities? Did these suspect people, open supporters of Pakistan until yesterday, and potential fifth columnists, have any right to remain in India?

Partition and Independence thus gave rise to an intense debate over the character of the new nation-states: should they be secular (which was to say multicommunity, with equal rights for all)? Socialist? Hindu? Muslim? Pakistan emerged, after the long drawn-out moment of Partition, with its communal holocaust and forced migration, as an overwhelmingly Muslim country, especially in its western half. As they saw this happening, sections of the Hindu nationalist press in India observed that Pakistan was on its way to establishing an *ekjatiya rashtra* (literally, a "one-nation nation," a homogenous, one-people nation) and lamented that India might never be able to achieve the same kind of unity (or, more accurately, homogeneity). Substantial sections of the north Indian population, especially Hindu and Sikh refugees from West Pakistan and those most directly affected by their influx, as well as sections of the political leadership, especially the Hindu right wing and leaders of the Sikh community, now demanded that India (or at least some parts of it, such as East Punjab, Delhi, and the neighboring districts of western U.P., where Hindu and Sikh refugees had flooded in in the weeks before and after 15 August 1947) should be cleared of Muslims: the latter should be sent to Pakistan and the territory handed over to the Sikhs and Hindus.

Could any substantial body of Indian Muslims stay on in India in these conditions? The answer to this question was perhaps provided in the end by sheer exhaustion, the recognition that killing and counterkilling, massacre and countermassacre could not go on endlessly without destroying everything and everybody, the fact that in some areas there was no one left to kill (except in fairly well-guarded refugee camps), and the awareness that the entire body of Muslims in India could not be driven out anyway. This growing exhaustion and awareness, however weak, was aided by the combined efforts of the governments on both sides to provide safe passage to all those who wished to migrate, especially from the two Punjabs; by the determination of a large section of India's nationalist (and left-wing) leaders and workers to support the goals of the Indian freedom struggle and fight for a secular republic where all of India's inhabitants could live, irrespective of religious denomination; and by the assassination of Mahatma Gandhi in January 1948 at the hands of a Hindu extremist, which seems to have brought a good deal of northern India back to its senses and marked a turning point in the debate over secular nation or Hindu nation.

The Muslims stayed, now constituting ten percent of the new nation-state's population.[8] But the question remained: can a Muslim really be an Indian? This is one of the enduring legacies of Partition in India, and it has more than a little to do with the way in which Indian nationalism and the Indian state have gone about the task of managing difference from that day to this.

Do Muslims Belong?

Which, if any, Muslims had the right to stay on in India? Gandhi, Nehru, and other top-ranking nationalist leaders answered the question categorically in 1947 and 1948: all those who wished to. However, there were doubts even in the minds of many who espoused this policy, and more than a little resistance from other quarters. The recriminations, calculations, bitterness, and heightened violence of the preceding year showed little sign of abating after 15 August 1947. Large numbers of politically conscious and mobilized Hindus felt betrayed, and openly moved to right-wing positions. The Sikhs, split down the middle by the partition of Punjab, were angry and bewildered almost as a community.[9] Muslim Leaguers in those provinces that remained in India, where Muslims were a minority—having obtained a partition they had probably never expected and about the practical implications of which they had certainly thought little—were at a loss.[10]

Few people now cared to differentiate carefully among the Muslims of India. The regional, caste, and occupational markers by which generations of Muslims had been known—and privileged, denigrated, or even declared to be only half-Muslims—seemed to lose much of their significance. The Muslims were now increasingly—in official documents, journalism, and common conversation—simply Muslims, and all of them were suspect as open or closet Pakistanis. When Gandhi declared it the duty of the central government and all provincial governments in India to ensure that "full justice" was done to the Muslims, there were many outraged protests. The comments of a Kanpur nationalist daily on 19 June 1947 provide an indication of the tone of much of this reaction. "We are prepared to deny our instinctive feelings," the editors wrote, "and go along with Mahatma Gandhi to the extent that we accept the good faith not only of Congress members but of all nationalist Muslims [though the same paper would observe a couple of months later that their numbers were "steadily declining"], and give to them the rights of Indian citizens. . . . But it would be a political blunder of a high order if we were to give these privileges to every Muslim living in India."[11] The undifferentiated category "Muslims" had been too greatly involved in the Muslim League demand for Pakistan: their sympathies were not likely to change overnight and their loyalty could not he counted upon.

The same suspicion spread, or already existed, among the ranks of the senior Congress leadership. An article published by Babu Sampurnanand, then education minister in the Congress government of U.P., two weeks before official Partition and Independence, illustrates the point very well indeed. Sampurnanand looked forward to 15 August with the mixture of excitement and sadness that was the common lot of many reflective nationalists at this time. He spelled out the reasons for his sadness as follows: "In earlier times too, India has for centuries been divided into small independent states, but overriding these political boundaries a cultural uniformity held these provinces together in a common bond. Today, this bond is breaking: the culture that the leaders [of Pakistan] have promised to develop for the provinces that are breaking away is utterly un-Indian."[12] Sampurnanand still expressed the hope that the "two halves" would come together again, but when or how this might happen he could not say.

In spite of this sorrow, *swa-raj* (self-rule, independence) was welcomed. India was losing something, wrote Sampurnanand, but what she was gaining was greater by far: "We are going to recover that [precious] thing that we lost a thousand years ago." Note how easily, not to say naturally, the *we* is constructed as Hindu: today we (Hindus/Indians) are going to recover that freedom which we lost with the coming of Muslim power. The Congress leader says this explicitly in the next sentence: "With the defeat of Prithviraj [at the hands of Mohammad Ghori] at the battle of Thanesar, Bharat [India] lost its *swa* [one's own, or self]. Look at the history of *our* science and *our* philosophy. Over the last one thousand years there has *not been even one development* [*aavishkar*, literally invention] which has contributed a mite to the sum of human knowledge."[13]

Finally, Sampurnanand mentioned a lurking fear about the potential loyalties of Muslims in independent India. To put this in context, it is necessary to reiterate that the theme of territorial integrity and the defense of our borders is a crucial ingredient of modern states and their nationalisms. This particular article was hardly an exception. The northwestern frontier of India was at the Khyber Pass, according to him. This was no political fantasy; it was "nature's arrangement"—very much in line with the propositions of natural nationhood discussed above. Now, unfortunately, Sampurnanand wrote, the burden of the defense of this frontier would fall on the young and inexperienced shoulders of Pakistan.

But there was more to it than that. If, "God forbid," there was ever a war between India and Pakistan, "*our* worries will be greatly increased, for it is not impossible that the sympathies of our Muslim population will veer towards Pakistan." The fear expressed here grew in strength in the weeks and months that followed, as Partition worked itself out and large numbers of Indian Muslims were pushed to the wall. Indeed the political history of India for some time afterward, and one might even say until today, has in no small part been the history of a struggle to control this fear.

In the later months of 1947, a wide range of India's nationalist leaders began to focus on the issue Sampurnanand had raised—war, and loyalty in war. The renowned Socialist leader Dr. Ram Manohar Lohia, speaking at a public meeting in Delhi on 11 October 1947, urged the people to "rally round the Nehru Government and make it strong enough to take, when necessary, effective measures against the Pakistan Government." This was an appeal to all communal forces, Hindu, Muslim, and Sikh, and to those who harbored doubts about the government's declared secular platform. But three days earlier, at another rally in Delhi, Lohia had pointedly asked India's Muslims to "surrender [their] arms and . . . be loyal citizens of India, ready to fight, if need be, against Pakistan or any other country."[14]

At the same time, Govind Ballabh Pant, Congress chief minister of U.P.—an accomplished parliamentarian, an able administrator, and a man of wide, secular, human sympathies—was driving home the same point. Every Indian Muslim should "realize clearly" what loyalty to the nation would mean if Pakistan invaded India, he declared. "Every Muslim in India would be required to shed his blood fighting the Pakistani hordes. Each one should search his heart now, and decide whether he should migrate to Pakistan or not."[15]

Muslim leaders who stayed on in India were clearly under some pressure to express themselves in similar terms. The Raja of Mahmudabad, secretary of the All-India Muslim League and Jinnah's right-hand man for much of the decade before 1947, provides a striking illustration. Like so many other Muslim League leaders of U.P. and Bihar, Mahmudabad had never contemplated leaving his native land. Broken by the experience of Partition, he resigned from the Muslim League in September 1947. The party had committed hara-kiri, he said. To keep it alive in India now was a cruel joke. Most of its leaders—Mahmudabad actually said all—had run away from India, leaving the Muslims to their fate. These opportunists should now be clear in their mind that they would never be able to mislead the Muslim masses again. "All Indian Muslims would go to war for India, even if they had to go to war against Pakistan."[16] Taking a similar tack, M. A. Salam, a member of the Madras Legislative Assembly and the All-India Muslim League Council, declared that his community of Andhra Muslims was loyal to the Indian Union and "shall defend it against anybody to the last drop of their blood."[17] That last contention had become a password to citizenship, as it were: a password that has been demanded of Muslims of India, in one form or another, ever since.

Partition produced a plethora of ideas on what would constitute adequate proof of Indian Muslims' loyalty to India. Many called for disbanding of the Muslim League and giving up any demand that smacked even remotely of separatism—such as appeals for separate electorates or an assured quota of legislative seats for Muslims. As the deputy prime minister of India, Vallabhbhai Patel, put it in the Constituent Assembly debate on minority rights, these measures had resulted in "the separation of the country": "Those who want that kind of thing have a place in Pakistan not here (applause). . . . We are laying the foundations of One Nation, and those who choose to divide again and sow the seeds of disruption will have no place, no quarter here. . . . (Hear, hear!)."[18] Today, a whole host of lower-caste groups have demanded and obtained reservations of various kinds to enable them to compete more equally in the administrative and political processes of India. But fifty years ago was a very different moment, and the Muslims were a very different minority.

After India became independent, the "Muslim League mentality" was declared to be completely unacceptable. Many nationalist observers declared that Muslim government officials in India needed monitoring, since Muslim professionals and educated urban youth had been especially enthusiastic about the Pakistan idea and Muslim civil servants had opted for Pakistan in substantial numbers where the option was available. Those who reversed an earlier option in favor of working in Pakistan and decided to stay on in India needed to be watched even more carefully, for this reversal might well be part of a plot hatched by the Muslim League and the leaders of Pakistan to plant spies in the corridors of power in India.

In support of this theory, the nationalist press gave much prominence to reports of documents recovered from passengers departing to or returning from Pakistan, of arms and machinery found on the persons or in the baggage of Muslim officials in transit, and of inefficient implementation of government orders by subordinate Muslim officials (as if they alone were guilty of such inefficiency!). In one instance, incriminating documents seized at Lucknow airport appear to have been handwritten letters sent by refugees in Pakistan to their relatives in India urging them to migrate as soon as possible because conditions in India were (from all reports) very bad and the future was unpredictable. Among reports of arms seizures, it is no surprise to find mention of batteries for flashlights, kerosene oil, bales of cloth, and air guns alongside swords, daggers, spears, guns, and more serious weapons. A Delhi paper reported in September 1947 that a "large number" of Muslim police officers were found trying to leave for Pakistan "without notice," taking with them their "uniforms and weapons."[19]

Muslims Leaguers and Muslim bureaucrats who remained in India amid these accusations and suspicions scarcely proved their loyalty in the eyes of their interrogators by making the difficult decision to stay on. They were called upon to swear oaths of loyalty to the new state, which they did. However, a demonstration of Muslim loyalty to the nation now required denial of any separate Muslim needs and of a Muslim perspective. Thus the *Aj* of Banaras, perhaps the most important Congress paper in the Hindi belt, welcomed the pledge of loyalty to the constitution taken by the Muslim League members of the Constituent Assembly, but asked why the same people had absented themselves at the time of the singing of "Bande Mataram," the "national song" (as *Aj* called it) composed by Bankimchandra Chattopadhyay, with its pronounced Hindu overtones. The Muslim legislators explained that they had abstained on grounds of religious sensibility. The editors of the Banaras daily shot back that while this anthem, unlike the flag, had not as yet been ratified by the Constituent Assembly, it nevertheless had the stamp of "historical legitimacy."[20]

As we have noted, several Muslim leaders in India demanded the disbanding of the League and the strengthening of the secular, democratic Indian National Congress as the one party that could guarantee the safety and rights of Muslims. Others argued that the League should continue, but as an unambiguously secular party working with other secular parties in India for the common advancement of the masses. The Muslim League leaders in India had readily sworn an oath of loyalty to the Indian flag and constitution. Yet many continued to travel frequently between India and Pakistan—as they had to, given that close relatives and associates were scattered because of the troubled conditions—and a few still looked to Jinnah for guidance on how to lead the Indian Muslims.[21] Their supporters and large numbers of other ordinary, nonpolitical Muslims hoisted the Indian tricolor and joined enthusiastically in the Independence Day celebrations on 15 August. Yet, in the prevailing circumstances, some prepared to defend themselves in case of attack, while many others sat ready to flee should developments make it even more dangerous to stay.

The swearing of oaths could scarcely be seen as adequate proof of loyalty in this context. "Loyalty is not established by mere verbal protestation," declared the *Vartman* on 27 September 1947. "How do we have any demonstration of it without deeds [*amal*]?" The proofs called for were curious and varied. Muslims alone could stop the killings in Punjab and other parts of northern India, it was said. All those who had links with the Muslim League should urge "their Pakistani brethren" to put an end to the violence. Leaguers must make an unqualified denunciation of the two-nation theory and campaign actively for reunification. Muslims generally must step forward to help Hindu and Sikh refugees and thereby demonstrate their patriotism. They should report fellow Muslims who collected arms or otherwise created trouble. They should be prepared to go to West Punjab and "take up the cudgels against their Pakistani brothers for their misdeeds." Indian Muslims would of course have to be prepared to lay down their lives for the country, as we have noted, but even before war broke out, they could prove their loyalty by taking up arms against "their Pakistani brothers."[22]

Two comments made during the debate on minority rights in the Constituent Assembly sum up the position of the Indian Muslims in the aftermath of Partition. One came from Mahavir Tyagi, a prominent congressman from western U.P., when the debate was being wound up on 26 May 1949: "The Muslims already know that they will not be returned [in elections to the various legislatures] for some time to come, so long as they do not rehabilitate themselves among the masses and assure the rest of the people that they are one with them. They have been separate in every matter for a long time past and in a day you can't switch over from Communalism to Nationalism."[23] The other was a straightforward statement from Vallabhbhai Patel to the Muslims, made in the course of the speech quoted earlier in this chapter: "*You* must change your attitude, adapt yourself to the changed conditions. . . . Don't pretend to say 'Oh, our affection is great for you.' We have seen your affection. Let us forget the affection. Let us face the realities. Ask yourself whether you really want to stand here and cooperate with *us* or you want to play disruptive tactics."[24]

Which of Us Are Indians?

It remains to scrutinize how the we/us of Indian nationalism was constructed at the moment of Partition and Independence. Some combination of political power and invisible presence has marked the emergence of the mainstream and natural citizen in nation-states the world over. Consider how naturally, invisibly, a certain kind of white Anglo-Saxon Protestant male became the representative American in the century or so following the Declaration of Independence and the American Revolution, or how Englishness became the core of British identity, or whiteness that of the Australian. The Indian case was not dissimilar. The we comes into play without any need for argument: it just happens to be that—the real, essential nation.

Many elaborations of the us and them of Indian nationalism during and immediately after Partition served to reinforce the conceptual split between the Hindu/Indian on the one hand, and the Muslim/foreigner on the other. Occasionally, this was presented as a division between the majority and the minorities, as in numerous Constituent Assembly speeches on the generosity of the majority toward the minorities. The easy, almost invisible, construction of the Hindus as the real Indians and the others—especially the Muslims—as communities that had to prove their belonging can also be found in other nationalist statements. The vernacular press speaking for the nonmetropolitan intelligentsia—provincial notables, small town professionals, teachers, journalists, traders, and clerks, who lent a great deal of the most vocal support to the nationalism of this period—provides numerous excellent illustrations.

Let me cite just one such example, from an editorial published in the Kanpur Hindi daily *Vartman* of 12 October 1947, which asks the question "Whose country is this?" in its first line. The answer is provided at once: "All those who can call India their native land [*swadesh*] in the real sense of the term, this country is theirs." The editors then proceed to argue that the Buddhists and Jains, Sikhs, Christians, Anglo-Indians, and Parsis all belong here because they think of India as their native land. Persecuted in early times, some Hindus became Buddhists and Jains. "However, they did not change their nationality. They did not leave the country. They did not start calling themselves Chinese or Japanese." Similarly, a Sikh *panth* (community or tradition) arose. "This Sikh community also recognizes India as their *janmabhumi* [land of their birth] and therefore their country."[25]

The analysis so far is simple. The Buddhists (even though they had practically disappeared from the land of the Buddha), Jains, and Sikhs treated India as the land of their birth because this is where they and their religious traditions were born. They are, in that sense original, natural Indians. The argument in the case of the other small religious (and racial) groupings—the Christians, Anglo-Indians, and Parsis—is not quite so straightforward. Many of the lowest castes and classes embraced Christianity in recent times, the editorial noted, to escape the oppression of untouchability as much as anything else. "Yet they did not forget that they could never go and settle in Europe; [they know that] India would always be their country."

The Anglo-Indians had, on the other hand, remained ambivalent for some time. They were after all Eurasian, both English and Indian by blood, and many of them had sought to migrate (as they would continue to do during the 1950s, and to some extent later). But there were two points in their favor, as *Vartman* saw it. First, their numbers were never very great; they would never constitute a demographic threat to the nation. Secondly, the departing British had left them to fend for themselves; "they came to their senses as soon as the British left" and recognized India as their native land.

The propositions here are patronizing and full of paradoxes. The Indian Christians could not dream of settling in Europe. The Anglo-Indians did dream of it but were left high and dry by the departing colonial rulers. In any case, the two communities were numerically small and widely dispersed. They had no other country to go to, and they constituted no threat to the nation or its culture. India could therefore be treated as their native land.

The argument was different again in the case of the Parsis. They came to the country from Iran, not as aggressors or missionaries, it is said, but as refugees, fleeing to save their lives (although one might note that some of them came as traders). Nor did they give up their religion, culture, or language on settling here. "Nevertheless, many of them have contributed to the economic, intellectual, social, and political development of India like true citizens." This is a line of reasoning with which we are not unfamiliar. Wealthy Japanese entrepreneurs, Arab sheikhs, and Indian computer whiz kids are welcome in the United States, Britain, and Australia because they contribute to the economic and intellectual development of these countries; not so the Bradford Muslims or Sikhs of Southall, Mexican and Cuban casual laborers, or Vietnamese boat-people. This was what went in favor of the Parsis in India, apart from the fact that they were a small, almost microscopic minority: because of the fairy privileged economic and social position they enjoyed in places like Bombay, many of them had—"like true citizens"—contributed to the economic, intellectual, social, and political development of India.

The case of the Muslims of India was another matter altogether. Conversions to Islam had taken place on a very large scale, and there were by the 1940s ninety million Muslims in the subcontinent, 25 percent of the population of undivided India. The majority of these Muslims had come from the depressed classes of the Hindu population, the paper acknowledged; they had become Muslims to escape the extreme sanctions and disabilities of the caste system. However, resisting the oppressiveness of the Hindu caste system was one thing and shedding one's national culture, religion, language, and dress another. "Flesh and blood of the Hindus though they were, these Hindavi Muslims came to think of themselves as belonging to the Arab and Mughal communities [or nations: the term *jati* can refer to either]. . . . Rulers like Aurangzeb, and later on the British, never tired of preaching that they [the Muslims] have been the governors of this country, and that their direct links are with Arabia, Persia, and Turkey. Their language, appearance, religion, and practices are all different from those of the Hindus."

The *Vartman* editorial refers to the tyranny and destructiveness of the Muslim invaders. It adds that the local converts had been even more tyrannical and destructive, attacking Hindu temples, images, and religious processions and making a point of sacrificing cows at the Baqr Id, precisely because the cow was sacred to the Hindus. But these sweeping and astonishing generalizations are by way of rhetorical flourish—well-known propositions (as we are told) that serve only to underline the basic argument that the Muslims of India are or may be suspected of being alien because "when they changed their religion, they also dreamt up schemes of changing their country." "They did not think of the [other] people living in India as their own. They thought of the local language [as if there were only one] as foreign. They cut themselves off from Indian civilization and culture."

In the course of the anticolonial struggle, the argument goes on, when people of every other community joined in a common fight for freedom, the Muslims stood in the way. They made separatist demands, played into the hands of the British, and were rewarded, finally, with the prize of Pakistan—from where Hindus were now being driven out. Many Indian Muslims had earlier tried to migrate to Persia, Arabia, Mesopotamia, and Turkey, only to return disappointed. Today, "if there was place in Pakistan, if there were agricultural lands, jobs, and if they had their way, [these Muslims] would undoubtedly go and settle there." On other occasions, the editors of *Vartman* declared that Pakistan was like Mecca, like paradise even, for every Indian Muslim, and Jinnah was their prophet.

Now, on 12 October 1947, the editorial continued, large numbers of Muslims had already gone to settle in Pakistan and many more sat waiting to go. As for the rest, who had decided to stay behind, did they show signs

of willingness to live in peace with the other communities of India—
"Sikh, Jain, Buddhists, Christians, Parsis and Anglo-Indians"? "These ma-
chine-guns, mortars, rifles, pistols, bombs, dynamite, swords, spears and
daggers, that are being discovered daily [in Muslim houses and localities],
are all these being collected for the defence of India?" The problem, in the
editors' view, was that there was just not enough room for all these Muslims in Pakistan. Yet the fact that so many stayed on in India was no reason to think of them automatically as Indian. Greater discrimination was
needed.

It would perhaps be a waste of time to point out all the errors of fact
and blatant half-truths that pepper *Vartman's* analysis of the Muslim condition.[26] One feature of the statement, however, requires comment. At
some stage in this articulation of the conditions of citizenship, an argument about culture gives way almost imperceptibly to an argument about
politics—or, more precisely, about political power. The Anglo-Indians, unable to attain the numerical strength of the Muslims, never constituted a
threat. The Parsis remained different in religion, culture, and "language,"
as the Hindi newspaper had it, but they contributed significantly to "our"
political, economic, intellectual, and social development. The Muslims
had, on the other hand, put forward separatist demands and had stood in
the way of the united struggle against the British. They had not accepted
"our" concept of India, and they were therefore not Indians.

There is another important aspect of this articulation. It is noteworthy that in the entire analysis, the Hindus appear only a couple of times, in
passing, as the people from whom the Muslims sought to differentiate
themselves. An editorial that elaborates the character and place of the religious communities of India in answer to the question "Whose country is
this?" does not even feel the need to mention the Hindu community as a
separate constituent of the nation. The Hindus are not a constituent; they
are the nation, the "we" who demand cooperation from the minorities, the
"us" that the Muslims have to learn to live with. Like the land and the
trees, the rivers and mountains, these invisible Hindus are the nation's natural condition, its essence and spirit. Their culture is the nation's culture,
their history its history. This does not need stating.

A poignant moment in the Constituent Assembly debates on the
question of minority rights came when Frank Anthony, the Anglo-Indian
leader, referred to a comment sometimes made to him that he should drop
the prefix *Anglo* from his description of his community if he was as

strongly committed to India as he claimed. Anthony's response was that, "good or bad," "right or wrong," the word *Anglo-Indian* "connotes to me many things which I hold dear." He went further, however: "I will drop it readily, as soon as you drop your label. . . . The day you drop the label of 'Hindu,' the day you forget that you are a Hindu, that day—no, two days before that—I will drop by deed poll, by beat of drum if necessary, the prefix 'Anglo.'" That day, he added, "will be welcome first and foremost to the minorities of India."[27]

The Anglo-Indian leader's argument was logical but misplaced. It would have appeared meaningless to many Hindus, who did not have to use the designation *Hindu* in any case. At Partition and for a long time afterward, they were the silent, invisible majority. They did not need to advertise the fact that they were Hindus. For some time after the assassination of Gandhi by a Hindu extremist, it was even a little difficult for the more militant among them to do so. Inasmuch as they were Hindu, they were automatically Indian. It was enough in this age of high nationalism to claim the latter designation. The question of what it meant to be a Hindu, what advantages such a classification brought to the lower castes and classes, and whether the Hindus as a whole were disprivileged, was not to be taken up in a sustained way until the 1980s and 1990s.[28]

To have given greater political visibility to the *Hindu* category at the moment of nationalist triumph in the 1940s would perhaps have meant running the risk of differentiating and problematizing it, and of having to recognize that history and culture and naturalness are not uncontested. This may also be the reason why the argument about whose country this is could not be acknowledged as a *political* argument. For to concede that the nation was a political project first and foremost would be to concede its historicity. To acknowledge that the nationalist struggle was a struggle for political power would be to open up the question of who should wield that power and to what end, for the progress of the nation did not mean the same thing to all parts of that imagined community.

There was a tacit agreement (it seemed) that, while these political questions would certainly be tackled in the constitution-making body and elsewhere, they must be kept separate from the sacred and natural history of nationalism. This set of questions therefore remained suspended in the nationalist debates at the moment of Partition and Independence. Thus, a particular conception of the Indian nation emerged, in which the Muslims had an unenviable place, the Dalits and other oppressed castes and classes were unseen or only symbolically present (as the backward parts of the nation, to be lifted up by those who ruled in the general interest, for the advancement of the nation as a whole), and other religious minorities and marginal nationalities had to work in collaboration with and subordination to that other invisible category, the mainstream Hindu majority.

Those Exceptional Times?

It may be argued that my analysis of nationalist discourse in India is skewed by the fact that I have drawn its features from an exceptional time, when all the extraordinary pressures and demands of Independence and, more particularly, Partition had distorted people's views. My response is simply this: all nations, all nationalisms and nationalist discourses, are made in exceptional (that is to say, particular, if not unique) historical circumstances. It was in the particular context of 1947—building on more than a century of colonial governance premised on a division between Hindus and Muslims and an extended (and oft-retold) history of Muslim adventurers raiding the land, settling, and setting up towns and kingdoms, in which the question of religious and ethnic identities became important political issues—that the "we" of Indian nationalism was elaborated and the Muslims were marked as a minority. Yet, even in 1947, and even with this historical baggage, there remained the distinct possibility that the identities of the nations (or nation) of the subcontinent might crystallize in a different way.

Partition and Independence (not only the divisions on the map, but the divisions on the ground and in the mind—the uprooting and looting, the rape, and the recovery operations) marked a moment of enormous uncertainty in the political and social life of the people of the region. It was a mark of the transitional character of this moment that the territories and peoples of northeast India continued to be classified for nearly three decades after Indian independence as the responsibility of the External Affairs rather than the Home Ministry—a fact that Indian commentators have generally not noticed.[29] As to the separation of Muslim majority areas, there was no knowing in 1947, or for some time afterward, who would belong where when things finally settled down. (It is often forgotten that the official announcement of where the new international boundaries would lie was not made until two days *after* the official transfer of power and establishment of the independent states of India and Pakistan.)

There was a redesignation of local castes and communities: those who had long adhered loosely to a label Muslim, Hindu, or Sikh were now categorically defined as one or the other. The Mevs of Mewat, the Momins of U.P. and Bihar, the Mapillas of Malabar all became simply Muslims, and for a while nothing else. There was, as we have noted, confusion about the meaning of Pakistan: Was it to be a Muslim or a secular nation? What were the minorities to do there? Could any Muslim from any part of the subcontinent go and settle in that country? Some of the same questions applied in the new India too—"this child of partition," as Sankaran Krishna has called it, "[which] has cartographic anxiety inscribed into its very genetic code."[30] There was uncertainty about the future of the princely states, about national boundaries—would Gurdaspur, or Khulna, or particular *tahsils* and even villages in those districts, be in India or Pakistan? where would Kashmir go?—and about whether people would be free to come and go between Karachi and Bombay, Dacca and Calcutta and Hyderabad, as they had so long done and continued to do for years after the official partition.

A few concrete examples will help clarify the point. In July 1947, Vallabhbhai Patel, home member in the interim government and acclaimed strong man of the Congress Party, wrote to an anxious Hindu correspondent from West Punjab that the matter of citizenship was under consideration by the Indian Constituent Assembly at that moment, but "whatever the definition may be, you can rest assured that the Hindus and Sikhs of Pakistan cannot be considered as aliens in India."[31] A remarkable comment in light of all the charges that were to be leveled in the next few weeks and months against Muslims living in India.

In September 1947, Pakistani Army Headquarters approached the authorities at Aligarh Muslim University, eighty miles east of Delhi, practically in the heart of the political and sectarian upheaval in India at the time, to provide appropriate candidates from the university for recruitment to regular commissions in the Pakistan army. That request, and the university authorities' innocent response—"Those interested in the above [call for applications] should see me in the Geography Department with a written application giving full particulars"[32]—indicates how little the idea had sunk in, even for people in government, that these were now separate countries, and that many existing lines of communication and supply would therefore have to be reconsidered, if not cut off.

Indeed it was in December 1947 that the government of India de-

clared Pakistan to be "foreign territory" for the purpose—and for this restricted purpose alone—of levying duties on raw jute and jute manufac-
tures exported from India.[33] Exit permits, passports, and visas for travel between India and Pakistan (at first a special "Pakistan passport," and only
later the standard passport needed for international travel) were some time
in the future. On the Indian side, in 1947–48, there was continued talk of
possible reunification, and many, even in high political circles, thought
Pakistan simply would not last.

Yet virtually from Independence Day, 15 August 1947, in the midst of
this unparalleled uncertainty, the Muslims of India were asked to make a
categorical declaration of which nation they belonged to: India or Pakistan.
Toward the end of September 1947, even Jawaharlal Nehru remarked that
only those men and women, Hindus or Muslims, were welcome to live in
India who considered it their own nation, gave it their undivided loyalty,
and refused to look to any outside agency for help. Removed from the confusion, suspicions, and violence of the time, this was an unexceptionable
statement. But as the Calcutta daily, *The Statesman*, commented editorially
on 5 October of that year, how were the Muslims of India to prove their
loyalty when fleeing in fear from their homes was interpreted as a sign of
disloyalty and extraterritorial attachment?

The consequences were hard, even for the more privileged among the
Muslims living in Indian territory. In October 1947, Choudhry Khaliquzzaman, the high-profile leader of the Muslim League in the Indian Constituent Assembly, long-time ally of Nehru and other Congress leaders in
U.P. and subsequently a vocal champion of the rights of India's Muslims,
unexpectedly and abruptly migrated to Pakistan, leaving behind a bewildered Muslim League rump. No one knew quite why he had suddenly
made this decision, and his own explanations—that he wanted to make
way for younger blood, that he could not reconcile himself to learning
Hindi, which had been made the official language of U.P., and (in his autobiography, ten years later) that he felt someone who had Jinnah's continued confidence should serve as the leader of the Indian Muslims—did not
put the controversy to rest.

Somewhat later, in 1949, Z. H. Lari, the deputy leader of the Muslim
League in the U.P. legislature, also left for Pakistan, although he had by
then spoken out strongly against the two-nation theory, separate electorates, reservations, and the accompanying baggage. It was, as many who
lived through those times recall, primarily a question of where one could
live in comparative mental and physical peace.

Ustad Bade Ghulam Ali Khan, the doyen of the Patiala *gharana* (school) of Hindustani music, moved to Pakistan, where he lived in relative obscurity for some years before returning to India—and to a successful re-vitalization of his musical career—many years before his death. Josh Mali-habadi, the great Urdu poet from Malihabad, near Lucknow, who had de-clared along with a host of other progressive writers that "we cannot partition Urdu,"[34] left and returned and left again, several times over, un-happy that he had no nation, no home now, and probably unclear to the end whether Urdu had been partitioned and what its fate would be in the two new countries.

The fact is that the choice between India and Pakistan could have no clear meaning for Muslims living in what were called the Muslim-minor-ity provinces of British India, especially in the immediate aftermath of Par-tition and Independence. The individuals mentioned in the preceding paragraphs belonged to the elite and possessed the resources, as well as the bureaucratic and political contacts, to move to and fro, at least for a time. There were innumerable others who did not have the luxury of such trial periods or the possibility of an appeal to Jawaharlal Nehru, yet moved one way and then the other in search of security and peace.[35]

In November 1947, for instance, it was reported that nearly five thou-sand Muslim railwaymen who had earlier opted for service in Pakistan had now "set the authorities a serious problem" by withdrawing their prefer-ence for Pakistan and refusing to leave India. They were, of course, by this change of decision, laying themselves open to the charge of being Pakistani agents engaged in a conspiracy, though their motives were almost certainly more mundane, the result of news of troubles on that side of the border as well as this, and of recognition that working in Pakistan would bring with it its own set of problems. Not even their coworkers in U.P. were inclined to be generous, however. Hindu railwaymen in Lucknow threatened to go on strike if the "Pakistan personnel" were allowed to stay, and the railway authorities insisted that those who had opted for service in Pakistan must go.[36]

A letter from one such railway worker, and the Indian government's response to it, may serve as an appropriate conclusion to this chapter. The letter was written in September 1947 by Safdar Ali Khan, "Guard, Morad-abad," to the secretary, Partition Department, Government of India. Headed "Permission to revise my decision to serve in India," it reads: "I had submitted my final choice to serve in Pakistan. . . . The persuasions of my fellow-workers and friends favoured [forced?] me to come to this decision at which I am rubbing my hands now. . . . My old mother is lying very seriously ill and she is not in a mood to allow me to go to Pakistan as she has no hope to survive her illness. . . . I have blundered in favour of Pakistan. Really speaking, as I have stated above, the decision was not my own but . . . made under compulsion. I am an Indian first and an Indian last. I want to live in India and die in India. . . . Hence I humbly request your honour to permit me to revise my decision and allow me to serve in India."[37]

Maulana Abul Kalam Azad, the education minister of India, forwarded this letter to Home Minister Vallabhbhai Patel, who responded briefly: "The Partition Council decision has been that once a final choice is made it should be adhered to. I [can] see no prospect, therefore, of the gentleman, whose application you have sent me, being allowed to change his option now."[38] There is a bureaucratic imperative at work here: two new state administrations are being set up, rules have to be made and followed. But there is a moral imperative as well. People simply have to decide where they stand and who they are, once and for all. This is a demand, as we have observed, that is made insistently of *one* part of the nation's inhabitants.

The point that needs to be underscored is the unrealizable character of the nationalist search for clarity, uniformity, and purity in the midst of manifest uncertainty, fluidity, and inequality—which is the actually existing condition of all nations and nationalisms. "Are we entitled to claim the status of true citizens, who have sacrificed family, caste, community, and religion in the name of the nation?" Indian nationalists repeatedly asked in 1947. Are *all* citizens asked to sacrifice the claims of family, caste, community, and religion? we might ask in turn.

There are perhaps two voices of nationalism audible in the above exchange between Azad and Patel. However, it was the second that won out, as it has so often done in our times, asserting certainty even in the midst of the intensely uncertain. Nationalist thought has always tended toward this end by its separation of public from private, of citizen from merchant from day laborer, landowner, religious person, and Jew, as Marx noted famously in "On the Jewish Question."[39] Partition produced a situation in which the private of one community (the Hindu in India and the Muslim in Pakistan) articulated itself as the public, while denying that possibility to other (minority) communities.

Patel and Azad represent, in the end, two orientations to the idea of the modern nation and the possibility of political community. One insists on homogeneity, lack of ambiguity, and a predestined national end. The other allows for its opposite: a political community in the making that consists of a multiplicity of selves and groups, all in the process of becoming. I pursue these twin orientations further in the last two chapters of this book, while underlining the paradox that the two can—and frequently do—coexist within the same person or program. I suggest this in relation to Gandhi in the chapter that follows, where I examine the conundrums it has led to in the struggle to define the place of the Dalits in independent India.

Cognizing Community

Like violence, community belongs to the category of the premodern. Let me explain what I mean by this. It will be agreed that the idea of community, in its modern sense, was constructed through the nineteenth and twentieth centuries in the course of assembling the modern: the state, nation, history. It was produced, one might say, in the same operation, as a necessary condition of the birth and advance of modernity. At the same time, it was produced as a singular and substantive entity seen as both primordial and antiquated—a relic of history. This happened not only in South Asia and other parts of the recently colonized world, but also in Europe, the so-called cradle of modernity. In the distribution of assets (or attributes) in the mirror of modernity, nationhood has been seen as the mark of the modern, what all great countries and peoples have achieved. Community is what existed before.[1]

There is a slight complication. The nation is also, after all, a community—*the* modern political community. So thoroughly has this community been naturalized, however, so widely has the nation been seen as the natural condition for the modern political existence of peoples, that it very quickly comes not to be referred to as community at all. The lesser term *community* is reserved for a description of the lesser, or smaller, groups within the larger category of the nation. So it has been in India, where the term *community* is applied above all to the religious groupings, but also to regional or linguistic communities, and sometimes to castes or caste conglomerations. The questions I ask in this chapter arise from an attempted entrenchment of claims to historical community by a lower-caste and lower-class category—a group of people who were (and are) parceled out into innumerable smaller castes, together now called untouchables, Harijans, Scheduled Castes, or Dalits.[2]

Affirmations of the greatness of India since ancient times have long been matched, as I have noted, by declarations of the uniquely accommodating character of the people and the country, its embrace of the most diverse communities, its celebration of unity in diversity. Nationalists have pointed to the coexistence in India of multiple cultural traditions and all the great religions of the world: Hinduism, Buddhism, Jainism, Christianity, Islam, Judaism, Zoroastrianism, and Sikhism. They have spoken of the amity that marked this coexistence over centuries (especially, it is said, before the coming of British colonial rule); and of the syncretism found in the religious practices of Hindus, Muslims, and others—at the level of both elites and common people. Interestingly, even self-described Hindu nationalists have shared this claim, in spite of their insistence on the axiomatically Hindu character of Indian history and Indian civilization. The country has been plural and secular and nonviolent, they argue, it has welcomed all these different faiths, beliefs, and practices, precisely because it is Hindu—hence tolerant and accommodating.

In the pages that follow, I seek to analyze the force of this particular set of claims regarding the tolerant, welcoming character of Indian/Hindu culture and civilization. However, I approach the question in a somewhat unconventional way. Rather than attempting once more to examine the evidence regarding relations and interactions between people belonging to different religious denominations (Hinduism, Islam, Christianity, or whatever), as numerous scholars have done,[3] I will ask, What is it that counts as community? In other words, what claims to community are seen as being deserving of political (and constitutional) recognition, and who decides these claims? And I will ask questions about coexistence or tolerance *within* the confines of a putative religion or religious tradition. The particular religious constellation I take up for discussion is that loose set of inherited beliefs, practices, and positions now described as Hinduism. I particularly want to examine, within the broad umbrella of Hindu society, the place of the Dalits.

Thus, this chapter continues the analysis of the status of minorities in the nation-state, but it does so through examination of a fairly unusual minority. The Dalit case is particularly interesting because of the historical location of Dalit groups and individuals on the boundaries of Hindu society—not apart from it, but not quite part of it either. We have noted earlier that, in the later nineteenth and early twentieth centuries, as movements for modern definitions of religion and religious community developed and the question of numbers gained importance, Hindu leaders and reformers became active in the effort to reclaim the Dalits and reeducate them in their identity as Hindus. Yet, given the character of Hindu society, the organization of classes and vocational groups into distinct castes, and the overriding concern with issues of purity and pollution, all the indications were that the Dalits would have to remain very *lowly* Hindus—a minority that could not be made part of the majority but that the majority would not treat as a minority either.

The Dalits themselves had an ambivalent, fragmentary relationship with this majority. The politics of colonial and postcolonial India gave them a new opportunity to challenge the inherited structures and relations of power around them. As the religious communities of the subcontinent went about purifying and reconstituting themselves and urbanization and migration, educational opportunities, and political consciousness grew, numerous Dalits responded with questions about existing social and political arrangements, demanding greater access to the resources of the modern society and state. Dalit leaders attempted to redefine the Dalits as a historically distinct community and to seek safeguards for it—such as separate electorates and the reservation of seats in legislative bodies and public services—of the kind that had been granted to other minority communities in the early twentieth century.

It was on the matter of separate representation for the Dalits that B. R. Ambedkar, perhaps the outstanding Dalit leader of the twentieth century, and Mohandas Gandhi, the primary leader of the Indian National Congress, disagreed most sharply. The differences between them reached a climax in 1932, when the British government announced a Communal Award that included separate electorates to untouchables in the areas of their greatest concentration. This award followed negotiations that had stalled—notably on the issue of separate electorates for untouchables—at the Round Table Conferences held in London to work out the details of a revised framework for the continued government of India under British control.

Gandhi, and others in the Congress, saw the grant of separate electorates—and the earlier demand for it by Dalit leaders—as a way of splitting and therefore weakening the Hindu community, a development that would only compound what the British had already accomplished through their institution of separate electorates for Muslims. Ambedkar, by contrast, saw separate electorates as an essential lever in the struggle to advance the downtrodden castes. He was forced to give in in 1932, unable to resist the pressure brought to bear upon him by the fast-unto-death that Gandhi launched against this extension of separate electorates. But the way the conflict played out left him deeply embittered, and he seems never to have forgiven Gandhi and the Congress for what he saw as their betrayal.[4]

The issues involved in the clash between Ambedkar and Gandhi were brought into even sharper focus with the extension of citizenship to all inhabitants, universal adult franchise, and the abolition of untouchability in the constitution of independent India, adopted in 1950. At one level, what was at stake in the Dalit struggle before and after Independence was differential access to the state and its resources. Equally at issue, however, was a question of pride and human dignity, of being equal citizens in a modern, democratic society. The struggle has shown no signs of abating; on the contrary, it has grown in strength at both levels.

In the following pages, I ask what it means to describe as members of one (Hindu) religion people who are denied access to central features of Hindu worship and practice, alongside people who deny them such access and force them to perform degrading and polluting work as a part of their social and religious duty, that is to say, of their religion? I ask, as numerous Dalit leaders have done, what it means in this context to deny recognition to the Dalits as a separate community. I go on to question the meaning of tolerance (or coexistence). It seems important to consider the practice of tolerance from the Dalit (or untouchable) point of view, and to ask what becomes of tolerance when untouchable groups opt out of the Hindu fold and convert to another religion, such as Buddhism or Islam.

Religion and Coexistence or Tolerance

Let me begin with a few observations regarding two terms that are central to the discourse of Indian nationalism and to the discussion in this chapter—*religion* and *coexistence*. I start with the latter. It will be clear that the coexistence of two or more individuals, groups, practices, or entities may refer to a variety of situations. These could cover a spectrum extending from benign neglect, on the one hand, through tolerance, to something like respectful interaction and mutual enrichment at the other end. I suspect, however, that in the historical situations and societies we usually study, the first of these is not a long-term possibility. By the same token, the concept of coexistence puts a certain limit on the possibilities of mutual enrichment, since an extended process of mutual enrichment is likely to transform and hence destabilize the bodies that are supposed to coexist. We are left, therefore, with a coexistence that hovers somewhere in the vicinity of the middle term in my suggested spectrum, tolerance, or more precisely, with a proposition about coexistence as a practice of recognition and tolerance between two or more fairly well established and recognizable assemblages.

Yet that is not the end of the matter, for the idea of tolerance can itself describe a multiplicity of conditions. One can think, for example, of an amused kind of tolerance—of the sort that adults sometimes practice in their dealings with children, or colonial regimes (and other ruling classes) have sometimes articulated in response to, say, a subject tribal population's "innocent" (child-like) performances, practices, or beliefs. One can conceive, by contrast, of a "grit one's teeth" kind of tolerance, where dominant classes or groups have to put up with alternative but unwelcome structures, practices, and nodes of power that cannot be easily wiped out—such as the Hindu Right's tolerance of Muslims in India today.

Or one may think of tolerance as a celebration of diversity, of richness, of alternative ways of being and believing—of the kind often advocated by M. K. Gandhi. It would be the end of Hinduism, this deeply religious political leader suggested in speech after speech in the last months of his life—and of Delhi, and India, as he knew them—if the Jama Masjid (Great Mosque) of Delhi no longer existed.[5] What would be left of India's mosaic of monuments, its complex of cultures, its claims to uniqueness, were that to happen? What would the city and the country be like without its Muslim heritage and its Muslim inhabitants? "Delhi has a long history behind it," Gandhi said in one of his prayer speeches in October 1947. "It would be madness even to try to erase that history."[6]

What lies behind this last kind of possibility—of tolerance as celebration—is of course a belief that the diverse paths and practices in question are in fact consonant and have (ultimately) the same kinds of goals. As social scientists or historians, one of our tasks is to consider what kind of tolerance or coexistence we (or others) are postulating in different times and places, but it will help to note at the outset what may well be one unvarying feature of the practice of tolerance: that it is only those in power who are in a position to practice it. Tolerance or coexistence is not a luxury permitted to the marginalized and subordinated, except in the obvious sense that they often have no choice. I will return to this point in my consideration of the place of the Dalits in India. Before I do that, however, it will help to introduce a question about the category of religion.

Several scholars of religion have made the point that the definition of religion as a transhistorical and transcultural phenomenon, and the (secular, liberal) understanding of it as quite separate from politics, law, science, economics, and so on—this "separation of religion from power"—is a relatively recent development. "It has become a commonplace among historians of modern Europe," Talal Asad writes, "to say that religion was gradually compelled to concede the domain of public power to the constitutional state, and of public truth to natural science. But perhaps it is also possible to suggest that in this movement we have the construction of religion as a new historical object: anchored in personal experience, expressible as belief-statements, dependent on private institutions, and practiced in one's spare time."[7]

W. C. Smith had made the same kind of point earlier, emphasizing that the concept of religion as a well-demarcated system of doctrines, scriptures, and beliefs, and that of the plural (religions), understood as different ideological communities, were modern European inventions. By the mid-sixteenth century, John Sommerville suggests, the term *religion* had begun to replace the medieval term *faith*. "But whereas faith had indicated a whole dimension of life and consciousness, religion now denoted an explanation of life or a set of propositions."[8] Religion is here objectified in a different way. It becomes an attribute of individuals or groups rather than an ethos or background that suffuses life and thought. It is something believed (or thought) rather than lived, something one *has* rather than something one *performs*. Finally, and perhaps most crucially for our purposes, it becomes a marker of identity, one of a series of similarly objectified (and more or less well demarcated) systems of belief and practice.

It is in this context that the Dalit place in Hindu society and tradition needs to be considered.

Dalits and Hindus

Whether the Dalits are Hindus or not has been the subject of lengthy controversy. I noted in Chapter 5 that various developments in the early twentieth century generated a fear among Hindu leaders that they might lose "sixty million" of their (untouchable) "coreligionists," which spurred them to recover "the wandering sheep who [had] strayed from the Hindu fold."[9] Dalit groups have responded in a number of ways to these developments.

The Dalits are looked upon as untouchables or ex-untouchables, of course, precisely in the context of Hindu society and the Hindu concern with practices that are polluting. Within the broader Hindu sphere, privileged, twice-born, upper-caste people live alongside a large population of lowly peasants, service communities, artisans, and workers (none of whom have the privilege of wearing the sacred thread) and, on the margins of the community, groups of menial workers and laborers who are decidedly unclean. In the reigning social system, as one student of caste has noted, "Everyone is to some extent impure, and . . . impurity is a relative concept." (It must be said that the distinction between the lowest touchable castes and the untouchables is not always very clear.) "But the impurity of Untouchables is peculiar to them, in that it is indelible and irreversible."[10]

Traditionally, Dalit oppression had several dimensions. It could be seen, and to a large extent still is seen, in their extremely low ritual status, frequently wretched economic conditions, and (until recently) the denial of access to common cultural and political resources. It was also to be seen in the sexual exploitation of Dalit women, which their alleged impurity and untouchability did nothing to prevent.[11]

Yet quite how, and to what extent, Dalit communities may be said to belong to Hindu society remains an open question. One striking illustration of the relevance of the question is to be found in accounts of the violence that characterized the Partition of the subcontinent in 1947. "We were neither Hindu nor Muslim, so we were not affected," a number of Dalits have suggested.[12] However, the records of the time—and the more detailed recollections of these interviewees themselves—tell a somewhat different tale.

Where locally dominant religious groups described themselves as Hindu or Muslim, those who were loosely tied to them (or otherwise in an ambiguous position, because they worshipped or venerated both Hindu and Muslim deities and saints or participated in other ways in both Hindu and Muslim festivals and practices) were asked to declare their allegiance clearly. Even those who had converted to Christianity were not always spared, for in this moment of crisis local communities sometimes failed to take account of what a Dalit Christian stood for or meant. And those who declared themselves Christians at this time—even if they escaped the worst of the attacks and bloodshed—were not free to choose where they wanted to live now that their land and, with it, their networks and families were being partitioned. Shortly after the official Partition and Independence of August 1947, the government of Pakistan announced that the work of removing night-soil, scavenging, and sweeping was an essential service (which of course it is, even if it is not acknowledged as such except at times of strikes and other emergencies) and banned the emigration of the lower castes (many of whom had converted to Christianity) who performed these jobs.

A leading Dalitbahujan intellectual from Hyderabad, Kancha Ilaiah (who uses the term *Dalitbahujan* to refer to the lower castes and classes at large) rejects the attempted assimilation of the Dalits into the Hindu fold. He writes in the context of the spread of an aggrandizing right-wing Hindu movement over the last two decades: "I, indeed not only I, but all of us, the Dalitbahujans of India, have never heard the word 'Hindu'—not as a word, nor as the name of a culture, nor as the name of a religion in our early childhood days. We heard about *Turukoollu* [Turks, or Muslims], we heard about *Kirastaanapoollu* (Christians), we heard about *Bapanoollu* (Brahmins) and *Koomatoollu* (Baniyas [merchants]) spoken of as people who were different from us," he says, using the terms of his native Telugu.

Of these several groups, those that were "most different" were the Brahmins and the Baniyas. There are several cultural practices that Ilaiah's Dalitbahujans are said to share with the Muslims and the Christians. "We all eat meat, we all touch each other." The Muslims and the lower castes also celebrated certain festivals jointly and worked together in the fields. "The only people with whom we had no relations, whatsoever, were the Baapanoollu and the Koomatoollu. But today we are suddenly being told that we have a common religious and cultural relationship with the Baapanoollu and the Koomatoollu."[13]

It was in the colonial period, as the counting and classification of India's diverse communities gathered speed and the issue of numbers became important for all kinds of claims on the resources of the state, that the question of the categorization of Dalit communities became particularly important. As we have already observed, census operations became one of the major sites for an extended contest over this matter. Were particular Dalit groups Hindu? Non-Hindu? Animist? Or something else altogether? Mark Juergensmeyer and Vijay Prashad have documented the struggle as it affected the fate of the Chuhras, Chamars, Sansis, and other low castes of Punjab in the late nineteenth and early twentieth centuries.

"In the case of depressed classes, such as Chuhras, Sansis, etc.," the census commissioner for Punjab and Delhi wrote in 1921, "it was laid down that they should be returned as Hindus if they did not profess to belong to any recognized religion." In the 1880s, a colonial official had written about the worship of Lal Beg in an attempt to describe the Chuhra religion, "a religion of their own," as he put it, "neither Hindu nor Musalman, but with a priesthood and a ritual peculiar to itself." Yet the claims of the Chuhras to be registered as belonging to a separate religion were denied. Prashad sums it up thus: "If the Chuhra[s] in question professed faith in Islam (as Musallis), in Sikhism (as Mazhabis) or in Christianity (as [low-caste] Indian Christians), then that Chuhra was to be returned as such." If they wished to be returned as Lal Begis or Bala Shahis (following another patron saint), that was not permitted. The requirements of colonial, or shall we say modernist, order could not accommodate such a multiplication of categories.[14]

However, politics has a way of upsetting the best laid plans of ruling classes. So, even as the colonial regime sought to restrict the number of admissible religions to a manageable and recognizable set, and Hindu reformers and organizations waded in to try and reclaim the Dalits who had fallen or even forgotten their Hinduness, a major Dalit caste of Punjab, the Chamars, found a leadership that was successful in its campaign to have the community registered not as a depressed caste within Hindu society but as a separate religious grouping—the Ad Dharmis (deriving from a notion of original inhabitants of the land professing the original religion). A "Report of the Ad Dharm Mandal" for the period 1926–31 declares, "We are not Hindus. . . . Our faith is not Hindu but Ad Dharm. We are not a part of Hinduism, and Hindus are not a part of us." It urges that "Ad Dharm should be listed separately in the census and in other ways be given rights equal to Hindus." "At first it seemed a brazen pretense," Juergensmeyer observes, "but in the census of 1931 the idea was voted into reality: the Scheduled Castes [or, more accurately, the Ad Dharmis] were declared a religious community."[15]

Yet, in spite of these occasional victories, the dominant Hindu culture has managed over time to appropriate (or reappropriate) most of these lower-caste religions of protest. The economic, political, and social power of the Hindus has so far been too great for lower-caste resistance. Juergensmeyer notes for Punjab, "The Ad Dharm and the Valmiki Sabha [a later movement among the Chuhras, renamed Balmikis after the seer who is supposed to have composed the *Ramayana*] have become a part of the texture of Hindu culture there."[16]

Much the same thing occurred in the case of an apparently more successful breakaway movement, the Satnampanth of Chattisgarh in central India. As early as the mid-nineteenth century, men of this major Dalit community of Chamars had used their relatively greater access to economic resources and the existence of their own separate villages to assert their independence and establish their own religious sect. A recent historian writes, "The sectarian endeavor . . . drew upon popular traditions and the ritual hierarchy of purity and pollution, rejected the divine and social hierarchies that centered on the Hindu pantheon, and repositioned old signs in a new matrix. . . . The Chamars who joined the sect were [supposedly] cleansed of their impurity and marks of ritual subordination and reconstituted as Satnamis." In the later nineteenth century and the decades that followed, the antagonism between upper-caste Hindu landowners and Chamar (or Satnami) cultivators expressed itself in a series of affrays and murders, a Satnami/Chamar refusal to pay rent, and court cases that became a new sign of lower-class and lower-caste assertiveness in Chattisgarh.[17]

The report that accompanied the first census in the region, in 1866, stated that the Chamars of Chattisgarh "have thrown off Brahmanical influence, have set up a new creed, possess a high priest and priesthood of their own." Yet, as another official noted two years later, while the Satnami sect accepted adherents from other castes, Chamars constituted the overwhelming majority of its members, and in the eyes of the Hindus all Satnamis were Chamars. Indeed, colonial administrators continued to use the terms *Chamar* and *Satnami* interchangeably. The position did not change appreciably in the twentieth century, in spite of the wider organization and self-consciousness of the Satnampanth. Satnamis in the villages could not enter the temples and shrines of the higher castes, use their wells, wear shoes, carry umbrellas, ride a horse or travel in a palanquin, or take a marriage procession through the village to the accompaniment of music.

The sexual exploitation of Satnami women also continued. An old Satnami woman put it this way: "As untouchables we could not enter the homes of clean castes, but women and girls were never left unmolested. . . . We had no escape. We had to accept our fate." And further:

"Women were specially vulnerable when their men folk went out on *begar* [forced labor]. When detected, this caused some flutter. But that was all. . . . Some officials demanded women, especially young girls. . . . To avoid trouble (and beating) some people sent their sisters, daughters, and daughters-in-law without much protest."

Community and Conversion

Called in 1919 to testify before a commission investigating what kind of franchise should be instituted for colonial India's next stage of training in representative government, B.R. Ambedkar declared that the country's social divisions were not Hindu, Muslim, Parsi, Christian, Jew, but touchable Hindu, untouchable Hindu, Muslim, Christian, Parsi, Jew.[18] In other words, just as Muslims, Christians, Parsis, Sikhs, Anglo-Indians, and so on had been recognized as identifiable communities with distinct histories and distinct needs, the untouchables too deserved recognition as a separate community.

Ambedkar's argument was that, like other minorities and even more obviously given the massive discrimination untouchables had suffered for centuries, the Dalits had their own cultural, economic, and political needs, and their own special claims on the state and its resources. The clearest formulation of this call for special treatment was a demand for positive discrimination—the reservation of seats in elective assemblies and education, and the establishment of separate electorates for untouchables like those for the Muslims.

The Indian constitution of 1950 reserved a percentage of seats in the legislatures, educational admissions, and public appointments for untouchables. This has contributed greatly to the rise of an educated elite, the emergence of a Dalit middle class, and the growing confidence of Dalit politics. However, Gandhi and the Congress were never able to accept the demand for separate electorates, thus recognizing Dalits as a historically separate community. It was seen as too much of a threat to existing social and political arrangements: to a political arithmetic that assured the numerical superiority of the Hindus, but also to a religious and cultural susceptibility that allowed the cultural and political dominance of certain (Hindu, upper-caste) groups and classes.

Through the 1920s and early 1930s, Ambedkar and other Dalit leaders sought to claim the religious status of caste Hindus through a series of well-publicized campaigns for temple-entry. In some of these, they were joined by upper-caste Hindu reformers like Gandhi. Even at this early stage, however, there were important differences in perceptions and approach between the Dalits and the upper castes, between Ambedkar and Gandhi. The latter described untouchability as "a curse, an excrescence on Hinduism, a poison, a snake, a canker, a hydra-headed monster, a great blot, a device of Satan, a hideous untruth, Dyerism and O'Dwyerism."[19] Ambedkar put the matter a little differently: "To the Untouchables, Hinduism is a veritable chamber of horrors," he wrote in the 1940s. "Inequality is the official doctrine of Brahminism." And later, the existence of communities labeled Criminal Tribes, Aboriginal Tribes, and Untouchables "is an abomination. The Hindu civilization, gauged in the light of these social products, could hardly be called civilization."[20]

For Gandhi, the crusade against untouchability was a religious affair internal to Hinduism. In contrast, Ambedkar saw the issue as one of civil rights—even during the years in which he argued for the Dalits' right to enter Hindu temples and public tanks. Gandhi's fast protesting the Communal Award announced by the British Government in 1932 was directed, in the words of one commentator, against "attempts to translate the problem of untouchables into the parlance of modern day democratic processes."[21] Such a translation, Gandhi believed, would prevent the natural growth of the Dalits in the organic community of Hinduism, and keep the upper castes from making honorable amends. "The evil [of untouchability] is far greater than I had thought it to be," he wrote in May 1933. "It cannot be eradicated by money, external organization and even political power for Harijans [his name for the Dalits], although all these three are necessary. . . . To be effective, they must follow . . . self-purification." His advocacy of a return to the roots—the harmonious village community, the simplicity of village life, and the ideal Bhangi (the respected and self-respecting sweeper)—was in line with this belief in the essential goodness of an organic Hinduism.

Ambedkar, who was born in a lowly Mahar family and suffered discrimination as a Dalit even after earning doctorates from Columbia University (New York) and the London School of Economics and rising to high professional and political positions, had little interest in this mythical past. He argued that the Mahars and other Dalits had to look to the future and for this purpose migrate to the towns, where they could (even at the start) escape from some of the worst disabilities of the caste system.[22] He wanted them to trust themselves rather than the mercy and benevolence of the upper castes and classes. In what was to become a battle cry for his followers, he advocated "Education, Organization and Agitation" in the struggle for equality. And in 1935, in a radical new move, he confronted the Gandhian (and upper-caste Hindu) position head on, announcing his decision to leave Hinduism. "I had the misfortune of being born with the stigma of [being] an Untouchable. . . . It is not my fault; but I will not die a Hindu, for this is in my power."[23]

The fact is that ritual impurity and religion could not be separated from economic dependence and political powerlessness. One student of caste and religion in a South Indian district writes: "There is no evidence that the Harijans' status is more clearly defined by their religious role as funeral servants, than by their economic role as labourers."[24] The opposite may perhaps be said with equal validity. Hence Ambedkar's insistent identification of caste, as another scholar has it, as "the most powerful vehicle of dominance—ritual as well as political and economic—in India."[25]

It is well established that Dalits were expected to perform functions—to follow paths, literally and metaphorically—that were symbolic of their very low status in ritual and social life, especially in the villages. Such is the weight of this history that many politically conscious Dalit youth shun the very instruments and expertise—say, in music or handicrafts—that they inherited as a mark of their lowly status. Thus the scholar D.R. Nagaraj described an activist friend, Krishna, for whom "the art of playing drums is linked with the humiliating task of carrying dead animals. The joy of singing oral epics is traditionally associated with the insult of the artist standing outside the houses of upper caste landlords with a begging bowl." He will have none of these, even when it is friends and activist colleagues who are celebrating. "I want to forget all this," he screamed one night: "I want to forget their gods, their folk epics, their violence."[26]

A Derridean double bind "characterize[s] the civilizational bind in which the Untouchable in fact exists," R.S. Khare writes at the end of his fine study of Dalit (Chamar) rickshaw pullers in Lucknow. The Dalit "continuously constructs and deconstructs himself in relation to the caste Hindu"—with deconstruction here being defined as having to do a thing *and* its opposite. The local Dalits' texts, speeches, and actions all work to disseminate a cultural argument, Khare observes, "sometimes along and sometimes across the caste Hindu's furrows and their 'cobweb' (a favorite expression with the Lucknow Chamar)." They have to let ideals and words multiply, to construct an ethic with "the ultimate goal of lifting caste morality above social injustice,"[27] or, as one might prefer to put it, an ethic of social justice and human dignity.

The cobweb is a significant metaphor. The Hindi word, *jaala*, is related to *jaal* (net). It is not easy to escape either, but the cobweb is more insidious, invisible, scary. "Hinduism is not ours," a group of Punjabi sweepers told Mark Juergensmeyer. Hinduism is a religion of oppression, the religion of the rich and the upper castes. At the same time, they went on to say, since untouchability is a religious concept, a change of religion would have to accompany economic and social progress to eliminate untouchability.[28] For this reason conversion has been central to Dalit politics.

I was born a Hindu, but I will not die as one, Ambedkar said in 1935. It would be another twenty years before he was ready to lead his followers into another religion. Much of this time was spent in studying various religions and discussing the options—Sikhism, Buddhism, Christianity, Islam—with members of those faiths and with his own close associates. Much has been written about Ambedkar's concern to choose a religion from the Indic tradition, to stay within the ambit of Indian civilization. After considerable study and deliberation, Ambedkar decided to convert to Buddhism. Daya Pawar's 1974 poem, "Buddha," explains part of the reason why:

I see you
Walking, talking,
Breathing softly, healingly,
On the sorrow of the poor, the weak;

Going from hut to hut
In the life-destroying darkness
Torch in hand[29]

Yet there were other matters that were at least as crucial to this conversion. In addition to a statement of traditional Buddhist beliefs regarding the noble eight-fold path, compassion, and equality,[30] for example, the vows administered by Ambedkar to his fellow converts at the Diksha Bhumi, Nagpur, on 14 October 1956, included the following: not to recognize or worship Brahma, Vishnu and Mahesh, Ram and Krishna, or other Hindu gods and goddesses; not to believe in the theory of incarnation or that the Buddha was an incarnation of Vishnu (which was "false propaganda and madness"); not to perform *shraaddha* or offer *pind-daan*, as the Hindus did for their dead; and not to allow any religious rites to be performed by Brahmin priests.[31]

Ambedkar was looking for "a broadly humanist and social religion," one scholar suggests. He found this in Buddhism. Deeply committed to a scientific outlook, he used "the yardstick of modern science, and its universalist claim to reason" to "test" the world religions, as he described it. "He did this," writes Martin Fuchs, "not in order to disown religion, but rather to find out and reclaim ancient moral insights—which had proved their trans-historical validity—and return them to his contemporaries."[32] "My social philosophy may be said to be enshrined in three words: liberty, equality and fraternity," Ambedkar declared on several occasions. However, as he went on to say, he derived these tenets not from the French Revolution (or "political science," as he put it), but "from the teachings of my Master, the Buddha."[33]

The mass conversion at Nagpur increased the number of Buddhists in India by half a million, a dramatic jump from the 141,426 Buddhists recorded in the census of 1951; the total increased again, to 3,206,142, in 1961. Most of the new converts were members of Ambedkar's Mahar community. The conversions have continued since and embraced many other Dalit groups, so that Buddhists numbered nearly six million in the 1990s.[34] Dalit groups also turned to the Christian church, in its various denominations, during the colonial period and to a lesser extent afterward, as they had done to Islam and various Sufi orders at an earlier stage.[35] And the effort to counter degradation and gain self-respect through conversion has hardly ended, as the widely publicized conversion of several thousand Dalits in and around Meenakshipuram (Tamil Nadu) in 1981–82 indicated.

The Tamil Nadu conversions were preceded by a sharpening of questions of caste inequality and positive discrimination (reservations) in national and regional politics, by violent clashes between caste Hindus and Dalits in Maharashtra in 1978 and a militant agitation in Gujarat in 1981 to protest reservations for untouchables in medical colleges. They were preceded too by long deliberation and planning on the part of local Dalits. In Meenakshipuram, for example, young Dalit converts reported that "their elders were thinking of converting to Islam for the last twenty years. They have been having this idea time and again. Since there was no support and unanimity three times earlier, they did not convert." The killing of two Thevars of the village in December 1980 brought "a new wave of police torture and harassment" directed against the Dalits (the Thevars were a low, but clean, landowning caste to which several local revenue and police officers belonged). In a gathering of Dalit villagers a short time afterward, a proposal to convert made by one of the young Dalits who had earlier converted to Islam was finally accepted. "This conversion came as a collective decision of converts," writes Mujahid in his detailed account of these conversions, "albeit in three installments."[36]

The 1956 conversion to Buddhism initiated by Ambedkar has become part of the inspiring mythology of the modern Dalit struggle. It was an act that gave memory to a "memoryless" people, as Nagaraj puts it—for the desire to look to the future alone must inevitably be a forlorn hope.[37] It has instilled new pride in millions of the downtrodden, and especially in the Dalit middle classes. The same claim to human dignity and self-respect has been made through conversions to Christianity, Islam, and Sikhism, in the recent as in the distant past, but the break from the past has been far from easy or complete.

A Return(?) to Politics

The experience of a Dalit woman schoolteacher from Tamil Nadu who gave up her career to join a Catholic religious order, and then gave up that order to pursue the fight for the dignity of her fellow beings by other means, illustrates the obstacles faced in the attempted break with the past. "If you look at our streets," she writes in her autobiography, "they are full of small children, their noses streaming, without even a scrap of clothing, rolling about and playing in the mud and mire, indistinguishable from puppies and piglets." In the churches, she tells us, "Dalits are the most, in numbers only. In everything else, they are the least. It is only the upper-caste Christians who enjoy the benefits and comforts of the Church." Of the convent she went into, she says: "The Jesus they worshipped there was a wealthy Jesus. . . . There was no love for the poor and the humble." "You can sit on your chair inside a convent, and say whatever you like about the struggling masses, about justice and the law. . . . But in that place you can never experience another people's pain." And further: "Now that I have left the order, I am angry when I see priests and nuns. . . . When I look at the Church today, it seems to be a Church made up of the priests and nuns and their kith and kin. And when you consider who they are, it is clear that they are all from upper-castes."[38]

Abdul Malik Mujahid describes the same kind of outcome, pointing to continued discrimination and the continued humiliation of converted Dalits through physical attacks in Maharashta, Gujarat, and elsewhere. "The term *neo-Buddhist* has become more or less synonymous with the terms *untouchable* or *Harijan.* . . . The Maharashtra riots of 1978 and a constant high rate of atrocities against them establish . . . the fact that the same stigmas are attached to this 'changed' identity as well."[39] There are indeed many striking illustrations of the discrimination that even well-to-do, relatively privileged, middle-class converts have to live with. Let me conclude this part of my argument with such an example, a story recounted to me by a talented young officer of the Indian Revenue Service—one of the Class I services of the government of India, entry into which used to be a matter of pride for the middle classes at large until the era of globalization produced another, international economic order for the most privileged of them to enter, with new international salaries and international aspirations.

A writer, a Buddhist preacher of some repute, a sophisticated and conscientious young man who had already gained considerable recognition in the service and been appointed to a number of challenging positions, this officer told me of a senior colleague, his boss, who treated him as a favorite junior, assigning him to numerous sensitive and difficult projects and showering him with praise. One day, his boss noticed an image of the Buddha in a corner of the younger man's office. Taken aback, the senior officer blurted out that he "could not have imagined that someone so brilliant was an SC [i.e. a member of the Scheduled Castes]." What is more, the Dalit officer said, "his whole attitude and interaction with me changed after that."[40]

It is scarcely surprising that the call for conversion, for getting away from the shadow of Hinduism, has often been articulated in militant terms. As Ambedkar put it in his emotional address to the gathering at Nagpur on 14 October 1956, "This conversion has given me enormous satisfaction and pleasure unimaginable. I feel as if I have been liberated from hell."[41] E. V. Ramaswami Naicker (Periyar, as he is fondly called), another remarkable—and fiery—leader of the lower-caste struggle in the twentieth century, put it this way: "Our disease of being Shudras is a very big monstrous disease. This is like cancer. . . . There is only one medicine for it. And that is Islam. . . . To cure the disease, [and] stand up and walk as worthy humans, Islam is the only way."[42] And, in line with these thoughts, some Buddhist converts in Maharashtra have been heard to say, "We should have become Muslims first, then Buddhists when we had won equality."[43]

A few points should have emerged clearly from the above discussion. Minorities are not automatically minorities; minorities, like communities, are historically constituted. This much is readily conceded. What is not always accepted is that claims to community are also subject to political scrutiny and, if I may use the word, censorship. Community or minority status is the product of political contest, which is sometimes recognized as being violent. Religious identity is also subject to this kind of contestation and violence. It makes little sense in this context to think of religion simply as a well-demarcated and stable system of doctrines, scriptures, and beliefs, when it is—at least as much—a ritual order and a social and political hierarchy that can be rearranged. In cases such as that of the Dalits, it calls out loudly for rearrangement.

Finally, it should be evident that the practice of coexistence, commonly promoted by political leaders and nation-states in our times, is not always benign. If coexistence implies a suggestion of adjacency or nextness—a spatial image—then it must be said that the adjacency at issue here is not merely horizontal but also vertical, that groups and communities are placed not only next to, but also on top of and underneath, one another. In a word, the idea of coexistence, in the form of tolerance, of unity in diversity, and the accommodation of multiple traditions and ways of being, means little or nothing from the Dalits' point of view—or for those who find themselves at the bottom of the heap.

What is missing from many modern notions of the imagined community—national, subnational, or international—is an adequate appreciation of the politics that goes into the making of community, and of the power relations and inequality that are part of the process of all political negotiations. It is this skewed condition of the terrain of politics and political negotiation that I take up in the final chapter of this book, dealing with the recent inclination of the nation-state in relation to the question of secularism and tolerance.

8

The Secular State?

Demographic changes and political developments in many parts of the world have reinvigorated the debate on the neutrality of the modern state and linked it with the issue of secularism—a political arrangement that is increasingly recognized as a necessary condition for the continuation of democratic life. We need to begin our discussion here with some consideration of what is at stake in the *new* project of secularism, in India and in other countries.

The concept of secularism has in recent times become detached to some extent from its filiation with the process of secularization and the expansion of the secular (as opposed to sacred) dimension of public life.[1] It is increasingly linked to the idea of the recognition and acceptance of difference. The question of secularism has been viewed as a question of pluralism, or of tolerance between diverse religious and cultural communities. In a more robust formulation, it has been represented as being about the possibility of "interreligious understanding," which, as T.N. Madan writes, "is not the same as an emaciated notion of mutual tolerance or respect, but also [about] opening out avenues of a spiritually justified limitation of the role of religious institutions and symbols in certain areas of contemporary life."[2] Underlying the politics of secularism, then, is a question of communication and understanding, a notion of give-and-take and compromise, between social groups identified by religion, race, or culture. This chapter is concerned with an examination of the conditions in which this parleying and communication is supposed to occur.

Recent political theory has been much occupied with a consideration of the conditions of possibility of political conversation between people who may have very different notions of the good life and the social and political institutions necessary for its realization. What are the grounds on which people with very different values and commitments can still communicate, interact, and arrive at commonly acceptable procedures (if not decisions) in the domain of the state? The matter of secularism has been a part of this larger inquiry, one that has come to occupy a pivotal position in the context of a new recognition of the explosive mix of populations inside and outside Europe and North America. "Either the civilized coexistence of diverse groups, or new forms of savagery," as Charles Taylor puts it. "Secularism in some form," he goes on to say, "is a necessity for the democratic life of religiously [and, one might add, culturally] diverse societies."[3] It is this concern that has lent a special importance and appeal to the kind of "overlapping consensus" that John Rawls put forward as the basis for political conversation between groups with different and even incommensurable views on many fundamental issues.[4]

In India, as elsewhere, the renewed debate on secularism has revolved around the necessity of *dialogue* between diverse *communities* in a *liberal, democratic regime*. In the pages that follow, I want to say just a little about each of the italicized terms in this sentence. The emphasis on dialogue (between Hindus, Muslims, Sikhs, and others) is an old, and persistent, feature of Indian political discourse. In particular instances, the proposition has been advanced in the form of a call for negotiation between these groups, although the term *negotiation* seems to have been less favored than *dialogue* or *conversation* in the vigorous academic exchanges of the last decade or so.[5] There is, however, in my view, an important difference between these terms. A failure to appreciate this difference may easily lead to a failure to understand that the conversation we are concerned with is a *political* conversation, and that the state is (or at least has been) at the very center of it.

In some versions of liberalism, *dialogue* refers to any talking, simple conversation as it were, between individuals and groups. This is not, however, what *political* implies. *Negotiation* comes closer to the heart of the matter. People with very different kinds of commitments and interests have to make concessions—and these negotiations are almost always between *unequals*. It is necessary to point to that dimension of dialogue or negotiation that rests on force. Inequality means that this element of (unequal) force is central to the dialogue. Open violence—that is to say, actions that are recognized as violence—is in this sense only a heightened form of what is always present in negotiations between different classes, communities, and sexes.

It is important to note too that the participants in such negotiations, the state among them, are recognized only through politics—both in the sense of being parties that are (often) legally or constitutionally recognized and of staking their own claims or the claims of interests they articulate. At the very outset, then, I suggest that we add the term *politicized* to the adjectives *religious* and *cultural* that are supposed to describe the communities or groups said to be parties to the dialogues on secularism. For, until it is politicized, the so-called religious/cultural community—or communities supposedly united by religious or cultural affiliation—would appear to be too differentiated and unorganized to enter into this kind of dialogue or conversation in the legal-constitutional domain of the state.

Even with that qualification, the communities involved in these national political debates are neither seamless nor obviously and easily identified. As in previous chapters, I will ask questions here about how they come to be established as historical actors and about the terms of the political interaction between them. Who establishes the boundaries between communities and posits an absence of boundaries within them? Who decides what is to be the language of negotiation between these different elements of a population? And when is it that this language of reasonable negotiation and persuasion breaks down and something called violence supervenes?

In connection with this, finally, I feel we need to query various suppositions about the liberalism of liberal-democratic states. Through the sacralization of nationalism and the identification of nation and state, the nation-states of our time have turned all too frequently to openly illiberal enforcement of particular demands, which are disguised as mainstream and nationalist. What one scholar calls the "violence of universalizing reason," expressed through the law, here transgresses its pretensions to civility and renders its own law irrelevant.[6] It is my argument that, in many so-called liberal and democratic regimes, the terms of negotiation between politicized religious/cultural communities, and between these communities and the state, have been radically—if quietly—altered at many junctures in the twentieth and twenty-first centuries. A recognition of this reversibility of liberal conditions is necessary to any rethinking of the requirements of a politics of secularism, pluralism, or pluralist democracy today.

A Dialogue on Secularism

The argument for Indian secularism is now built largely on an appeal for communication and tolerance between religiously differentiated segments of the country's population. I begin by pointing to a number of assumptions that underlie this argument: among them, that we are dealing with bounded communities, that the parties to the dialogue as well as their commitments are fairly easily identified, and that the state may be treated as neutral (or even, in the extreme case, irrelevant). These assumptions bear closer scrutiny, especially since—as I will try to show—they mark in various ways some of the best academic writing on the subject too.

Ashis Nandy, one of the most prominent contributors to the academic debate, is perhaps the leading advocate of the view that "religious communities in traditional societies" knew how to live with one another. He suggests by implication that these communities shared a common language and a basic understanding, in spite of the differences between them and the scarcely surprising occurrence of periodic conflicts. Nandy has frequently expressed the opinion that state systems in South Asia need to "learn something about religious tolerance from everyday Hinduism, Islam, Buddhism or Sikhism."[7] "In rural India, where communities have not yet fully broken down," he writes, "the ideology of Hindutva [right-wing Hindu militancy and aggression] faces resistance from everyday Hinduism." Hence a cautious optimism: apart from the ideology of secularism, which Nandy doesn't especially care for, "there are other, probably more potent and resilient ideas within the repertoire of cultures and religions of the region that could ensure religious and ethnic co-survival, if not creative inter-faith encounters."[8]

I have suggested that we need to keep the adjective *politicized* at hand whenever we talk about religious communities in this context. Nandy would probably claim that his everyday or traditional religious community is—precisely—*not* politicized. If that were the case, however, he would have to explain what constitutes this community and how it is to take part in modern political dialogue. Who occupies the subject position of the everyday Hindu, Muslim, Buddhist, or Sikh in legal-constitutional practice? This is a point to which I will return.

Partha Chatterjee also works with a fairly sharp state/community distinction in his writings on secularism. The communities he writes about are seen as being more recent and more political articulations than Nandy's. Nonetheless, they are fairly secure and stable entities in the analysis. Chatterjee argues, for instance, that "the minorities are unwilling to grant to a legislature elected by universal suffrage the power to legislate the reform of their religions." He urges the need to establish "other institutions which have representative legitimacy to supervise such a process of reform," observing that "even while resisting the idea of a uniform civil code on the ground that this would be a fundamental encroachment on the freedom of religion and destructive of the cultural identity of religious minorities, the Muslim leadership in India has not shunned state intervention altogether." His prescription for the present is "a strategic politics of toleration" that would "resist homogenization [of communities] from the outside, and push for democratization inside."[9]

Akeel Bilgrami, while seeking to distinguish his position carefully from Chatterjee's and even more carefully from Nandy's, puts forward his own proposal for dialogue between communities as the way forward for Indian secularism. Noting the pre-1947 Congress's rejection of the Muslim League demand that the League should represent Muslims, a Sikh leader the Sikhs, and an untouchable the untouchable community, he concludes: "Secularism thus never got the chance to *emerge* out of a creative dialogue between these different communities." What he would want from the state is that it "bring about reform in a way that speaks to the value commitments of communities whom it is seeking to reform . . . (i.e.) speaks to them internally." The state needs to provide "a field of force of internal reasons addressing different communitarian perspectives from within their own internal substantive commitments and unsettling them into awareness of their own internal inconsistencies so as to eventually provide for a common secular outcome, each on different internal grounds."[10]

There is an interesting echo of Gandhi in several of these arguments, even though none of the writers I have quoted uses the kind of religious language that Gandhi consistently employed. Like these scholars, Gandhi stressed the importance of *conversation* as a means toward the resolution of the great political problems of his day. Ideally, these conversations would take place between parties on the basis of an absolute difference and an equality that were the condition of neighborliness and friendship. However, Gandhi proposed different kinds of dialogue as being necessary to po-

litical negotiation between people placed at different levels in the social-po-
litical hierarchies of the actually existing real world. He advocated the
mode of *mitrata* (*friendship*) toward equals, as for example between Hindus and Muslims; of *seva* (service) toward subordinates (or, in Gandhian
terms, "unfortunates"), as in the relations between upper castes and untouchables—Gandhi's Harijans (children of God); and of *satyagraha* (appeal for justice, through noncooperation) toward the dominant, as in the
case of the Indian population in relation to their British rulers.[11]

The problem with Gandhi's approach, as I see it, was an all too easy
fixing of groups of people in a specified place in the social hierarchy—that
of equal, dominant, or subordinate, to be met with *mitrata, satyagraha,* or
seva—and the homogenization of whole groups of people in order that
they could be thus fixed. Were the Muslims of British India such an undifferentiated category? Could they be unified into one seamless bloc, allowing absolute difference and full equality" between them and the (similarly
undifferentiated and seamless) Hindus? And why were they to be treated
as equals and not, say, as *daridranarayan* (God in the form of the poor),
which was another Gandhian appellation for the untouchables or Dalits?
Finally, while there is perhaps greater justification for this, is it adequate for
purposes of political negotiation to classify Dalits as unfortunates (*daridra*,
Harijan, part of divinity, subalterns to be transformed through *darshan*)
and nothing else? Who indeed has the right to assign people a place in this
amazingly unambiguous hierarchy? Is there not a remarkable arrogance in
the Gandhian position not only in arrogating that place to itself, but also
in declaring that it knows so clearly, so indubitably, and forever, where people belong? How would—and did—Jinnah and Ambedkar, to take only
two obvious examples, respond to this?

The same kinds of questions might be raised in response to recent
commentaries on the negotiations (or dialogue) necessary to secularism.
What marks the boundaries of the identified communities? Who is to represent their voice (or multiple voices), interests, values, "internal" reasons?
How do we determine that these spokespersons have the status they claim
(of belonging to the community, let alone being representative of it)?

Bilgrami has argued that this kind of objection is misplaced. What he
is proposing, he stresses, is the idea of "an emergent and negotiated secularism." For this, we require a "minimal and *descriptive* acknowledgement"
of communities, which can "giv(e) internal reasons to one another [and
presumably to liberal secularist political forces] in a political disagree-

ment." The possibility of advancing such "internal" reasons in the dialogue arises precisely because "agents and communities . . . are not monsters of consistency, their desires and values are often [indeed, in a sense, always] in conflict."[12] Yet his position begs the question: who names and identifies the communities to be involved in the dialogue on secularism or on the constitution and arrangements of the modern political community? Why this set, identified in this way, and not some other, identified differently? How do we come to have these notions of a (permanent) Hindu majority, and (similarly permanent) Muslim, Christian, Sikh, and even untouchable minorities?

One can see that contemporary politics itself provides a part of the answer. Chatterjee says as much when he speaks of "minority groups" as "an actually existing category of Indian citizenship—constitutionally defined, legally administered and politically invoked."[13] In other words, a discourse of state, which gives us our constitutional provisions, government policy, and legal practice, also gives us our notions of majority and minorities, alongside the list of communities that occupy the domain of national politics. The communities in question, the parties to particular political dialogues, are conjured up to a large extent by this powerful political discourse.

It is necessary to note, however, that this privileged discourse is itself the enunciation (or an outgrowth of the enunciation) of particular powerful classes and communities with considerable leverage within the institutions of the state. Besides, there are communities other than these apparently stable religious groups that appear in this same political discourse, even in its more restricted legal-constitutional form: the "weaker sections of society," "backward classes (or castes)," poor and marginalized groups like the Scheduled Tribes (whom it is necessary to distinguish from the now politically more prominent Scheduled Caste untouchables or Dalits), women, and so on. It is not by accident that we have arrived at the set said to make up the (long-term) majorities and minorities of Indian democracy, and hence the parties to the most important national political debates. Nor, as the recent assertiveness and electoral advances of Backward Caste and Dalit parties has shown, is this a stable set. Political parties, associations, and movements are central to the negotiations that produce the particular distribution and hierarchical arrangement of communities that mark contemporary Indian discourse. So of course is the state and its legal apparatus.

It is certainly the case that in situations of massive and prolonged bloodshed (such as that found in many recent civil wars) and resulting political impasse, the state's representatives have occasionally opted to talk to what might be identified as the most extreme and best organized of dissenting political groups (the African National Congress in preliberation South Africa, the Irish Republican Army in Northern Ireland, the Liberation Tigers of Tamil Ealam in Sri Lanka, Khalistani, Kashmiri, and ULFA[14] militants in India). Yet things are hardly as clear-cut as all that, even in times of civil war, for there is often a multiplicity of parties involved in any major conflict, as well as many internal divisions and fractions among each of the parties. The identification of representative parties and positions is no less complicated in other persistent and difficult, if less violent, disputes. Secular feminists have not found it easy to reach agreement on a model uniform civil code, and on rules for opting in or out of it. Consider, again, the status of the protests by women, including many Muslim women, in the context of the new Muslim Women's Act passed by Rajiv Gandhi's government to defuse what it saw as Muslim anger in the Shah Bano case. Who would have been the appropriate parties to the debate on secularism at that particular moment? And how do we resolve the question of a quota of reserved seats for women in Parliament, on which upper-caste women members of Parliament and elected representatives of the Backward Castes and Dalits have taken strongly opposed positions?

Let me move from this to another, related question—that of the language of communication between people who live by very different kinds of beliefs and values. Gandhi accepted these beliefs and values as different, not to say entirely different, versions of truth ("One person's truth may appear as another's untruth") and urged everyone to follow the dictates of his or her own truth. He did this in the name of a higher Truth, that of nonviolence and love, which for him formed the basis of all religions and hence of the religious politics he advocated. *Ahimsa*—nonviolence and love—was to serve as the protocol for relationships and conversations among all political antagonists.[15]

The difficulty is that some truths (including perhaps that of Enlightenment rationality and modern secularist politics) do not conceive of or allow the coexistence of multiple truths in this way, and some (including Enlightenment rationality!) have believed in the need to obliterate other truths in order to establish the Truth.[16] What of those who will not or perhaps cannot define God in the nebulous, always open way preferred by

Gandhi or accept his proposition about the fundamental identity of all religions? How are conversations to be developed between such groups?

This is why the protagonists in the current debate on Indian secularism have returned to urging state intervention in promoting communication, dialogue, and understanding between the religious communities,
with the state itself acting as neutral arbiter. Bilgrami's is probably the most
robust and forthright articulation of the position. "Internal reform" needs
to take place on a "statist site." Unlike Chatterjee, he notes, he has "made
no commitment to ... intracommunity democratic institutions," but
rather insisted on the "necessity for statist reform." The state must "bring
about reform in a way that speaks to the value commitments of communities whom it is seeking to reform." It should provide "a field of force of internal reasons addressing different communitarian perspectives from
within their own internal substantive commitments."[17]

Gauri Vishwanathan speaks from the same sort of position when she
observes that the provisions of the Indian constitution provide no ground
for "religious communication between groups."[18] Nandy too continues to
hope (against hope) that the state systems of South Asia will learn something about tolerance from the "traditional religious communities."[19]
Chatterjee, who in my view comes closest to Gandhi in conceding the possibility that different parties in this conflict may in fact hold incommensurable positions ("a group could insist on its right not to give reasons for doing things differently, provided it explains itself adequately in its own
chosen forum"), nevertheless calls for the institution—presumably by the
state—of "other institutions which have the representative legitimacy" to
supervise a process of reform *within* the religious communities.[20]

I have underlined the centrality in Chatterjee's account of legal-
constitutional arrangements, and of politics more generally, in giving rise
to the groups that need to be party to the dialogue on secularism. This is
an important departure from Gandhi's position, which seems to have been
premised on natural communities constituted by birth. On the other
hand, Gandhi would seem to have the stronger of the argument when it
comes to thinking about the possibility of dialogue between two incommensurable positions—in the absence, that is, of placing one's hopes in an
impartial state.

Gandhi responded to the problem of reconciling incommensurable
views, as a recent study puts it, not through an advocacy of democratic negotiation and compromise, but by "working out the politics of neighborli-

ness in myriad singular situations, some of extremely local concern," an approach that led to great frustration among nationalist colleagues who bemoaned his "lack of [a] sense of priorities."[21] Pared down to the basics, this invocation of *tapasya* (self-sacrifice and suffering) by every human amounts to a search for the truth of neighborliness and the ground for dialogue. Here, I would suggest, relations of dominance, subordination, or inequality are not posited in advance, but rather sought to be established—both comprehended and laid down—in the moment of interaction. In this form, the Gandhian formula is perfectly consistent, but its utopianism is evident.

The Gandhian *mantra* becomes much less feasible as soon as we recognize that not every individual body in the real world can isolate itself in the way Gandhi prescribed for *tapasya* or dialogue. For most individual bodies come as components of more or less well-defined if changing constellations of kin, clan, group, age, gender, and class, organized into relations of dominance and subordination that are themselves subject to continuous challenge. Modern states and economies have underlined and complicated the fault lines of our individual and collective existences. There is going to be no easy escape from them—which is why the analyst is compelled to turn back to the state in the search for justice, fairness, impartiality, and patience.

Communities and Nations

Before we consider the possible response of states and state institutions, it will help to approach the question of secularism from another direction—that of the nation and the communities it allows to exist (or wills into existence). In India, secularism made its appearance not only as a concomitant of modernity and nationalism, but also as a necessary part of the answer to communalism, another modern political development with its own pretensions to nationalism. "Hindu nationalism was a natural growth from the soil of India," Jawaharlal Nehru wrote in a classic articulation of the secular, modernist position, but, like Muslim nationalism, "inevitably it comes in the way of the larger nationalism which rises above differences of religion or creed." "*Real* or *Indian* nationalism was something quite apart from these two religious and communal varieties of nationalism, and strictly speaking is the only form which can be called *nationalism in the modern sense of the word.*"[22]

In the plural societies of many parts of Asia and Africa, where neither an absolutist nor a conquest state had emerged in the early modern period to homogenize religious traditions and cultural practices, the politics of communalism (or what has been called communalism) arose in the colonial period to become a major factor in political debates.[23] For all their violent and unfortunate consequences—and these were not trifling—communalisms, no less than nationalisms, had their life in the context of wider debates about the future political community: Indian, Nigerian, Malaysian, Sri Lankan, or other. They acquired their meaning in a contest over the nature of an imagined national community. What would be the character of that community? Should it be unitary or federal? What power should the federating units have? What would be the basis of elections and the delimitation of constituencies? What would be the language (or languages) of the nation, its history, its culture, its flag, and its anthem? What would be its civil code, its marriage and property laws, and the character of the economic development that it would seek? Should there be special safeguards for minorities and marginalized communities—in education, public service, the electoral arena, or the matter of religious and cultural practices?

With the establishment of the independent nation-state, that relation to nationalism largely disappears. Nationalism no longer inhabits quite the same kind of vigorously argued, *imaginative* moment. While the ideals and images, policies and practices of the nation and its state continue to be contested, the nation-state now exists as a powerful and tangible material, legal, and political force. It lays down the terms of debate in a different way, setting out what is politically acceptable and unacceptable, legal and illegal. What emerges in this context are fairly well defined notions of "good" and "bad" community.

The nation of course becomes the supreme example of the good.[24] People may still belong to sundry communities apart from the nation, but permission to belong and to proclaim such belonging depends to a large extent on the lesser community's conformity or lack of conformity to the current state of the national project or, to put it more bluntly, whether it is seen as threatening to the nation(al) community or not. Members of marginal, subordinated, or politically disadvantaged communities, who were and often continue to be the proponents of communalist standpoints and the makers of communalist demands, are now formally citizens. At the same time, they are seen as belonging to politically or constitutionally recognized minority communities that are preconstituted, unchanging, and in that sense unhistorical. These communities may continue to participate in political affairs, but their culture and interests, inclinations and "passions" are already known from the start. They appear as frozen entities, which are denied the possibility of internal difference, political agency, and change, even as they become objects of political manipulation and governmentality in a new way.

It may help to further investigate this process of the freezing of communities (or minorities), for it obviously did not begin with the nation-state. In the nineteenth century, as we have observed, propagandists and publicists among the Hindu, Muslim, Sikh, and other religious groupings in India moved to appropriate marginal populations (the untouchables came to be classified as unambiguously Hindu for the first time by Hindu leaders), to purify their communities (Muslims must not be contaminated by Hindu practices and vice versa), and to establish distinct and separate identities (among religious groupings, most notably in the case of the Sikhs). In this way, notions of an all-India Hindu community, an all-India Muslim community, and a new Sikh community distinct from the Hindus gradually took hold in the later nineteenth and early twentieth centuries.

Partition significantly hastened these processes, and for some time in 1947–48 it was as if great numbers of people all over northern India were marked by nothing but their Muslimness, Hinduness, or Sikhness. Communities like the large peasant caste of Mevs in the Mewati region south and west of Delhi, which had worn their Islam lightly for centuries and were described by observers (and sometimes by themselves) as "half-Hindu and half-Muslim," were now treated as Muslims plain and simple who in the view of many were best dispatched to Pakistan.[25] Hindu and Muslim politics and the continuation of open violence in subsequent decades have only exacerbated these tendencies.

Even after the experience of Partition, the identification of Muslim and foreigner was not automatic in many parts of the country. Anthropologist David Pocock's account of a Gujarat village illustrates the point very well indeed. There were four poor Muslim households in the village Pocock studied in the mid-1950s. Two of them were called Vora, derived from the Shia sect (the Bohras), the other two Sipai, indicating that some ancestor had been a soldier. One or two pictures in the houses suggested Shia allegiance, but (says Pocock) these Muslims knew nothing of Shia-Sunni or other sectarian differences. "Similarly the Prophet was represented as a holy man, one of many, who was born in India and was the originator of the sect to which they belong." The children were given Muslim names and sons were circumcised, but the families followed customary Hindu rules of property and succession, participated in Hindu ceremonies in the village, and were treated much as a Hindu caste by the other villagers.[26]

Throughout western India, Bohras and Khojas were recognized as Muslim groups of a special kind: practical businessmen, speakers of Gujarati, well integrated into the local society and culture—more like the Parsis of Bombay than the allegedly turbulent Muslims of north and northwestern India (and Pakistan).[27] But sustained campaigns of anti-Muslim propaganda and the major conflicts of the last two decades have nullified the benefits of such exceptionalism. In March and April 2002, not even the rural Muslims of Gujarat, Bohras and Khojas among them, were spared by the Hindu assailants who spread terror and death among Muslims throughout the state.

Thus the forging of entirely new kinds of Muslim, Sikh, and Hindu identity provided the basis for new kinds of struggles for Muslim and Sikh homelands in the middle and later twentieth century (to be matched, in the last couple of decades, by the most ironic of all—the movement for a Hindu homeland in the Hindu majority country of India). Since the 1980s, arguments have been advanced to the effect that the Hindu majority must unite to avoid being overwhelmed by the minority, that the minority (tied to international forces of various kinds) must not be allowed to hold the nation to ransom and that it must certainly no longer be appeased.

In India, the immediate context was the collapse of earlier constituencies (most notably, perhaps, the alliance between the highest castes and the lowest, along with the Muslims, that had returned the Congress to power in several elections), and the appearance of a new politics of coalitions, pragmatism (or *realpolitik*), and a "make your fortune while you can" mentality. In this situation, Hindu right-wing forces—but not these forces alone, for the entire political spectrum has shifted to the right, in India as in other parts of the world—were able to generate a heightened rhetoric of natural national unity, based now not on a political vision and program for the future, but on religious symbols described as the nation's fundamental heritage. The new commercialization and the much more evident flattening of cultures that came with neoliberalism contributed to this. An increasingly influential group of nonresident Indians, seeking identity and self-definition, now became ardent, long-distance nationalists—fervent supporters of the battle for new Sikh and Muslim homelands and the destruction of a disused (but beautiful) sixteenth-century mosque in Ayodhya—based not on any historical debate or political struggle, but rather on the most excessively invested and reductionist symbols of nation, community, and religion.[28]

With such support and the backing of well-entrenched and well-trained police and paramilitary forces on the one hand, and of major international organizations on the other, and facing widely scattered, poor, and largely unarmed minorities, right-wing parties have more or less successfully reinvented the nation-state in a chauvinist Hindu image and successfully intimidated the minorities—except in the border regions of Kashmir and the Northeast. Muslims in India, and increasingly the very small community of Christians too, come under suspicion because of their link to foreign (antinational) religions, hence foreign (antinational) forces, and more recently—in the case of the Muslims—to what is widely proclaimed as a worldwide terrorist network. All of this has substantially altered the world of Indian politics, and with it the conditions of struggle for secularism and democracy. This is best demonstrated through a consideration of the altered inclination of the Indian state.

The State of the State

A very brief outline of the characteristics of the colonial and postcolonial state may be useful at this point, before we note the dangerous contemporary trend toward the reemergence of colonial conditions within national borders. The colonial state was marked by a clear and sharp distinction between subjects and citizens. The former, who comprised the vast majority of colonial populations and indeed of the population of the world until the middle of the twentieth century, were in the colonial dispensation supposedly being trained for citizenship—presumably in the distant future. They were, in Foucauldian terms, populations to be disciplined, educated, fashioned, so that they might be infused with increased productive capacity and a greater respect for law and order.

The early nationalist states of the postcolonial era announced their arrival by granting citizenship rights to all who inhabited their territories, with perhaps just the occasional question mark over the status of marginal individuals or groups. These were professedly developmental states, under which the national population was to be made fit (and equal) in a modern world. The focus was supposed to be on education and all-round economic growth as a means to establishing the necessary underpinnings of democracy and modernity.

The neoliberal regime of our own time appears to have reverted to a colonial conception of productive citizens on the one hand, who provide the elements of enterprise and modernity in our societies, and populations on the other, who are lacking in resources, education, and initiative and to that extent unworthy of the privileges accorded proper citizens. This version of the postcolonial state leaves large sections of the population fundamentally without rights. However, there is no escape from these populations: unwelcome and sometimes illegal or barely legal immigrants, slum dwellers, vagrant children and youth, and so on. They cannot easily be moved out. All the state can do is discipline them in such a way as to maintain, and if possible improve, conditions for the rapid economic advance of the country and its citizens (that is to say, its more prosperous and privileged classes).

This is not a developmental state any more, even theoretically. Terms like *poverty, the poor,* and *economic democracy* (or *economic and social justice*) have largely disappeared from ruling-class discourse. Nevertheless, while the development or welfare of the people at large seems to matter less and less, legitimacy is still sought and obtained in the name of the nation. Trade unions, secessionist movements, and disruptive opposition groups are all quickly pronounced antinational. Minorities are targeted for alleged deviation from national and modernist norms. Muslims in India become even more uncertain political quantities. Since the partition of the subcontinent in 1947, the Muslims of India have lived, especially at times of open violence between the religious communities, under the suspicion of harboring loyalties to Pakistan. The situation has worsened in some ways over the last two decades.

For a long period in the nineteenth and twentieth centuries, the state's claim to neutrality formed a large part of the argument for the perpetuation of colonial government in Asia and Africa. It is a claim that many postcolonial regimes continued to put forward with greater insistence, and for a while in democracies like India and Sri Lanka, perhaps with somewhat greater success. This did not remain the case. In India and Sri Lanka, the state became a much more active (and openly partisan) party to intercommunity conflicts that, once upon a time, it was supposed to have mediated, although there are some signs in both countries now of political forces attempting to pull back from the brink. If communalism refers to a condition of conflict and negotiation between two or more politicized religious communities, the Indian and Sri Lankan states—or, at least, important parts of these states—have in recent years acted rather like politicized religious communities themselves. And the communal riot, once thought of as the quintessential expression (and upshot) of communalist politics, has given place to a very different kind of violence.

On the partisanship of state forces, let me cite the comment of a senior officer of the Indian Police Service, made in the wake of the anti-Muslim pogrom in Gujarat in 2002. "Since 1960," he writes, "in almost all [communal] riots that have occurred, the same picture has been painted in the same colours, a picture of a helpless and often inactive police force that allowed wailing members of the minority community to be looted and killed in its presence, that remained a mute witness to some of their members being burnt alive." Further: "For an average policeman, collection of intelligence is limited to gathering information about the activities of communal Muslim organizations. It is not easy to make him realize that the activities of Hindu communal organizations also come under the purview of anti-national activities. . . . Similarly, preventive arrests, even in riot situations in which Muslims are the worst sufferers, are restricted to members of the minority community."[29]

As for communal riots, it is enough to say that the worst examples of violence against minority racial or religious communities, over the last two decades and more, fail to fit that description in any commonly understood sense of the term. It is unnecessary to recount details of the carnage that occurred in Colombo in 1983, Delhi in 1984, Bombay and other places in 1992–93, or Gujarat in 2002. Suffice it to recall that, in these as in other instances, hundreds if not thousands of people from the majority community congregated at will for days (sometimes weeks) on end, to attack and loot the persons, property, and wealth of the targeted community. The habitations, houses and shops, vehicles and machines, fields and hand pumps that belonged to members of the minority community were identified and marked out in advance, with the assistance of electoral registers, tax rolls, census data, and local informants.

The attacks took place with the acquiescence (if not active encouragement) of the police, the political leadership, and even leading ministers in the government, and with almost no fear of counterattack or loss of life (since the police were at hand to ward off and shoot any counterattackers), or indeed of punishment (since the police and the existing political leadership were on their side, and even the judiciary seemed mindful of the views of the political leadership, if not in agreement with them). These were not riots; they were organized political massacres, feeding on and fanning the hatred and prejudices of a growing segment of the majority community, pogroms sanctioned by the government, and examples of a new brand of state terrorism.

I would like to add one word, finally, on state terrorism and the prospects for democracy. Let me stay with the example of Gujarat for a moment to clarify the reason for this digression. An attack on 27 February 2002, carried out (it was claimed) by some Muslims at Godhra on a train bearing Hindu pilgrims from Ayodhya, became the occasion for the launching of widespread and barely controlled violence against Muslims in the towns and villages of Gujarat over the next few weeks. A press note issued by the state government on the evening of 27 February described the torching of the train and the killing of passengers as a "pre-planned inhuman collective violent act of terrorism." Chief Minister Modi spoke of Pakistan's proxy war and its "clandestine role . . . behind the Godhra genocide," and referred to the latter as "the pre-planned collective terrorism against Gujarat." Modi in his turn has been hailed as "the Sardar opposed to terrorism."[30] Six months later, following what might much more reasonably be described as a terrorist attack on a Hindu temple in Gandhinagar, then prime minister Atal Behari Vajpayee declared from the Indian Ocean island of Male where he was attending a SAARC meeting that terrorism was "on its last legs," the Taliban and Al-Qaeda were finished, and there was a global war against terrorism in which India was fully playing its part.[31]

Since the terrorist attacks on New York and Washington on 11 September 2001, the war against terror has become an instrument in the hands of numerous powerful groups and states in various parts of the world, India, Russia, and Israel among them, to settle old scores and make easy (financial and political) gains. There was large-scale international public opposition at one point to the war against Iraq, but opposition to the longer-term strategies adopted by governments far and wide in their efforts to combat terror has been muted at best—and there has been little challenge to the nationalist, even humanitarian, arguments advanced to justify their actions. Governments and bureaucracies have over time accumulated increasing power to do as they want largely unchallenged—because of their invisibility, their access to information, and easy recourse to arguments about the sanctity of national interests, above all, that of national security. Over the last three years, this exercise of bureaucratic state power has been particularly arbitrary and unquestioned.

Today this is a notable condition of politics in democratic India, as well as in the United States. Opposition, especially from organized mainstream political parties, has been restricted to condemnations of the government for its poor timing or its failure to pursue vigorously enough nationalist policies (such as antiterrorist measures, militarization, or nuclearization). Large sections of the population have lived in a kind of security state even in these leading democracies, with increasing restrictions on what official policies may be debated, let alone combated.

In many parts of the world, I submit, religious belief and observance, and more generally cultural practice, is very much subject to this new illiberal regime. These must now, perhaps more than ever before, conform to the definitions (and prescriptions) of the mainstream. Instead of a constitutionally guaranteed right to diversity of faith and worship and a struggle for tolerance and understanding based upon that right, what we have had in India recently is an *intolerance* not so much of particular religious practices or beliefs as of the very existence of people belonging to other religious denominations. Two slogans widely touted in Ayodhya (in 1990 and 1992) and Gujarat (in 2002) sum up the new politics of violence that comes with this intolerance. The first, *Musalman ke do hi sthaan, Pakistan ya kabristan*, left no space at all for the existence of Muslims in the nation-state of India. The second, *Pahle Qasai, phir Isai*, extended the argument to the small Christian community as well.

Concluding Thoughts

In its exploration of the continuing dominance of the ideology of nationalism—one people, one culture, one history, one nation—this book has engaged with the question of natural and not-so-natural belonging. In this chapter, I have focused on the issue of secularism (and its supposed counterpoints, dubbed communalism, fundamentalism, and religious bigotry), which has been central to the project of building modern democratic polities throughout the world. Nationalism and secularism have both derived their political force in large part by occupying the high moral ground—*above* the play of sectional, parochial, or party interests, and *above* the dirtiness and greed of petty politics and money.[32] In that sense, they have sometimes even claimed to be *apolitical,* beyond politics—the natural condition of a civilized people, or at any rate, the natural and obvious goal of any modern, civilized society.

I argue the opposite. My aim is to reveal the *politics* necessary to the realization of nationhood or secularism, and indeed to the very articulation of these as appropriate goals for a people. Today, many would question the continued value or validity of the nation form, even if they recognize the need for the establishment of something like secularism everywhere. Yet, whether we support them or not, the political nature of these projects and of the violence informing them needs to be underscored.

I have argued that the kind of dialogue between religious groups that is invoked by many proponents of secularism requires questioning. It is necessary, first, to recognize the proposed exercise as a *political* dialogue— a negotiation, in which the parties are not always (or even usually) equal, and in which the state also participates, as an interested and of course privileged party. Second, the statement is based on assumptions about the liberal state within which this negotiation is supposed to occur that are no longer valid and probably never were. The democratic states of our time have been quite prepared, when the need has arisen, to give up their pretences to liberalism or to a Habermasian commitment to rational dialogue between legally equal parties in a neutral public sphere. They have shown themselves more than willing to negotiate through undisguised violence— within the borders of their countries as well as outside them.

What is it that authorizes the kind of extreme violence I have outlined in the preceding pages? The answer, I have suggested, lies in the routine violence practiced all along to constitute certain groups as majorities and others as minorities, to deny yet other groups even the status of minorities, and to create special targeted minorities that then live under constant suspicion of disloyalty. Behind this lies a very widely accepted view of the sanctity of nationalism and the nation-state and an all too easy equation of the interests of the state with those of the nation.

An argument about the primacy, naturalness, and supreme legitimacy of the nation has led to demands for exclusive, unambiguous, unquestioning loyalty to the state and those (temporarily?) in command of it. This has facilitated the leveling of charges of antinational conduct, treason, and even terrorism against a whole range of political opponents of the ruling groups and classes—from peasant rebels fighting for land rights to disadvantaged minority communities struggling to preserve some sense of self.

Anyone or any group that mounts a challenge to the proclaimed national interest is denounced as an enemy. The charge is commonly brought against members of minority communities who have what are described as foreign links. No particular argument is required to demonstrate their enemy status. It is demonstrated by their very being, their foreign religions or languages, the mosques they congregate in, their links with people (sometimes relatives) in other countries, and by the simple fact of loud and repeated assertion. These are enemies and terrorists almost by definition, wreckers of peace in the nation ("in every country they inhabit," it is commonly said), wreckers of the nation. It is up to them to prove that they no longer harbor weapons and drugs, that they have renounced criminal intentions, and that they will now begin to be like us.

As a result of the unchecked advance of such arguments about threats to our nations, frequently portrayed as threats to civilization, the ground for any politics of difference, not to say the practice of democracy in general, has shrunk considerably. In this context, an unyoking of the pair state and nation is an urgent task. This seems to me crucial for two reasons. First, so that the state does not mask its own particular interests (and the interests of ruling classes and factions) as the interests of a sacred community called the nation. Secondly, so that no community can permanently claim for itself the status of mainstream, and hence majority, and hence (since the majority is generally invisible, and presents itself as the nation) neutrality—much like the proclaimed neutrality of the liberal state.

Thus we might be able to hold the state to account as a party to political engagement that must justify the disposition and policies it adopts in favor of particular groups, classes, and sections. This would be a fight for the recognition of all communities—secularists, modernists, conservatives, Christians, Buddhists, Hindus, working people, or middle classes—as minorities, with no place for an unquestioned, permanent majority, a natural mainstream (or natural nation).[33] There can be no place in such a scheme for an Other. Instead, one might expect a proliferation of others in a multiplicity of spaces, citizens with many affiliations who would be German, Indian, Rwandan, American "among other things."[34] In time perhaps our states too will be able to celebrate a new society of plural belonging.

Notes

CHAPTER 1

1. G. W. F. Hegel, *Introduction to "The Philosophy of History,"* trans. Leo Rauch (Indianapolis, Ind., 1988), pp. 65–66 (emphasis added).

2. "Africa proper, as far as History goes back, has remained . . . the land of childhood, which lying beyond the day of self-conscious history, is enveloped in the dark mantle of Night. . . . The Negro . . . exhibits the natural man in his completely wild and untamed state;" G. W. F. Hegel, *The Philosophy of History,* trans. J. Sibree (Buffalo, N.Y., 1991), pp. 91, 93, and *passim.* Peter Geschiere recalls English historian Hugh Trevor-Roper's observation in a radio address in the 1960s that African history began with the coming of the white man; before that, according to him, there were only the "unrewarding gyrations of barbarous tribes."

3. Hegel, *Introduction to "The Philosophy of History,"* p. 64.

4. Cf. Frantz Fanon, *The Wretched of the Earth* (New York, 1963); Jean Suret-Canale, *French Colonialism in Tropical Africa, 1900–1945* (New York, 1971); Hannah Arendt, *Eichmann in Jerusalem: A Report on the Banality of Evil* (New York, 1977); Zygmunt Bauman, *Modernity and the Holocaust* (Ithaca, NY, 1989).

5. Fanon, *Wretched of the Earth,* pp. 40, 93.

6. David Herman, "Bloody History," *Prospect Magazine,* no. 99 (June 2004).

7. For a few of the most widely cited, see Mushirul Hasan, ed., *India Partitioned: The Other Face of Freedom,* 2 vols. (Delhi, 1995); Urvashi Butalia, *The Other Side of Silence: Voices from the Partition of India* (Delhi, 1998); Ritu Menon and Kamla Bhasin, *Borders and Boundaries: Women in India's Partition* (Delhi, 1998); Veena Das, *Critical Events: An Anthropological Perspective on Contemporary India* (Delhi, 1995), ch. 3; Shail Mayaram, *Resisting Regimes: Myth, Memory and the Shaping of a Muslim Identity* (Delhi, 1997); and Gyanendra Pandey, *Remembering Partition: Violence, Nationalism and History in India* (Cambridge, 2001).

8. Herman, "Bloody History." The information and quotations in the next two paragraphs are taken from this review article.

9. W. G. Sebald, *On the Natural History of Destruction* (New York, 2003), pp. 4 and 104.

10. Simon Schama, *Citizens: A Chronicle of the French Revolution* (New York, 1989), pp. 787 and 791–92.

11. Suret-Canale, *Essays on African History: From the Slave Trade to Neocolonialism* (London, 1988), pp. 63–65 and *passim.*

12. For an examination of the estimates of Partition casualties, see Pandey, *Remembering Partition,* ch. 4.

13. Marcel Mauss, *The Gift: The Form and Reason of Exchange in Archaic Societies* (London, 1990), pp. 3 and 78–79.

14. Michael Billig, *Banal Nationalism* (London, 1995), p. 12 and *passim.*

15. E. Kedourie, *Nationalism* (rev. ed., London, 1985), pp. 73–74.

16. Billig, *Banal Nationalism,* p. 6.

17. Ibid., pp. 158–61.

18. Ibid., pp. 6, 11.

19. Achille Mbembe, *On the Postcolony* (Berkeley, Ca., 2001), pp. 174–75. The italics are his.

20. Ibid., p. 74 and *passim.*

21. Donald Carter, *Navigating Diaspora* (Minneapolis, forthcoming), pp. 108–109. Carter writes that "the proliferation of ethnic militias and the attempt of the state to displace 'traditional' local administrations have resulted in a battle over control of a number of regions and an overall militarization of Sudanese society. But many of these features of the postcolonial state including the structure of its particular orchestration of violence date back to the colonial period" (p. 116).

22. Jonathan Glover, *Humanity: A Moral History of the Twentieth Century* (London, 1999), p. 88 and *passim.*

23. Sebald, *On the Natural History of Destruction,* p. 33.

24. On the reemergence of these categories as significant elements in African politics, see Peter Geschiere, "Ecology, Belonging and Xenophobia: The 1994 Forest Law in Cameroon and the Issue of Community," in Harri Englund and Francis B. Nyamnjoh, eds., *Rights and the Politics of Recognition in Africa* (London, 2004).

25. Ajay Skaria and others have made this point to me on the basis of extended work and stay in Gujarat since 2002.

26. For one discussion of this kind of reaction, see Ruby Lal and Gyan Pandey, "Who are We?" in their column "North American Notes and Queries," *Economic and Political Weekly* 39, no. 19 (8–14 May 2004).

CHAPTER 2

1. The same point needs to be made about the kind of historical and social science writing discussed in this chapter. I have deliberately taken my examples from some of the best left and liberal scholars writing in India. This is because it is among them, rather than among chauvinist "Hindu," "Muslim," or "Sikh" historians and social scientists, that there is serious debate about "secularism" versus "communalism" and the meaning of sectarian violence. It seems to me also that a critique of their writings is not only harder to make but, in terms of building up

an alternative to the dominant (chauvinist) political and ideological tendencies in India today, also more necessary.

2. Numerous reviews of the early *Subaltern Studies* volumes (the first three of which were published between 1982 and 1984) and of Ranajit Guha's *Elementary Aspects of Peasant Insurgency in Colonial India* (Delhi, 1983) argued that these works concentrated far too much on the moment of open revolt and violence. Exactly the same thing has been said about recent work on the partition of British India in 1947, which again "concentrates too much on violence." Indeed, it is the non-violent character of the Indian national movement led by Gandhi that is supposed to represent the truth of Indian history, as several examples in the following pages will show.

3. See Lata Mani, *Contentious Traditions: The Debate on Sati in Colonial India* (Berkeley, Ca., 1998), which makes a similar point about agency and the moment of suffering.

4. See, for example, contributions by Partha Chatterjee, Ashis Nandy, T.N. Madan, and others in Rajeev Bhargava, ed., *Secularism and Its Critics* (Delhi, 1998); Dipesh Chakrabarty, *Provincializing Europe: Postcolonial Thought and Historical Difference* (Princeton, N.J., 2000); and Gyanendra Pandey, *The Construction of Communalism in Colonial North India* (Delhi, 1990).

5. For a discussion of the peculiar usage of this term in India, see Pandey, *The Construction of Communalism*, pp. 6ff.

6. Bipan Chandra, *Modern India* (New Delhi, 1971), pp. 305–306. Page numbers for subsequent quotations are provided in the text.

7. Ibid., pp. 296–97 and *passim*.

8. Sumit Sarkar, *Modern India, 1885–1947* (New Delhi, 1983), p. 438. Page numbers for subsequent quotations are given in the text.

9. This might be said to have applied also to Bangladesh before the violence, looting, and rape perpetrated by the Pakistan army in 1971 overshadowed even the Partition experience.

10. See James Knowlton and Truett Cates, ed., *Forever in the Shadow of Hitler? Original Documents of the 'Historikerstreit,' the Controversy Concerning the Singularity of the Holocaust* (Atlantic Highlands, N.J., 1993). See also Theodor Adorno, *Minima Moralia: Reflections from a Damaged Life* (London, 1974).

11. See, for example, Mushirul Hasan, *Legacy of a Divided Nation: India's Muslims since Independence* (London, 1997); Butalia, *The Other Side of Silence;* Menon and Bhasin, *Borders and Boundaries;* Das, *Critical Events*, ch. 3; Mayaram, *Resisting Regimes;* and Pandey, *Remembering Partition*.

12. Over the last two decades, contributions in *Subaltern Studies*, in a variety of feminist studies, and more recently in Dalit writings, as well as the new corpus of research on the violence of Partition, have raised new questions about the nationalist paradigm. See, for example, Chatterjee, *The Nation and Its Fragments;* Shahid Amin, *Event, Metaphor, Memory: Chauri-Chaura, 1922–1992* (Berkeley, Ca., 1995); G. Aloysius, *Nationalism without a Nation in India* (Delhi, 1997); Mri-

nalini Sinha, *Colonial Masculinity: The "Manly Englishman" and the "Effeminate Bengali" in the Late Nineteenth Century* (Delhi, 1997); Tanika Sarkar, *Hindu Wife, Hindu Nation: Religion and Cultural Nationalism* (Delhi, 2001); in addition to the references cited in the previous note.

13. This includes the great Partition poems of Faiz Ahmad Faiz, which have gained extraordinary popularity in both India and Pakistan.

14. See Alok Bhalla, *Stories on the Partition of India* (New Delhi, 1994), 3 vols.; Hasan, *India Partitioned*; Muhammad Umar Memon, ed., *An Epic Unwritten: The Penguin Book of Partition Stories* (Delhi, 1998); Jason Francisco, "In the Heat of the Fratricide: The Literature of India's Partition Burning Freshly," review article, *Annual Review of Urdu Studies* (1997); Aijaz Ahmad, "Urdu Literature in India," *Seminar* 359 (July 1989); Alok Rai, "The Trauma of Independence: Some Aspects of Progressive Hindi Literature, 1945–47," and Surjit Singh Hans, "The Partition Novels of Nanak Singh," in Amit Kumar Gupta, ed., *Myth and Reality: The Struggle for Freedom in India, 1945–47* (Delhi, 1987).

15. Tapati Chakravarty, "The Freedom Struggle and Bengali Literature of the 1940s," in Gupta, ed., *Myth and Reality*, p. 329.

16. The incidents of strife in Delhi in 1984, in Meerut in 1987, and in Bhagalpur in 1989 were reported precisely in this way. Tavleen Singh's report on the Gonda riots in *Indian Express* (Delhi), 14 October 1990, provides a less familiar example. The violence that followed the December 1992 destruction of the Babari Masjid in Ayodhya and the 2002 Gujarat carnage are other well-known and well-documented examples.

17. The details in the next two paragraphs are taken from the PUDR report *Bhagalpur Riots* (Delhi, 1990) and the notes upon which it is based.

18. While many local people put the death toll at not less than two thousand, the official figure was 414 dead as of April 1990. The most careful unofficial calculations suggested that perhaps one thousand people lost their lives, over 90 percent of them Muslims; ibid., p. 1.

19. I refer here to our own efforts as a team of investigators. Satish Sabherwal and Mushirul Hasan also note the "wholly unjustified confidence" of the mass media in the official version of events in recent instances of strife; "Moradabad Riots, 1980: Causes and Meanings," in Asghar Ali Engineer, ed., *Communal Riots in Post-Independence India* (Hyderabad, 1984), p. 208.

20. As the PUDR report notes, the support given to its ten-member team by local activists of the Communist Party of India (Marxist) "effectively doubled our strength"; PUDR, *Bhagalpur Riots*, p. 70.

21. It is worth noting that we were repeatedly pressed to go and see those places where Hindus had been the victims of attacks—notably, a village named Jamalpur and a few sections of Bhagalpur city. We had decided to visit these places in any case, even before our on-the-spot investigations began in Bhagalpur, precisely in order that we might see and hear "both sides."

22. The "First Information Report" is a formal report registered at a local police station as the first record of a crime or disturbance reported to the police.

23. PUDR, *Bhagalpur Riots*, p. 57.

24. Ved Prakash Vajpayee, *Navbharat Times* (Delhi), 19 November 1989 (translation mine).

25. Ibid.

26. PUDR, *Bhagalpur Riots*, p. 6.

27. Engineer, "Causes of Communal Riots," in *Communal Riots*, pp. 36–37.

28. Sumitra Kumar Jain, "Economy of Communalism," *Times of India* (Delhi), reproduced in *India-Pakistan Times*, May 1990.

29. See, for example, A.S. Raman, "Leaders to Blame for Communalism," *Sunday Mail*, 14 October 1990: "In India the basic material is very good. I mean, the people. They are honest, intelligent and generous. They are only waiting to be drawn into the national mainstream. What is absent is leadership of the right type."

30. This issue is taken up for lengthier discussion in Chapters 5 and 6 below.

31. All of these instances are from Bhagalpur (see PUDR, *Bhagalpur Riots*), but examples could be cited from other events, and have unfortunately been bested—if that is the word—in the experience of Gujarat in 2002.

32. The rumor was, in fact, malicious and baseless. Most students living in the boardinghouses left as soon as the disturbances broke out, if they had not already left earlier, and many were helped to get away safely by their Muslim landlords. The number of students killed or missing was subsequently found to be six; of these, the bodies of only two students (one Hindu and one Muslim) had been found when the PUDR team visited Bhagalpur (PUDR, *Bhagalpur Riots*, p. 12). However, in the disturbed and dangerous condition of the city and district in the first few days after the outbreak of violence, many students appear not to have been able to reach their homes. During this time, and indeed for long afterward, the story of the massacre of students was neither investigated nor countered by the district or the university authorities. On the contrary, it was publicized in the press, even aired on the radio (both local and BBC), and was readily and widely accepted. It was still widely believed when we visited Bhagalpur at the end of January 1990.

33. For a discussion of this mass conversion, see Chapter 7 below.

34. See Asghar Ali Engineer, "On the Theory of Communal Riots," in Engineer and Moin Shakir, eds., *Communalism in India* (Delhi, 1985), p. 62; and leaflets and pamphlets collected by the PUDR team in Bhagalpur. The two preceding quotations in this paragraph are from a leaflet entitled "*Bhagalpur ka sampradayik danga kyon?*" issued in the name of the "People of Bhagalpur"; and Vinayak Damodar Savarkar, *Six Glorious Epochs of Indian History*, trans. S.T. Godbole (Bombay, 1971), p. 175.

35. Dr. Rajeshwar, Akhil Bharat Hindu Mahasabha, *Hindu bandhuon, socho aur sambhalo*, which is among the leaflets mentioned in the previous note (translation mine).

36. The English word is used in the Hindi text.

37. A Muslim religious foundation set up for charitable purposes, and in places supported by government.

38. The slogan *Bande Mataram* is controversial because of its Hindu religious connotations. The political wrangling over this is discussed further in Chapter 6 below, where I also discuss the construction of the invisible national "mainstream."

39. See A. Shankar, *Chetavni 2: Desh ko khatra* (n.p., n.d.). On some of the logical problems arising out of the declaration that Indian Muslims are converts (forcibly converted) and the descendants of Babar at the same time, see Alok Rai, "Only Bigots Feel That Conversions Follow Invasion," *Times of India* (Lucknow), 13 August 1990.

40. The malleability of Hindu traditions and practices is discussed further in Chapter 5.

41. Anuradha Kapur, "Deity to Crusader: The Changing Iconography of Ram," in Gyanendra Pandey, ed., *Hindus and Others: The Question of Identity in India Today* (New Delhi, 1993), pp. 74–109. See also Sudipto Kaviraj's discussion of the nineteenth-century reconstruction of the image of Lord Krishna in a new, masculine mode ("The Myth of Praxis: The Construction of the Figure of Krishna in *Krishnacharitra*," *Nehru Memorial Museum and Library Occasional Papers on History and Society*, no. 50 [1987]). For a fuller account of the movement to destroy the mosque and liberate Ram's claimed birthplace in Ayodhya, see Chapter 4 and its appendix below.

42. As one commentator observed in the 1960s, who would have thought in the 1940s that the Jews would become an aggressive, militaristic nation in the Middle East, and the Japanese would become the shopkeepers of the world!

43. For some reports on these, see Engineer, *Communal Riots*; Engineer and Shakir, *Communalism in India*; PUCL and PUDR, *Who Are the Guilty? Report of a Joint Inquiry into the Causes and Impact of the Riots in Delhi from 31 October to 31 November* (Delhi, 1984); Uma Chakravarti and Nandita Haksar, *The Delhi Riots: Three Days in the Life of a Nation* (Delhi, 1987); Stanley J. Tambiah, *Sri Lanka: Ethnic Fratricide and the Dismantling of Democracy* (Chicago, 1986); and Veena Das, ed., *Mirrors of Violence: Communities, Riots, Survivors in South Asia* (Delhi, 1990).

44. Interview with Shri Arun, Bhagalpur, 20 January 1990.

45. Budaun and Bhagalpur provided examples in 1989.

46. "Five Rallyists Crushed to Death," *Hindustan Times* (Delhi), 9 October 1990.

47. The protests followed a government announcement on 7 August 1990 reserving a percentage of government jobs for the "Other Backward Classes," in addition to those already reserved for the "Scheduled Castes and Tribes." For detailed reports on the agitation and protest immolations, see *Economic and Political Weekly*, *India Today*, and newspapers for September and October 1990.

48. Manazir Aashiq Harganvi, *Ankhon dekhi: Bhagalpur ke bhayanak fasad ko dekhne ke baad* (Bhagalpur, 1989) (translations mine).

49. Cf. Antonio Gramsci: "Is it possible to write (conceive of) a history of Europe in the nineteenth century without an organic treatment of the French Revolution and the Napoleonic Wars . . . ? One can say, therefore, that [Croce's] book on the *History of Europe* is nothing but a fragment of history." *Selections from the Prison Notebooks of Antonio Gramsci,* edited by Quintin Hoare and Geoffrey Nowell Smith (London, 1971), pp. 118, 119. It will be clear, of course, that I am not advocating the kind of objective, integral history that Gramsci called for.

50. See William E. Connolly, *Why I Am Not a Secularist* (Minneapolis, Minn., 1999), p. 3 and *passim.*

51. *Hindustan Times,* 23 July 1990.

52. Constitution of India, preamble.

APPENDIX TO CHAPTER 2

1. See Appendix to Chapter 4 below.

2. The reference is to a forced sati (wife-burning on the pyre of a recently deceased husband) that took place amid much fanfare in this Rajasthani village in 1987, and that became a focus of major political contention between women's groups and other progressive forces on the one hand, and the local elite supported by right-wing elements in the provincial and national governments on the other. For an illustration of some of the positions taken in the debate, see Madhu Kishwar and Ruth Vanita, "The Burning of Roop Kanwar," *Manushi,* nos. 42–43 (September–December 1987); K. Sangari and S. Vaid, "Institutions, Beliefs, Ideologies: Widow Immolation in Contemporary Rajasthan," in *Economic and Political Weekly* 26, no. 17 (27 April 1991); and Rajeswari Sunder Rajan, *Real and Imagined Women: Gender, Culture and Postcolonialism* (London, 1993), ch. 1.

CHAPTER 3

1. See the references cited in n. 11 of Chapter 2.

2. In Bangladesh, nationalist historiography has had a more checkered career, with the Partition of 1947 now seen as the "first stage" in a struggle for liberation that reached its goal only in 1971.

3. François Furet, *Interpreting the French Revolution* (Cambridge, 1981), pp. 18 and 22 (emphasis in original).

4. For a classic discussion of the standard colonial idea of Muslim conspiracies, see W.W. Hunter, *The Indian Musalmans: Are they bound in conscience to rebel against the Queen* (1876; rpt. Delhi, 1969).

5. For a detailed discussion of this colonialist proposition, see my *Construction of Communalism in Colonial North India,* ch. 2.

6. See Dadabhai Naoroji, *Poverty and UnBritish Rule in India* (London, 1901); R.C. Dutt, *The Economic History of India,* 2 vols. (London, 1908); and for a more recent synthetic statement, Bipan Chandra, *Rise and Growth of Economic*

Nationalism in India: Economic Policies of Indian National Leadership, 1880–1905 (Delhi, 1966).

7. See the discussion of this point in my response to a right-wing journalist, reproduced here as the Appendix to Chapter 2.

8. K.N. Panikkar, "In Defence of Old History," *Economic and Political Weekly* 29, no. 40 (October 1994).

9. Irfan Habib, *Reason and History* (Delhi, 1994).

10. On this point, see especially Dipesh Chakrabarty, *Provincializing Europe*; Partha Chatterjee, *The Nation and Its Fragments*; and Ranajit Guha, *Dominance without Hegemony: History and Power in Colonial India* (Delhi, 1998).

11. I refer to E.P. Thompson's classic work, *The Making of the English Working Class* (London, 1963), as well as his and his collaborators' work on the eighteenth century, published in volumes such as Douglas Hay et al., eds., *Albion's Fatal Tree: Crime and Society in Eighteenth Century England* (New York, 1975). For further debates and extension of the argument about the making of new classes and cultures, see, for example, Louise Tilly and Joan Scott, *Women, Work and Family* (New York, 1987); and Carolyn Steedman, *Landscape for a Good Woman: A Story of Two Lives* (New Brunswick, N.J., 1987).

12. Ranajit Guha, *Elementary Aspects of Peasant Insurgency in Colonial India* (Delhi, 1983).

13. Cf. Gayatri Chakravarty Spivak, "Can the Subaltern Speak? Speculations on Widow Sacrifice," in L. Grossberg and C. Nelson, eds., *Marxism and the Interpretation of Culture* (Chicago, 1988). As should be evident, the following pages owe a great deal to my reading of this classic essay.

14. It should be unnecessary here to dwell on the status of facts, but historians as a tribe perhaps need periodic reminders that there are no preconceptual, prelinguistic facts. Cf. Alasdaire Macintyre: "Facts, like telescopes and wigs for gentlemen, were a 17th century invention. In the sixteenth century and earlier 'fact' in English was usually a rendering of the Latin 'factum,' a deed, and action, and sometimes in scholastic Latin an event or an occasion. . . . It is of course . . . harmless, philosophically and otherwise, to use the word 'fact' of what a judgement states. What is . . . not harmless, but highly misleading, was to conceive a realm of facts independent of judgement or of any other form of linguistic expression." *Whose Justice? What Rationality?* (London, 1988), pp. 357–67.

15. Gramsci, *Selections from the Prison Notebooks*, pp. 54–55.

16. Das, *Critical Events*, p. 79.

17. For one outstanding example of the attempt to write such a transgressive history, see Ranajit Guha, "Chandra's Death," in Guha, ed., *Subaltern Studies: Writings on South Asian Society and History*, vol. 5 (Delhi, 1987).

18. Religion, Guha notes, is the "oldest of archives," and (one might add) among the most neglected in large parts of the world. Ranajit Guha, "The Career of an Anti-God in Heaven and on Earth," in Ashok Mitra, ed., *The Truth Unites: Essays in Tribute to Samar Sen* (Calcutta, 1985), p. 1.

19. Ibid., p. 2.

20. W. E. B. Du Bois, *The Souls of Black Folk* (New York, 1995), p. 43.

21. Du Bois writes: "It is a peculiar sensation, this double-consciousness, this sense of always looking at one's self through the eyes of others, of measuring one's soul by the tape of a world that looks on in amused contempt and pity. One ever feels [one's] twoness—an American, a Negro; two souls, two thoughts, two unreconciled strivings; two warring ideals in one dark body, whose dogged strength alone keeps it from being torn asunder." Ibid., p. 45.

22. Ibid.

23. I refer to the idea that a daughter is a stranger in her natal home, on the reasoning that she is only growing up to go away, or rather be given away, to a husband and his family. The tragedy is that the married woman is not always easily assimilated into her new home either, however much it may be said that this is her real, destined home.

24. Das, "Composition of the Personal Voice," p. 69.

25. Guha, "Chandra's Death." "To wear a Boishnob habit, that is, to adopt the dress, ornaments and body markings which make up the semiotic ensemble called *bhek*, is to move out of caste," writes Guha. Over time, *bhek* came to signify loss of caste by "expulsion" rather than by "abdication." Some observers spoke of the *akhras*, where such outcaste women were frequently confined, as "abortion centres," others of how religion was being used to "corrupt" women—ignoring their own complicity in this exploitation of harassed women. Guha notes that the largest group of female outcastes placed in this situation was made up of "Hindu widows ostracized for defying the controls exercised on their sexuality by the local patriarchies." Ibid., pp. 156–59.

26. Lawrence Stone, "The Revival of Narrative: Reflections on a New Old History," *Past and Present* 85 (1979).

27. E. J. Hobsbawm, "The Revival of Narrative: Some Comments," *Past and Present* 86 (1980).

28. David Lowenthal, *The Past Is a Foreign Country* (Cambridge, 1985), pp. 223–24.

29. Joan Scott, "The Campaign against PC: What's Really at Stake," *Radical History Review* 54 (1992), p. 71.

30. Ranajit Guha, "The Small Voice of History," in Shahid Amin and Dipesh Chakrabarty, eds., *Subaltern Studies: Writings on South Asian History and Society*, vol. 9 (Delhi, 1996).

31. Ibid.

32. Das, *Critical Events*, p. 177.

33. Cf. Foucault's distinction between "exhaustiveness" and "intelligibility" as alternative ideals in dealing with historical evidence. What follows from that, I suggest, is the possibility of two kinds of history: one that looks for evidence of "all that happened" in the past or in a designated part of the past, and one that exam-

ines evidence of how a particular discourse or field came to be constituted, even thinkable.

CHAPTER 4

1. While this attack clearly has a great deal to do with the Muslim identity of the painter, that is not the stated reason. It is notable that Muslim artisans and artists have contributed to Hindu festivals and prayers in significant ways: in Ayodhya, even today, the sacred wooden sandals worn by Hindu devotees and priests are often made my local Muslims.

2. Girilal Jain, "Vexing Ayodhya Issue," *Times of India*, 14 August 1992.

3. Much of my investigation of the history and politics of Ayodhya took place in collaboration with Professor Sudhir Chandra. I owe thanks to him, as well as to Drs. Anuradha Kapur and Geetanjali Shree, for numerous insights and suggestions that have gone into the writing of this chapter.

4. Pratap Narayan Mishra, *Kya Kahti Saryu Dhara? Shri Ram Janmabhumi ki Kahani* (2d ed., Lucknow, 1990), appendix and p. 144. To the battles listed in this appendix, I have added events 1, 3, and 13–15, which appear regularly in these histories of Ayodhya. The date of event 3 varies, being given as late as the fifth century in Radhey Shyam Shukul's *Sachitra, Pramanik Itihasa*, which identifies Vikramaditya with the Gupta king Skandagupta, who ruled at Pataliputra (modern Patna) from A.D. 455 to 467.

5. *Ham Mandir Vahin Banayenge* (New Delhi, 1989).

6. A *lakh* = 100,000; a *crore* (from the Hindi *karor*) = 10,000,000.

7. The story is told in the great epic, the *Ramayana*, which has been reproduced in numerous recensions in India over the centuries. Perhaps the most popular of these is Tulsidas's *Ramcharitmanas*, the colloquial Hindi version written in the sixteenth century.

8. The reference is to *Lucknow Gazetteer*, part 26, p. 3.

9. *Ham Mandir Vahin Banayenge*, pp. 10–11. It is noteworthy that while the attacks by Ravana and Milind (Menander) appear in these opening paragraphs, not even the latter is among the 77 battles listed by the author as having taken place for the protection/liberation of RJD. The reference to "the historian Cunningham" is to the civil servant who compiled the Lucknow *District Gazetteer* in the later nineteenth century. As with so many other references in these Hindu histories, this is fraudulent in its failure to make an accurate identification, its modification of quotations, and its failure to acknowledge, in this instance, that unidentified local oral sources were the authority for the author's statements and statistics.

10. Ramgopal Pandey Sharad, *Shri Ram Janmabhumi ka Romanchkari Itihasa* (Ayodhya, n.d.), pp. 3–4.

11. The so-called RJB temple in Ayodhya, the Vishwanath temple in Banaras, and the site of the Krishna Janmabhumi (birthplace of the god Krishna) in Mathura have been listed as the three most sacred sites, on which there can be no

compromise with Muslims: the mosques at these sites have to be destroyed (or moved) and the sites returned to the Hindus.

12. R. Koselleck, *Futures Past: On the Semantics of Historical Time* (Cambridge, Mass., 1985), p. 18. The writing on the question of the "modern" in Indian history is now considerable: see, for example, Ashis Nandy, *The Intimate Enemy* (Delhi, 1983); Ranajit Guha, *An Indian Historiography for India: A Nineteenth-Century Agenda and Its Implications* (Calcutta, 1988); Uma Chakravarti, "Whatever Happened to the Vedic Dasi?" in Kumkum Sangari and Sudesh Vaid, eds., *Recasting Women: Essays on Colonial India* (New Delhi, 1989); Sudhir Chandra, *The Oppressive Present: Literature and Social Consciousness in Colonial India* (Delhi, 1992); Chatterjee, *The Nation and Its Fragments*; Partha Chatterjee, *Our Modernity* (Rotterdam, 1997); and Sarkar, *Hindu Wife, Hindu Nation.* See also the writings and speeches of Tilak and Syed Ahmad Khan; *Bal Gangadhar Tilak: His Writings and Speeches,* enlarged ed. (Madras, 1919), especially his comments on the *Gita,* 231ff.; and Christian W. Troll, *Sayyid Ahmad Khan: A Reinterpretation of Muslim Theology* (New Delhi, 1978). For a fascinating comment on changing traditions in iconography, see Anuradha Kapur, "Deity to Crusader: The Changing Iconography of Ram," in Pandey, ed., *Hindus and Others.*

13. I have discussed this local history in my *Construction of Communalism in Colonial North India,* ch. 4.

14. I take this articulation regarding modernists as purifiers from Jane Bennett's summary of Bruno Latour's arguments. I have also adapted for my purposes other comments that she makes on the relationship between the modern and the premodern; see Bennett, "Modernity and Its Critics" (forthcoming).

15. Jain, "Vexing Ayodhya Issue."

16. See S. Gopal, R. Thapar, et al., "The Political Abuse of History," *Seminar,* no. 364 (Dec. 1989); A. Bakker, *Ayodhya* (Groningen, 1984); P. van der Veer, "'God must be liberated!' A Hindu Liberation Movement in Ayodhya," *Modern Asian Studies* 21, no. 2 (1987); Sushil Srivastava, *The Disputed Mosque* (Delhi, 1990).

17. The following discussion is based on two articles on Ayodhya by Girilal Jain, "A Glorious Time to Break Free," *Sunday Observer,* 9–15 August 1992; and "Vexing Ayodhya Issue."

18. See Chapter 6 below for a discussion of some of the wider context of these migrations.

19. To take only two fairly well documented twentieth-century instances, the 1912 and 1934 riots, one in Ayodhya and the other nearby, automatically became wars over the Ram Janmabhumi in the Hindu account, even though neither was directly related to control of this site, but rather to other matters of property and local control.

20. One of the earliest formulations of this argument is Romila Thapar et al., *Communalism and the Writing of Indian History* (Delhi, 1967).

21. Harbans Mukhia, "Communalism and the Writing of Medieval Indian History: A Reappraisal," *Social Scientist* 123 (August 1983), pp. 63–64.

22. It is worthwhile pointing to the poisonous reporting that characterized the very large and far-reaching Hindi press during the Ayodhya mosque/temple controversy in the 1980s and 1990s. The Gujarati press played an equally, if not more, harmful role in the course of the anti-Muslim violence in Gujarat in 2002, although it is notable that along with the English-language national media, the north Indian Hindi press presented a much more critical and balanced account of events during the latter period.

23. Further examples of this argument, and the context for it, are provided in the next chapter.

24. Cf. M.S. Golwalkar, *Bunch of Thoughts* (Bangalore, 1966), p. 164. As it happens, Hindu (and Muslim) nationalists are not alone in constructing the history of the subcontinent along these lines. In relation to the question of the naturalness of Muslim nationalism in the subcontinent, note the title of Francis Robinson's important study, *Separatism among Indian Muslims: The Politics of the United Provinces' Muslims, 1860–1923* (Cambridge, 1974); also the comments of John McLane in *Indian Nationalism and the Early Congress* (Princeton, N.J., 1977).

25. This paragraph has benefited greatly from Ajay Skaria's comments on an earlier version of this chapter.

APPENDIX TO CHAPTER 4

1. *Seminar*, no. 364, "Mythifying History" issue (December 1989). I have kept references to a minimum in this appendix; references are given simply to indicate the sources of direct quotations.

2. See P. van der Veer, "God must be liberated!"; also his *Gods on Earth: The Management of Religious Experience and Identity in a North Indian Pilgrimage Centre* (Delhi, 1989).

3. R.S. Shukul, *Shri Ram Janmabhumi: Sachitra, Pramanik Itihasa* (Ayodhya, 1986), p. 2. Emphasis added.

4. It is of some interest that in Thailand, where the legend of Ram has been powerful, the dynastic capital was renamed Ayutthaya during the premodern period for precisely this reason. I am grateful to Professor Romila Thapar for reminding me of this.

5. P. Carnegy, *Historical Sketch of Tahsil Fyzabad, Zillah Fyzabad including Haveli-Oudh and Pacchimrath, with the Old Capitals Ajudhia and Fyzabad* (Lucknow, 1870), p. 6.

6. Shukul, *Shri Ram Janmabhumi: Sachitra, Pramanik Itihasa*, p. 6.

7. Ibid., p. 7. Emphasis added.

8. Carnegy, *Historical Sketch of Tahsil Fyzabad*, p. 20.

9. Ibid., p. 21.

10. David Hardiman, "Power in the Forests: The Dangs, 1820–1940," in David Arnold and David Hardiman, eds., *Subaltern Studies: Writings on South Asian Society and History*, vol. 8 (Delhi, 1994).

11. Shukul, *Shri Ram Janmabhumi*, p. 16n.

12. This translation of the *farman* comes from Bharat Kala Bhawan, Banaras Hindu University, where both a Hindi and an English translation may be seen. I have modified the last sentence in light of the Hindi version. A translation of this *farman* is also to be found in R. R. Sen, *The Holy City (Benares)* (Chittagong, 1912), Appendix. Sen gives the date Hijri 1061 (1653–54 A.D.) for the *farman*.

13. Van der Veer, "God must be liberated!" p. 288.

14. Ibid., p. 285.

15. This paragraph draws primarily on A. G. Noorani, "The Babari Masjid Case," *Economic & Political Weekly*, 17 January 1987. Noorani cites several reports from which he obtained his information.

16. By this act, which followed a major agitation organized by right-wing Muslim organizations, Muslim women lost their right to appeal to the uniform civil code in order to obtain support and alimony on the dissolution of a marriage. See Asghar Ali Engineer, ed., *The Shah Bano Controversy* (Bombay, 1987); Vasudha Dhagamwar, ed., *Towards the Uniform Civil Code* (Bombay, 1989); Zakia Pathak and Rajeswari Sunder Rajan, "Shahbano," *Signs: Journal of Women in Culture and Society*, 14, no. 3 (Spring 1989); and Flavia Agnes, *Law and Gender Inequality: The Politics of Women's Rights in India* (Delhi, 1999).

CHAPTER 5

1. Radhakumud Mookerji, *The Fundamental Unity of India* (London, 1914), p. 6. Burma was part of British India at this time.

2. D. R. Goyal, *Rashtriya Swayamsevak Sangh* (Delhi, 1979), p. 40, citing C. P. Bhishikar, *Keshav: Sangh Nirmata* (Delhi, n.d.), p. 31. It seems almost unnecessary to make the point that there has been nothing like automatic agreement about the identity of the nation in France, Germany, or for that matter England.

3. M. S. Golwalkar, *We, or Our Nationhood Defined* (Nagpur, 1949), p. 49.

4. Ibid., p. 48; Nathuram Godse, *May It Please Your Honour: Statement of Nathuram Godse* (Pune, 1977), p. 119; V. D. Savarkar, *Hindutva* (Poona, 1949), pp. 95, 136.

5. Ibid., p. 74; Golwalkar, *We*, p. 10.

6. V. D. Savarkar, *Hindu-Pad-Padshahi or a Review of the Hindu Empire of Maharashtra* (Madras, 1925), pp. 246–47 and 281.

7. Examples are legion and too numerous to list, but for a particularly lurid one, see V. D. Savarkar, *Six Glorious Epochs of Indian History* (Bombay, 1971; reprint 1980).

8. Golwalkar, *Bunch of Thoughts*, pp. 404–405.

9. Golwalkar, *We*, pp. 16–17 (emphasis added).

10. See Harjot Oberoi, *The Construction of Religious Boundaries: Culture, Identity and Diversity in the Sikh Tradition* (Delhi, 1994).

11. Before this time, the term itself is not used: witness the writings of Dayanand Saraswati and Bal Gangadhar Tilak, for example.

12. Swami Shraddhanand, *Hindu Sangathan: Saviour of the Dying Race* (n.p., 1924), pp. 13 and 140–41 (emphasis added). Page numbers for subsequent quotations are given in the text.

13. Indeed, as Shraddhanand plainly states on p. 14, his pamphlet was at least partly inspired by a meeting with Col. U.N. Mukerji, who in 1909 had written a series of articles entitled "A Dying Race" in the newspaper *Bangalee*. Mukerji used the census data from 1872 to 1901, province by province, to make the alarming case that within a given number of years the Hindus would disappear altogether from India; see K.W. Jones, "Religious Identity and the Indian Census," in N.G. Barrier, ed., *The Census in British India: New Perspectives* (Delhi, 1981), p. 91. Hindu propagandists have continued to repeat this argument to the present day.

14. See, for example, Sudhir Chandra, *The Oppressive Present.*

15. Sudipto Kaviraj makes this point with reference to Bankim Chandra Chattopadhyaya, who defined the "we" sometimes as Bengalis, at other times as all Hindus, and at yet other times as all Indians; see his *The Unhappy Consciousness: Bankimchandra Chattopadhyay and the Formation of Nationalist Discourse in India* (Delhi, 1995).

16. Savarkar, *Hindutva*, p. 84.

17. Sudhir Chandra, *The Oppressive Present*, p. 125.

18. See my *Construction of Communalism in Colonial North India*, p. 216 and note.

19. Bhai Parmanand, *The Story of My Life* (Lahore, 1934), p. 66.

20. E.A. Gait, *Census of India, 1911, Volume I, Part I—Report* (Calcutta, 1913), p. 117.

21. R.V. Russell and Hiralal, *Tribes and Castes of the Central Provinces*, vol. 3 (London, 1916), p. 315.

22. Page numbers in brackets in the following paragraphs refer to the 4th ed. (Poona, 1949).

23. The translation is taken from the title page of the 4th ed.

24. Prithviraj Chauhan, king of Delhi and Ajmer, who was defeated by Muhammad Ghori at the second battle of Tarain in 1192 A.D.

25. *Amritsar*, the name for the holy city of the Sikhs and the site of the Golden Temple, means "the lake of [eternal, life-giving] nectar."

26. Perhaps the most barbaric indication of this is found in the slogan accompanying many recent instances of sectarian violence, "*Musalman ke do hi sthaan, Pakistan ya kabristan* [Muslims belong in one of two places—Pakistan or the grave]" or, in an earlier version, "*Babar ki santaan, jaao Pakistan ya kabristan* [Progeny of Babar, go to Pakistan or to the grave]."

27. Page numbers in brackets in the text refer to the 2d ed. (Bangalore, 1980).

28. *The Statesman*, 29 October 1947.

29. *Hindustan Times*, 28 September 1947, cited in *People's Age*, 12 October 1947.

30. Cited in Ashish Nandy, *At the Edge of Psychology: Essays in Politics and Culture* (Delhi, 1980), p. 91.

31. Cf. his comments on Africa, p. 341.

32. The same argument is now put forward with regard to secularism. It is notable that no such objection is ever raised when it comes to nationalism, industrialism, or capitalism.

33. Golwalkar, *Bunch of Thoughts*, p. 263.

34. Golwalkar, *We*, p. 62.

35. Lajpat Rai, *A History of the Arya Samaj* (rpt., Delhi, 1967), pp. 124–25.

36. Ibid., p. 120 (emphasis added).

37. J.T.F. Jordens, *Dayanand Saraswati: His Life and Ideas* (Delhi, 1978), p. 170 and note on p. 322.

38. Lajpat Rai, *History of the Arya Samaj*, p. 120n.

39. Savarkar, *Six Glorious Epochs*, pp. 154–57, 188, 192–93, and *passim*.

40. J.T.F. Jordens, *Swami Shraddhananda: His Life and Causes* (Delhi, 1981), p. 142.

41. Ibid., p. 143.

42. Veer Bharat Talwar, *Jharkhand ke Adivasi aur R.S.S.* (Chhaibasa, n.d.)

43. Ibid.

44. Lajpat Rai, *History*, pp. 123–24.

45. Savarkar, *Hindutva*, pp. 120–01 (emphasis added).

46. Dayanand Saraswati, "My Beliefs and Disbeliefs," a condensed version of his thoughts appended to the second edition of the *Satyarth Prakash* and reproduced in K.C. Yadav, ed., *Autobiography of Dayanand Sarasvati* (Delhi, 1978), p. 87; see also Jordens, *Dayanand*, p. 226.

47. *Hindu Sangathan*, pp. 136–37.

48. On the historical controversy regarding the so-called Aryan invasion of India, see Romila Thapar, "Which of Us Are Aryans?" in *Seminar*, no. 364 (December 1989); and Thomas A. Trautmann, *Aryans and British India* (Berkeley, Ca., 1997).

49. I owe this reference and the points arising out of it to Veer Bharat Talwar. See his *Jharkhand ke Adivasi*.

50. *We*, p. 62.

51. Ibid.

52. *Hindu Sangathan*, p. 141 (emphasis added).

53. An ancient Hindu prayer approvingly cited by Shraddhanand in ibid., p. 93.

54. Golwalkar, *Bunch of Thoughts*, p. 48.

55. Ibid., pp. 120–1.

56. See, e.g., Uma Chakravarti, "Whatever Happened to the Vedic Dasi?" in Sangari and Vaid, eds., *Recasting Women*; Sarkar, *Hindu Wife, Hindu Nation*; Partha Chatterjee, *Nationalist Thought and the Colonial World* (Delhi, 1986); and his "The Nationalist Resolution of the Women's Question," in Sangari and Vaid, eds., *Recasting Women*.

57. These quotations come from two leaflets circulated in Bhagalpur during the sectarian violence of October–November 1989. The emphases are mine.

58. *Hindu Sangathan*, pp. 93 and 138.

59. See my *Construction of Communalism*, Appendix 2.

60. For this very reason, abducted women were often reluctant to return to

their original families and communities. The recent literature dealing with these issues includes Butalia, *The Other Side of Silence*; Menon and Bhasin, *Borders and Boundaries*; Das, *Critical Events*, ch.3; and Pandey, *Remembering Partition*.

61. For details, see Uma Chakravarti, "Whatever Happened to the Vedic Dasi?"

62. See, e.g., R. Guha, *An Indian Historiography of India: A Nineteenth Century Agenda and Its Implications* (Calcutta, 1988); Chandra, *The Oppressive Present*; and Sudipto Kaviraj, *The Myth of Praxis: The Construction of the Figure of Krishna in the Krishnacharitra* (Occasional Paper No. 50, Nehru Memorial Museum and Library, New Delhi).

63. Golwalkar, *Bunch of Thoughts*, pp. 317–18 (emphasis added); cf. the sections entitled "Be Men with a Capital M" and "Potent Men vs. Patton Tanks."

64. Golwalkar, *Bunch of Thoughts*, p. 377; Savarkar, *Six Glorious Epochs*, p. 55. This last slogan is also found in leaflets circulated in Bhagalpur in 1989.

65. Savarkar, *Hindutva*, p. 19; Godse, *May It Please Your Honour*, p. 7.

66. V.D. Savarkar, *Presidential Address at the 22nd Session of the Akhil Bharatiya Hindu Mahasabha* (Madura, 1940), p. 41.

67. Savarkar, *Six Glorious Epochs*, p. 169.

68. Ibid., p. 169 (emphasis added); see also pp. 185 and 394–95. Cf. the repeated pronouncements in the RSS journal, the *Organizer*, since at least the 1980s that "the need of the hour" now is "not tolerance, but courage."

69. This fits in very well with the reconstruction of the figures of the Hindu deities, Ram and Krishna, in a new militaristic image, as discussed in Chapter 2 and earlier in this chapter.

CHAPTER 6

1. Brackette F. Williams makes the same point in discussing ethnicity in the context of territorial and cultural nationalism. Like tribe, race, or barbarian, she notes, the label *ethnicity* identifies those at the borders of empire or nation. "Within putatively homogenous nation-states, this border is an ideologically produced boundary between 'mainstream' and peripheral categorical units of this kind of 'imagined' social order." Williams, "A Class Act: Anthropology and the Race to Nation across Ethnic Terrain," *Annual Review of Anthropology* 18 (1989), p. 439.

2. J. Nehru, *Glimpses of World History* (Bombay, 1961), pp. 1129–30.

3. Talal Asad, *Genealogies of Religion: Discipline and Reasons of Power in Christianity and Islam* (Baltimore, Md., 1993), p. 257.

4. See Chapter 1, n. 12.

5. Shahid Javed Burki, *Pakistan: A Nation in the Making* (Boulder, Colo., 1986), p. 42.

6. Ibid. See also Stanley Wolpert, *Jinnah of Pakistan* (New York, 1984), pp. 339–40.

7. *Civil and Military Gazette*, 21 October 1947.

8. The same held true in East Pakistan, which was to become Bangladesh in 1971, where the Hindu population has remained as high as 10 percent.

9. See, for example, Nehru Memorial Museum and Library, New Delhi, AICC Papers, G-34/1947, Resolutions from several villages of Ferozepur and "Hindu and Sikh Public of Campbellpur," sent to President, Indian National Congress, 9 July 1947; also India Office Records, London, T.W. Rees Collection (uncatalogued at the time I saw it), "A Note on the Communal and Political Situation in the Punjab" (Appendix A to Lahore Area Op. Instr. No. 6, dated 23 July 1947); "Punjab Boundary Force Intelligence Summary No.1," 6 August 1947; and "Report of the Punjab Boundary Force, 1 August–1/2 September 1947" (New Delhi, 15 November 1947), ch. 2 and *passim*. (I am grateful to Professor Robin Jeffrey for first drawing my attention to these papers, which have now been acquired by the India Office Library and Records.)

10. See the U.P. governor's report to the viceroy in early June, after the public announcement that India was to be partitioned into the two new states of India and Pakistan. The Muslim League legislators in U.P. are "coo[ing] like doves," he reported, now that a "national home" for the Muslims has been conceded: "the whole attitude now is that in the U.P. we must forget the past and become all brothers together" (India Office Records, London, Mss. Eur. F200/168, Wylie-Mountbatten, 9 June 1947).

11. *Vartman*, 19 June 1947. (I am grateful to Saumya Gupta for giving me access to her photocopies of the files of this newspaper.)

12. Ibid., 30 July 1947.

13. Ibid., emphasis added.

14. *The Statesman*, 9 October and 12 October 1947. At the end of September, at a public meeting of prominent citizens addressed by Gandhi, one person declared that "the citizens of Delhi were ready to live in peace with the Muslims provided they were loyal to the Union and surrendered all arms and ammunition which they possessed without a license" (*The Statesman*, 2 October 1947).

15. Ibid. See *Aj*, 22 September 1947, for a report of another, very similar speech by Pant.

16. *Aj*, 7 October 1947.

17. *Pakistan Times*, 8 October 1947.

18. *Constituent Assembly Debates: Official Report*, vol. 5, p. 271.

19. *Tej* (Urdu), 18 September 1947.

20. *Aj*, 20 August 1947.

21. Cf. Choudhry Khaliquzzaman's *Pathway to Pakistan* (London, 1961), p. 411, on his reasons for resigning from the leadership of the Muslim League in the Indian Constituent Assembly.

22. See the comments of the U.P. [Uttar Pradesh] Congress leaders, A.P. Jain and Charan Singh, reported in *Aj*, 26 September, and *Pakistan Times*, 11 October 1947, respectively; also reports in *Aj*, 7 October, and *Vartman*, 27 September 1947.

23. *Constituent Assembly Debates*, vol. 8, p. 346.

24. Ibid., vol. 5, p. 271 (emphasis added).

25. *Vartman*, 12 October 1947.

26. In connection with the proposition that the "language, appearance, religion, and practices" of the Muslims were "all different" from those of the Hindus, I might note only that all the Indian Muslims I know or have heard of speak the Bengali, Gujarati, Marathi, Malayalam, Punjabi, Hindi, Urdu (or to break the vernaculars down further, the Awadhi, Bhojpuri, Magahi, etc.) of their regions. I should add that Urdu—designated the language of the Indian Muslims, which is also my language, and the language of very large numbers of Hindus and Sikhs of my parents' and grandparents' generations—whatever else it might be, is not a foreign language but distinctively Indian (or, now, subcontinental). Just as Indian intellectuals claim, with considerable justification, that English is now one of the languages of India, I would also want to assert that Islam is now (and has long been) one of the religions of India.

27. *Constituent Assembly Debates*, vol. 8, p. 329.

28. Ambedkar and other Dalit leaders had of course already initiated a significant debate about the relevance of the category *Hindu* for their followers, and similar questions had been raised in connection with the *adivasis* in the work of anthropologists like G. S. Ghurye and Verrier Elwin.

29. See T. N. Kaul, *Diplomacy in Peace and War: Recollections and Reflections* (Delhi, 1979), p. 111; and Ramchandra Guha, *Savaging the Civilized: Verrier Elwin, His Tribals and India* (Delhi, 1999), pp. 238–39, 255, 257.

30. Sankaran Krishna, "Cartographic Anxiety: Mapping the Body Politic in India," in Michael J. Shapiro and Hayward R. Walker, eds., *Challenging Boundaries: Global Flows, Territorial Identities* (Minneapolis, 1996), p. 196.

31. See Patel's letter of 16 July 1947 to Parmanand Trehan, in Durga Das, ed., *Sardar Patel's Correspondence, 1945–50*, vol. 5 (Ahmedabad, 1973), p. 289.

32. Ibid., vol. 4 (1972), pp. 426–27.

33. *Hindustan Times*, 23 December 1947; see Ganda Singh's "Diary of Partition Days," cited in Mushirul Hasan, ed., *India Partitioned*, vol. 2, p.87.

34. *People's Age*, 7 September 1947.

35. Thus a member of the staff of the British High Commission in Delhi, on tour on 17 November 1947, learned of a convoy of eighty thousand Mev peasants on their way to Pakistan along the Alwar road, which was likely to delay his motor car by several hours between Sohna and Gurgaon. On his homeward journey the next day, he saw that "the return movement of refugees had greatly increased"; the returnees included a group of some ten thousand Mevs at Sohna who had decided against going to Pakistan after all, judging that the dangers of going forward were greater than those of turning back (India Office Records, London, L/P & J/7/12589, R. C. Hadow's report on his visit to Alwar).

36. *Statesman*, 23 November 1947. Cf. *Statesman*, 15 October 1947, in which the Lucknow correspondent reports, "By an interesting unanimity of purpose, backed, no doubt, by a firm administration of law and order, [the Muslims of U.P.,

who, he notes, form the largest concentration of Muslims outside the Pakistan areas] have been determined hitherto to stay put."

37. Das, ed., *Patel's Correspondence*, vol. 4, p. 421.

38. Ibid., p. 422.

39. "The difference between the religious man and the citizen is the [same as the] difference between the merchant and the citizen, between the day-labourer and the citizen, between the landowner and the citizen, between the *living individual* and the *citizen*." Karl Marx, "On the Jewish Question," in *Early Writings* (London, 1975), pp. 220–21 (emphasis in the original).

CHAPTER 7

1. For an elaboration of the argument presented in this and the next paragraph, see my "The Politics of Community: Some Notes from India," in Gerald Creed, ed., *The Seductions of Community* (Santa Fe, forthcoming).

2. There is no universally agreed name for the castes at the bottom of society which I am concerned with here. Many are still referred to, and refer to themselves, by locally specific caste names—Chamar, Jatav, Pasi, Namasudra, Mahar, Mang, Nadar, etc. For a long time, they were referred to collectively as outcastes, depressed castes (or classes), or untouchables. Gandhi chose to describe them as Harijans, or children of God, as we will see later in this chapter. The Government of India Act of 1935 and the Indian constitution of 1950 called them Scheduled Castes, in reference to a "schedule" of the lowest castes that was drawn up in both documents. The chosen term of self-description by many of the most militant and outspoken of the former untouchables is *Dalit*, which means the downtrodden or oppressed.

3. For a variety of examples over time, see K.M. Ashraf, *Life and Conditions of the People of Hindustan* (2d ed., Delhi, 1970); C.A. Bayly, "The Pre-history of 'Communalism'? Religious Conflict in India, 1700–1860," *Modern Asian Studies* 19, no. 2 (1985); Mayaram, *Resisting Regimes*; and Shahid Amin's forthcoming work on Ghazi Mian.

4. See Ambedkar's writings of the 1940s, especially his *What Congress and Gandhi Have Done to the Untouchables* (Bombay, 1945).

5. *The Collected Works of Mahatma Gandhi*, vol. 89 (New Delhi, 1983), pp. 181, 201, 206, 223, and *passim*. Gandhi spoke a religious language, arguing that it would spell the end of Hinduism or Sikhism if the Jama Masjid was ever converted into a Hindu or Sikh temple (ibid., p. 201). I think it is clear that this was a question about India's future too.

6. Ibid., p. 393.

7. Asad, *Genealogies of Religion*, pp. 28 and 207.

8. Both Smith and Sommerville are cited in David Scott, *Refashioning Futures: Criticism after Postcoloniality* (Princeton, N.J., 1999), pp. 55 and 67.

9. See Chapter 5, section entitled "Untouchables: The Fallen Hindus."

10. Robert Deliege, *The Untouchables of India* (Oxford, 2001), p. 50.

11. As an old Dalit of the Satnami (or Chamar) caste from Chattisgarh said bitterly to a senior anthropologist in 1985, "The upper castes would not touch us. They would never eat with us. But they were always ready to fornicate. For 'doing it' our women were not untouchable. . . . Even after licking the privates of Satnami women, they would not lose their purity." Saurabh Dube, *Untouchable Pasts: Religion, Identity, and Power among a Central Indian Community, 1780–1950* (New Delhi, 2001), p. 171.

12. For one example of this kind of argument, see the interview with Maya Rani in Butalia, *The Other Side of Silence*, esp. p. 256.

13. Kancha Ilaiah, *Why I Am Not a Hindu: A Sudra Critique of Hindutva Philosophy, Culture and Political Economy* (Calcutta, 1996), p. xi.

14. The quotations in this paragraph are all taken from Vijay Prashad, *Untouchable Freedom: A Social History of a Dalit Community* (Delhi, 2000), pp. 67–69.

15. The information in this paragraph comes from Mark Juergensmeyer, *Religion as Social Vision: The Movement against Untouchability in Twentieth-Century Punjab* (Berkeley, Ca., 1982), pp. 277 and 301.

16. Ibid., p. 280.

17. This and the following two paragraphs draw on Dube, *Untouchable Pasts*, pp. 25, 50, 57, 96–97, 107–108, and *passim*.

18. See Eleanor Zelliot, *From Untouchable to Dalit: Essays on the Ambedkar Movement* (Delhi, 1996), p. 97.

19. Ibid., p. 154.

20. A.K. Narain and D.C. Ahir, eds., *Dr. Ambedkar, Buddhism and Social Change* (Delhi, 1994), pp. 5 and 85; and B.R. Ambedkar, *The Untouchables: Who They Were and Why They Became Untouchables* (Shravasti, 1977), p. ix.

21. D.R. Nagaraj, *The Flaming Feet: A Study of the Dalit Movement in India* (Bangalore, 1993), p. 19. This paragraph draws heavily on Nagaraj's argument. The following quotation from Gandhi appears in ibid., p. 19.

22. Nagaraj writes of the motif of escape from persecution and the journey to the promised land, "This time the promised land is the modern city" (ibid., p. 58).

23. Zelliot, *From Untouchable to Dalit*, p. 206.

24. D. Mosse, "Caste, Christianity and Hinduism: A Study of Social Organization and Religion in Rural Ramnad" (D.Phil. diss., Institute of Social Anthropology, Oxford, 1985), p. 247, cited in Deliege, *The Untouchables*, p. 67.

25. N.B. Dirks, *Castes of Mind: Colonialism and the Making of Modern India* (Princeton, N.J., 2001), p. 7.

26. Nagaraj, *The Flaming Feet*, pp. 74–75.

27. R.S. Khare, *The Untouchable as Himself: Ideology, Identity, and Pragmatism among the Lucknow Chamars* (Cambridge, 1984), p. 147.

28. Juergensmeyer, *Religion as Social Vision*, p. 1.

29. Narain and Ahir, eds., *Ambedkar, Buddhism and Social Change*, p. 203.

See also the poem by Namdeo Dhasal and Zelliot's commentary on it, which appear on the same page.

30. In his posthumously published *The Buddha and His Dhamma* (Bombay, 1957), Ambedkar wrote: "Inequality is the official doctrine of Brahminism. The Buddha opposed it root and branch. He was the strongest opponent of caste and the staunchest upholder of equality. There is no argument in favour of caste which He did not refute" (p. 340).

31. Anand, *The Buddha: The Essence of Dhamma and Its Practice* (Mumbai, 2002), pp. 123ff.

32. Martin Fuchs, "A Religion for Civil Society? Ambedkar's Buddhism, the Dalit Issue and the Imagination of Emergent Possibilities," in Vasudha Dalmia et al., eds., *Charisma and Canon: Essays on the Religious History of the Indian Subcontinent* (Delhi, 2001), pp. 252–53.

33. See, for example, his address on All India Radio, 3 October 1954, quoted in D.C. Ahir, *Dr. Ambedkar on Buddhism* (Bombay, 1982), p. 156.

34. Gauri Viswanathan, *Outside the Fold: Conversion, Modernity, and Belief* (Princteon, N.J., 1998), p. 225; Narain and Ahir, eds., *Ambedkar, Buddhism and Social Change*, pp. 12–13.

35. For some indication of the process, see Deliege, *The Untouchables*, pp. 157ff; Juergensmeyer, *Religion as Social Vision*, pp. 26–27 and 181ff.

36. Abdul Malik Mujahid, *Conversion to Islam: Untouchables' Strategy for Protest in India* (Chambersburg, Penn., 1989), p. 55 and *passim*.

37. Nagaraj, *The Flaming Feet*, p. 58.

38. Bama, *Karukku*, trans. Lakshmi Holmstrom (Chennai, 2000), pp. 68, 69, 91–92, 93, and 102.

39. Mujahid, *Conversion to Islam*, p. 86.

40. Interview, Bombay, 24 November 2003.

41. Ahir, *Ambedkar on Buddhism*, p. 35.

42. *Periyarana*, pp. 115–16, cited in Anand, *Buddha*, p. 190.

43. Eleanor Zelliot, "New Voices of the Buddhists of India," in Narain and Ahir, eds., *Ambedkar, Buddhism and Social Change*, p. 201.

CHAPTER 8

1. These distinctions have of course been usefully problematized in recent debates. Talal Asad has reminded us that the modern category of the secular itself produces the sacred and the religious in new ways, just as Benedict Anderson and others have underlined the reinvention of the sacred in modern, nationalist contexts. Talal Asad, *Formations of the Secular: Christianity, Islam, Modernity* (Stanford, Ca., 2003); Benedict Anderson, *Imagined Communities: Reflections on the Origin and Spread of Nationalism* (London, 1983). However, the commonly understood distinction between these terms will suffice for my purposes at this point.

2. T.N. Madan, "Secularism in Its Place," in Rajeev Bhargava, ed., *Secularism and Its Critics*, p. 314.

3. Charles Taylor, "Modes of Secularism," in ibid., pp. 46, 48.

4. See John Rawls, "Justice as Fairness: Political not Metaphysical," *Philosophy and Public Affairs* 14, no. 3 (Summer 1985). For an indication of the range of thinkers who turn to the idea of "overlapping consensus" even if they disagree with particular details in Rawls's version of it, see Charles Lamore, "Political Liberalism," *Political Theory* 18, no. 3 (August 1990); Amy Gutman, "The Challenge of Multiculturalism in Political Ethics," *Philosophy and Public Affairs* 22, no. 3 (Summer 1993); and Taylor, "Modes of Secularism," Akeel Bilgrami, "Secularism, Nationalism and Modernity," and Rajeev Bhargava, "What Is Secularism For?" in Bhargava, ed., *Secularism and Its Critics*.

5. Several of the most important contributions in this exchange are reproduced in Bhargava, ed., *Secularism and Its Critics*.

6. Asad, *Formations of the Secular*, pp. 59–60.

7. Ashis Nandy, "The Politics of Secularism and the Recovery of Religious Tolerance," in Bhargava, ed., *Secularism and Its Critics*, pp. 336, 338.

8. Ashis Nandy, "The Twilight of Certitudes: Secularism, Hindu Nationalism and Other Masks of Deculturation," in Veena Das, Dipankar Gupta, and Patricia Oberoi, eds., *Tradition, Pluralism and Identity: In Honour of T.N. Madan* (New Delhi, 1999), pp. 402, 414, 416n.

9. Partha Chatterjee, "Secularism and Tolerance," in Bhargava, ed., *Secularism and Its Critics*, pp. 363, 364, 378.

10. Akeel Bilgrami, "Secularism, Nationalism and Modernity," in ibid., pp. 395, 410, 411 (emphasis author's).

11. I take this formulation of Gandhi's approach to political negotiation from Ajay Skaria, "Gandhi's Politics: Liberalism and the Question of the Ashram," *South Atlantic Quarterly* 101, no. 4 (Fall 2002).

12. Bilgrami, "Secularism, Nationalism and Modernity," pp. 406, 408, 409.

13. Chatterjee, "Secularism and Tolerance," p. 375.

14. United Liberation Front of Assam, a guerrilla movement that has been active in northeastern India for some time.

15. Cf. Skaria, "Gandhi's Politics."

16. See, in this connection, Connolly, *Why I Am Not a Secularist*.

17. Bilgrami, "Secularism, Nationalism and Modernity," pp. 406, 408, 410, 411.

18. Gauri Vishwanathan, "Literacy, Conversion and Hindu Nationalism," in *Race and Class* 42, no. 1 (2000), p. 8.

19. Nandy, "The Politics of Secularism," p. 338.

20. Chatterjee, "Secularism and Tolerance," pp. 375 and 364.

21. Skaria, "Gandhi's Politics."

22. J. Nehru, *The Discovery of India* (Bombay, 1961), p. 286; and *Glimpses of World History* (Bombay, 1962), pp. 1129–30 (emphases added). Also cited in Chapter 6, n. 2.

23. For a fuller discussion of this term and its politics, see my *Construction of Communalism.*

24. Cf. the important discussion of this theme in Chatterjee, *The Nation and Its Fragments,* ch. 11.

25. See my *Remembering Partition.* For a detailed treatment of the Mevs, see Mayaram, *Resisting Regimes;* also the section entitled "Those Exceptional Times?" in Chapter 6 above.

26. David F. Pocock, *Kanbi and Patidar: A Study of the Patidar Community of Gujarat* (Oxford, 1972), p. 44.

27. Cf. Asghar Ali Engineer, *The Bohras* (New Delhi, 1980); J.C .Masselos, "The Khojas of Bombay," in Imtiaz Ahmad, ed., *Caste and Social Stratification among the Muslims* (Delhi, 1973).

28. For the recent Gujarat case, see Upendra Baxi's comments on "cosmopolitan" versions of Gujarati *asmita,* "The Second Gujarat Catastrophe," *Economic and Political Weekly,* 24 August 2002, p. 3523 and *passim.* For earlier comments on Ayodhya, Khalistan, and other battles, see S. Gopal, ed., *Anatomy of a Confrontation* (New Delhi, 1991); G. Pandey, ed., *Hindus and Others;* and Achin Vanaik, *The Furies of Indian Communalism: Religion, Modernity, and Secularization* (London, 1997).

29. Vibhuti Narain Rai, "An Open Letter to My Fellow Police Officers," reprinted in Siddharth Varadarajan, ed., *Gujarat: The Making of a Tragedy* (New Delhi, 2002), pp. 211–12.

30. Aakar Patel et al., *Rights and Wrongs: Ordeal by Fire in the Killing Fields of Gujarat* (New Delhi, 2002), p. 13. "Sardar" refers to Sardar Vallabhbhai Patel, a close follower of Gandhi and leader of the independence struggle in Gujarat, the "iron-man" of India, as he was dubbed when he served as the country's first home minister.

31. *The Hindu,* 25 Sept 2002.

32. I take this formulation from Thomas Blom Hansen, who speaks of religion and culture in India being "elevated to an ostensibly apolitical level, above the profanities of the political." *The Saffron Wave: Democracy and Hindu Nationalism in Modern India* (Princeton, N.J., 1999), pp. 11–12.

33. Cf. William E. Connolly, "Europe: A Minor Tradition" (unpublished).

34. R. Giordano, "Auschwitz—and Life! Why I Have Remained in Germany," in Susan Stern, ed., *Speaking Out: Jewish Voices from United Germany* (Chicago, 1995), cited in Carter, *Navigating Diaspora,* pp. 87, 307, 407. Cf. Michel-Rolph Trouillot, *Global Transformations: Anthropology and the Modern World* (New York, 2003), pp. 38–39 and *passim.*

Further Reading

Agnes, Flavia. *Law and Gender Inequality: The Politics of Women's Rights in India* (Delhi, 1999).

Aloysius, G. *Nationalism without a Nation in India* (Delhi, 1997).

Arendt, Hannah. *Eichmann in Jerusalem: A Report on the Banality of Evil* (1963; New York, 1977).

Asad, Talal. *Formations of the Secular: Christianity, Islam, Modernity* (Stanford, Ca., 2003).

———. *Genealogies of Religion: Discipline and Reasons of Power in Christianity and Islam* (Baltimore, Md., 1993).

Bauman, Zygmunt. *Modernity and the Holocaust* (Ithaca, N.Y., 1989).

Beevor, Antony. *Berlin, the Downfall: 1945* (New York, 2002).

Bhargava, Rajeev, ed. *Secularism and Its Critics* (Delhi, 1998).

Billig, Michael. *Banal Nationalism* (London, 1995).

Butalia, Urvashi. *The Other Side of Silence: Voices from the Partition of India* (Delhi, 1998).

Carter, Donald. *Navigating Diaspora* (Minneapolis, Minn., forthcoming).

Chakrabarty, Dipesh. *Provincializing Europe: Postcolonial Thought and Historical Difference* (Princeton, N.J., 2000).

Chakravarti, Uma, and Nandita Haksar. *The Delhi Riots: Three Days in the Life of a Nation* (Delhi, 1987).

Chandra, Sudhir. *The Oppressive Present: Literature and Social Consciousness in Colonial India* (Delhi, 1992).

Chatterjee, Partha. *Nationalist Thought and the Colonial World* (London, 1986).

———. *The Nation and Its Fragments: Colonial and Postcolonial Histories* (Princeton, N.J., 1994).

Connolly, William E. *Why I Am Not a Secularist* (Minneapolis, Minn., 1999).

Daniel, E. Valentine. *Charred Lullabies: Chapters in an Anthropography of Violence* (Princeton, N.J., 1996).

Das, Veena. *Critical Events: An Anthropological Perspective on Contemporary India* (Delhi, 1995).

————, ed. *Mirrors of Violence: Communities, Riots, Survivors in South Asia* (Delhi, 1990).

Deliege, Robert. *The Untouchables of India* (Oxford, 2001).

Dirks, Nicholas B. *Castes of Mind: Colonialism and the Making of Modern India* (Princeton, N.J., 2001).

Dube, Saurabh. *Untouchable Pasts: Religion, Identity, and Power among a Central Indian Community, 1780–1950* (New Delhi, 2001).

Du Bois, William E.B. *The Souls of Black Folk* (1903; New York, 1995).

Engineer, Asghar Ali, ed. *Communal Riots in Post-Independence India* (Hyderabad, 1984).

————, ed. *The Shah Bano Controversy* (Bombay, 1987).

Fanon, Frantz. *The Wretched of the Earth* (New York, 1963).

Figes, Orlando. *A People's Tragedy: The Russian Revolution, 1891–1924* (London, 1996).

Glover, Jonathan. *Humanity: A Moral History of the Twentieth Century* (London, 1999).

Golwalkar, M.S. *Bunch of Thoughts* (Bangalore, 1966).

Gopal, Sarvepalli, ed. *Anatomy of a Confrontation* (New Delhi, 1991).

Gramsci, Antonio. *Selections from the Prison Notebooks of Antonio Gramsci*, edited by Quintin Hoare and Geoffrey Nowell Smith (London, 1971).

Guha, Ranajit. *Dominance without Hegemony: History and Power in Colonial India* (Delhi, 1998).

————. *Elementary Aspects of Peasant Insurgency in Colonial India* (Delhi, 1983).

————, ed. *Subaltern Studies: Writings on South Asian Society and History*, vols. 1–6 (Delhi, 1982–89).

Hansen, Thomas Blom. *The Saffron Wave: Democracy and Hindu Nationalism in Modern India* (Princeton, N.J., 1999).

Hasan, Mushirul, ed. *India Partitioned: The Other Face of Freedom*, 2 volumes (Delhi, 1995).

————. *Legacy of a Divided Nation: India's Muslims since Independence* (London, 1997).

Hegel, G.W.F. *Introduction to 'The Philosophy of History,'* trans. Leo Rauch (Indianapolis, Ind., 1988).

Herman, David. "Bloody History," *Prospect Magazine*, no. 99 (June 2004).

Ilaiah, Kancha. *Why I Am Not a Hindu: A Sudra Critique of Hindutva Philosophy, Culture and Political Economy* (Calcutta, 1996).

Juergensmeyer, Mark. *Religion as Social Vision: The Movement against Untouchability in Twentieth-Century Punjab* (Berkeley, Ca., 1982).

Kaviraj, Sudipto. *The Unhappy Consciousness: Bankimchandra Chattopadhyay and the Formation of Nationalist Discourse in India* (Delhi, 1995).

Khare, R.S. *The Untouchable as Himself: Ideology, Identity, and Pragmatism among the Lucknow Chamars* (Cambridge, 1984).

Knowlton, James, and Truett Cates, eds. *Forever in the Shadow of Hitler? Original Documents of the 'Historikerstreit,' the Controversy Concerning the Singularity of the Holocaust* (Atlantic Highlands, N.J., 1993).

Lata Mani, *Contentious Traditions: The Debate on Sati in Colonial India* (Berkeley, Ca., 1998).

Mamdani, Mahmood. *When Victims Become Killers: Colonialism, Nativism, and the Genocide in Rwanda* (Princeton, N.J., 2001).

Mauss, Marcel. *The Gift: The Form and Reason of Exchange in Archaic Societies* (1950; English translation, London, 1990).

Mayaram, Shail. *Resisting Regimes: Myth, Memory and the Shaping of a Muslim Identity* (Delhi, 1997).

Mbembe, Achille. *On the Postcolony* (Berkeley, Ca., 2001).

Menon, Ritu, and Kamla Bhasin. *Borders and Boundaries: Women in India's Partition* (Delhi, 1998).

Mujahid, Abdul Malik. *Conversion to Islam: Untouchables' Strategy for Protest in India* (Chambersburg, Penn., 1989).

Nagaraj, D.R. *The Flaming Feet: A Study of the Dalit Movement in India* (Bangalore, 1993).

Nandy, Ashish. *At the Edge of Psychology: Essays in Politics and Culture* (Delhi, 1980).

———. "The Twilight of Certitudes: Secularism, Hindu Nationalism and Other Masks of Deculturation," in Veena Das, Dipankar Gupta, and Patricia Oberoi, eds., *Tradition, Pluralism and Identity: In Honour of T.N. Madan* (New Delhi, 1999).

Narain, A.K. and D.C. Ahir, eds. *Dr. Ambedkar, Buddhism and Social Change* (Delhi, 1994).

Pandey, Gyanendra. *The Construction of Communalism in Colonial North India* (Delhi, 1990).

———. *Remembering Partition: Violence, Nationalism and History in India* (Cambridge, 2001).

———, ed. *Hindus and Others: The Question of Identity in India Today* (New Delhi, 1993).

Prashad, Vijay. *Untouchable Freedom: A Social History of a Dalit Community* (Delhi, 2000).

PUDR, *Bhagalpur Riots* (Delhi, 1990).

Rai, Vibhuti Narain. *Shahar mein curfew* (New Delhi, 1987).

Sangari, Kumkum, and Sudesh Vaid, eds. *Recasting Women: Essays on Colonial India* (New Delhi, 1989).

Sarkar, Tanika. *Hindu Wife, Hindu Nation: Religion and Cultural Nationalism* (Delhi, 2001).

Scott, David. *Refashioning Futures: Criticism after Postcoloniality* (Princeton, N.J., 1999).

Sebald, W.G. *On the Natural History of Destruction* (1999; English trans., New York, 2003).

Sinha, Mrinalini. *Colonial Masculinity: The "Manly Englishman" and the "Effeminate Bengali" in the Late Nineteenth Century* (Delhi, 1997).

Skaria, Ajay. "Gandhi's Politics: Liberalism and the Question of the Ashram," *South Atlantic Quarterly* 101, no. 4 (Fall 2002).

Spivak, Gayatri Chakravarty. "Can the Subaltern Speak? Speculations on Widow Sacrifice," in L. Grossberg and C. Nelson, eds., *Marxism and the Interpretation of Culture* (Chicago, 1988).

Sunder Rajan, Rajeswari. *Real and Imagined Women: Gender, Culture and Postcolonialism* (London, 1993).

Suret-Canale, Jean. *Essays on African History: From the Slave Trade to Neocolonialism* (London, 1988).

Tambiah, Stanley J. *Sri Lanka: Ethnic Fratricide and the Dismantling of Democracy* (Chicago, Ill., 1986).

Thapar, Romila. "Which of Us Are Aryans?" *Seminar*, no. 364 (December 1989).

Trouillot, Michel-Rolph. *Global Transformations: Anthropology and the Modern World* (New York, 2003).

Van der Veer, Peter. *Gods on Earth: The Management of Religious Experience and Identity in a North Indian Pilgrimage Centre* (Delhi, 1989).

Vanaik, Achin. *The Furies of Indian Communalism: Religion, Modernity, and Secularization* (London, 1997).

Varadarajan, Siddharth, ed. *Gujarat: The Making of a Tragedy* (New Delhi, 2002).

Viswanathan, Gauri. *Outside the Fold: Conversion, Modernity, and Belief* (Princeton, N.J., 1998).

Williams, Brackette. "A Class Act: Anthropology and the Race to Nation across Ethnic Terrain," *Annual Review of Anthropology* 18 (1989).

Zelliot, Eleanor. *From Untouchable to Dalit: Essays on the Ambedkar Movement* (Delhi, 1996).

INDEX

bureaucracy, 4,31, 62, 151f, 188f, 202
Burma, 103, 205

Calcutta, 21, 88, 149f
Cambodia, 3
Canada, 58
Cariappa, General, 116, 127
Carr, E. H., 6
Carter, Donald, 11, 194
capitalism, 57f, 84, 90, 113, 206
caste, 2, 18, 35, 39, 43, 47f, 57ff, 69, 113,117,
   122ff, 135, 147, 149, 152, 154–71; and
   census, 163; and Hinduism, 110, 118,
   119–23, 156; among Muslims, 137, 183;
   conversion from, 119, 143, 144f, 168f,
   183f; "criminal castes" 29, 165; lower, 31,
   108, 111, 147, 155, 161f, 170, 178f, 198; 211;
   upper, 62f, 118, 123, 127, 164, 167, 169,
   177, 179; molestation of backward caste
   women, 163f, 211f. *See also* Dalits;
   reservations
censorship, 68f, 171
census, 108, 110, 118, 161ff, 168, 187, 206
Chamars, 111, 162f, 166f, 211f. *See also*
   Dalit; caste, lower
Chandra, Bipan, 20
Chatterjee, Partha, 176, 178, 180
Chattisgarh, 163, 211f
child marriage, 107
China, 116f
Christianity, 3, 36f, 69, 77, 79, 87, 115f,
   118f, 122f, 129, 132, 143f, 146, 155, 160ff,
   164, 167ff, 178, 185, 189, 191
citizenship, 9f, 44, 56, 67, 92, 109, 157, 178,
   184ff, 191, 209, 211; conditions of, 90,
   115; marked and unmarked, 13, 92,
   129–53 passim; second-class, 10, 185f
civilization, 7, 15, 117, 122, 173, 190f;
   Hindu, 104, 113, 121, 124, 145, 165f;
   Indian, 18, 32, 155, 167
class, 4, 6, 18, 48f, 57f, 118, 123, 156, 164,
   174, 181, 191; lower, 39, 58f, 62f, 122, 143,
   147f, 155, 161, 163; middle, 13, 17f, 40, 48,
   60, 63, 124, 164, 169f, 191; upper, 62, 123,
   116, 178, 186; ruling, 4, 14, 18f, 26, 34,
   47f, 53, 59f, 82, 158, 162, 186, 190f. *See
   also* peasants; workers; Dalits

Colombo, 38, 187
colonialism, 13f, 17, 19–23, 29, 33, 51, 53ff,
   58, 79ff, 85, 100f, 109, 111, 148, 155f, 158,
   162f, 194; British in India, 13f, 26, 56,
   72, 80, 95, 99–106 passim, 117, 121, 127f,
   131, 144ff, 151, 155ff, 165, 177, 195, 210;
   colonial modernity, 4, 162, 185f; and
   violence, 4f, 7–11 passim, 194. *See also*
   historiography; state
"Communal Award," 156, 165. *See also*
   reservations
communalism, 17, 19ff, 30–33, 43, 48f, 52,
   57, 59, 61, 70, 87, 91, 101, 131, 139, 142,
   149, 181–84, 187, 189, 194; violence of, 2,
   5, 13f, 16f, 19ff, 23–42 passim, 45f, 49,
   53f, 68f, 80, 95, 100f, 125, 127, 135, 187f,
   194, 196, 203f, 206f
communism, 6, 21, 102, 116ff, 123. *See also*
   left-wing; socialism
Communist Party (Marxist), 38, 196
community: conceptions of, 13ff, 49, 149,
   154–57, 161, 171, 177f, 181–85 passim, 191.
   See also majority; minority
Congo, 5, 7
Connolly, William E., 43
conversion, 61, 108, 197; to Buddhism,
   167ff; to Christianity, 119, 161; to Islam,
   34, 36, 115, 119f, 144f, 169, 198; to
   Sikhism, 61. *See also* Dalits
cow protection, 107f
creative writing, 9, 16f, 22f, 42, 47. *See also*
   film
crowd, 6, 13, 38, 68, 96, 127

Dalits, 13, 35, 48, 59, 63, 69, 108, 132,
   154–71, 176–78, 195, 210; attempted
   appropriation of, 69, 107f, 111, 118–23,
   147, 153, 160, 162; naming of, 111, 155,
   162, 170, 177, 178, 211; conversion of, 34,
   108, 120, 144, 157, 160, 166–70; sexual
   exploitation of, 163–64, 211–12. *See also*
   women
Das, Veena, 63, 66
Dayanand Saraswati, 104, 121, 126, 205
Delhi, 17, 25, 29, 37ff, 43f, 50, 61, 88, 93,
   105f, 136, 139, 141, 149, 162, 183, 206,
   209f; Muslim monuments in, 60, 90,
   158; violence in, 5, 38f, 43, 187

162–71 passim; Hindu law, 121, 123. *See also* caste; tolerance
Hindutva, 89, 113f, 121, 175; Savarkar's *Hindutva*, 109–15 passim
Hiroshima, 5, 12
historiography, 5f, 15, 17–24 passim, 42, 50–67 passim, 74, 84, 194; colonial, 53–56, 80, 82, 87, 100, 109, 111, 126, 199; disciplinary, 39, 42f, 46f, 51–55, 64f, 67, 70, 85, 200f; Hindu, 34f, 68–92 passim, 96–99, 114, 194, 202; minority, 50, 56, 64; nationalist, 10, 13, 32f, 43, 53–59 passim, 62, 64, 87, 91, 199; Marxist, 5, 20ff, 55f, 58, 64f, 87, 91; of Partition, 5, 7, 12, 19–22, 51ff, 91, 195; secular, 18ff, 43, 54, 57, 85, 87f, 91f. *See also* subaltern studies; state
Hobsbawm, E. J., 55, 64
Hochschild, Adam, 5
Hyderabad, 134, 149, 161

Ilaiah, Kancha, 161
Independence: *see* Partition and Independence
Indian National Congress, 35, 69, 109, 116, 137, 141, 156f, 164, 176, 184; leadership, 61, 86, 137ff, 142, 149f, 156f, 164
Indian People's Front, 39
Iqbal, Mohammad, 109
Iran, 86, 144f
Iraq, 3, 188
Irish Republican Army, 179
Israel, 3, 188

Jain, A.P., 209
Jain, Girilal, 203
Jainism, 110f, 114, 128, 132, 143, 146, 155
Japan, 3, 21, 58, 198
Jews, 14, 129, 152, 155, 164, 198, 211
Jinnah, Mohammad Ali, 85, 131, 134f, 139, 141, 145, 150, 177
Josh Malihabadi, 86, 151
journalism: *see* media
Juergensmeyer, Mark, 161f, 167

Kanpur, 21, 137, 143
Kapur, Anuradha, 37

Karachi, 21, 149
Kashmir, 36, 44, 47, 149, 179, 185
Kaviraj, Sudipto, 198, 206
Kedourie, Elie, 9f
Khalistan, 47, 179, 215
Khaliquzzaman, Choudhry, 150, 209
Khan, Khan Abdul Ghaffar, 131
Khare, R.S., 166
Kosambi, D.D., 62
Koselleck, Reinhardt, 82
Kosovo, 6
Krishna (Hindu deity), 78, 94, 126, 167, 198, 202, 208
Kshatriya, 123, 127. *See also* caste, upper

Lajpat Rai, Lala, 105, 118
landlordism, 58, 117f, 152, 211; in India 81, 123, 163, 166, 197
language: and identity, 88f, 107, 114f, 144ff, 150, 182, 184, 191, 209f
Lari, Z. H., 150
law, 2, 100, 117, 121, 123, 159, 169, 174, 182, 194
left-wing, 8f, 19, 27, 55, 69, 86, 89, 91f, 136, 194. *See also* communism; socialism
liberalism, 15, 30, 51, 65, 89, 92, 159, 173ff, 177, 189ff; liberal scholars, 19, 91, 194; neo-liberalism, 184, 186
Liberation Tigers of Tamil Ealam, 179
Lohia, Ram Manohar, 138f
London, 78, 156, 165
Los Angeles, 3
Lowenthal, David, 64
Lucknow, 78, 140, 151, 166f, 202, 210
Ludhianvi, Sahir, 86

Macaulay, Lord, 42, 47
Macintyre, Alasdaire, 200
Madan, T.N., 172
Madras, 88, 105, 110, 139
Mahabharata, 94
Mahar, 165, 168, 211. *See also* Dalits
Maharashtra, 105, 168, 170
majorities, 15f, 36, 43, 83f, 90, 129–52 passim, 156, 174, 178, 187ff, 197; construction of, 1, 8, 13, 50, 178, 190, 198, 208; Hindu, 18, 36f, 83, 115, 120, 132, 147f, 178, 184; permanent, 14, 191

Cultural Memory | in the Present

Jacques Derrida, *Eyes of the University: Right to Philosophy 2*

Nanette Salomon, *Shifting Priorities: Gender and Genre in Seventeenth-Century Dutch Painting*

Jacob Taubes, *The Political Theology of Paul*

Jean-Luc Marion, *The Crossing of the Visible*

Eric Michaud, *The Cult of Art in Nazi Germany*

Anne Freadman, *The Machinery of Talk: Charles Peirce and the Sign Hypothesis*

Stanley Cavell, *Emerson's Transcendental Etudes*

Stuart McLean, *The Event and its Terrors: Ireland, Famine, Modernity*

Beate Rössler, ed., *Privacies: Philosophical Evaluations*

Bernard Faure, *Double Exposure: Cutting Across Buddhist and Western Discourses*

Alessia Ricciardi, *The Ends Of Mourning: Psychoanalysis, Literature, Film*

Alain Badiou, *Saint Paul: The Foundation of Universalism*

Gil Anidjar, *The Jew, the Arab: A History of the Enemy*

Jonathan Culler and Kevin Lamb, eds., *Just Being Difficult? Academic Writing in the Public Arena*

Jean-Luc Nancy, *A Finite Thinking*, edited by Simon Sparks

Theodor W. Adorno, *Can One Live after Auschwitz? A Philosophical Reader*, edited by Rolf Tiedemann

Patricia Pisters, *The Matrix of Visual Culture: Working with Deleuze in Film Theory*

Andreas Huyssen, *Present Pasts: Urban Palimpsests and the Politics of Memory*

Talal Asad, *Formations of the Secular: Christianity, Islam, Modernity*

Dorothea von Mücke, *The Rise of the Fantastic Tale*

Marc Redfield, *The Politics of Aesthetics: Nationalism, Gender, Romanticism*

Emmanuel Levinas, *On Escape*

Dan Zahavi, *Husserl's Phenomenology*

Rodolphe Gasché, *The Idea of Form: Rethinking Kant's Aesthetics*

Michael Naas, *Taking on the Tradition: Jacques Derrida and the Legacies of Deconstruction*

Herlinde Pauer-Studer, ed., *Constructions of Practical Reason: Interviews on Moral and Political Philosophy*

Jean-Luc Marion, *Being Given: Toward a Phenomenology of Givenness*

Theodor W. Adorno and Max Horkheimer, *Dialectic of Enlightenment*

Ian Balfour, *The Rhetoric of Romantic Prophecy*

Martin Stokhof, *World and Life as One: Ethics and Ontology in Wittgenstein's Early Thought*

Gianni Vattimo, *Nietzsche: An Introduction*

Jacques Derrida, *Negotiations: Interventions and Interviews, 1971–1998*, ed. Elizabeth Rottenberg

Brett Levinson, *The Ends of Literature: Post-transition and Neoliberalism in the Wake of the "Boom"*

Timothy J. Reiss, *Against Autonomy: Global Dialectics of Cultural Exchange*

Hent de Vries and Samuel Weber, eds., *Religion and Media*

Niklas Luhmann, *Theories of Distinction: Redescribing the Descriptions of Modernity*, ed. and introd. William Rasch

Johannes Fabian, *Anthropology with an Attitude: Critical Essays*

Michel Henry, *I Am the Truth: Toward a Philosophy of Christianity*

Gil Anidjar, *"Our Place in Al-Andalus": Kabbalah, Philosophy, Literature in Arab-Jewish Letters*

Hélène Cixous and Jacques Derrida, *Veils*

F. R. Ankersmit, *Historical Representation*

F. R. Ankersmit, *Political Representation*

Elissa Marder, *Dead Time: Temporal Disorders in the Wake of Modernity (Baudelaire and Flaubert)*

Reinhart Koselleck, *The Practice of Conceptual History: Timing History, Spacing Concepts*

Niklas Luhmann, *The Reality of the Mass Media*

Hubert Damisch, *A Childhood Memory by Piero della Francesca*

Hubert Damisch, *A Theory of /Cloud/: Toward a History of Painting*

Jean-Luc Nancy, *The Speculative Remark (One of Hegel's Bons Mots)*

Jean-François Lyotard, *Soundproof Room: Malraux's Anti-Aesthetics*

Jan Patočka, *Plato and Europe*

Hubert Damisch, *Skyline: The Narcissistic City*

Isabel Hoving, *In Praise of New Travelers: Reading Caribbean Migrant Women Writers*

Richard Rand, ed., *Futures: Of Derrida*

William Rasch, *Niklas Luhmann's Modernity: The Paradox of System Differentiation*

Jacques Derrida and Anne Dufourmantelle, *Of Hospitality*

Jean-François Lyotard, *The Confession of Augustine*

Kaja Silverman, *World Spectators*

Samuel Weber, *Institution and Interpretation: Expanded Edition*

Jeffrey S. Librett, *The Rhetoric of Cultural Dialogue: Jews and Germans in the Epoch of Emancipation*

Ulrich Baer, *Remnants of Song: Trauma and the Experience of Modernity in Charles Baudelaire and Paul Celan*

Samuel C. Wheeler III, *Deconstruction as Analytic Philosophy*

David S. Ferris, *Silent Urns: Romanticism, Hellenism, Modernity*

Rodolphe Gasché, *Of Minimal Things: Studies on the Notion of Relation*

Sarah Winter, *Freud and the Institution of Psychoanalytic Knowledge*

Samuel Weber, *The Legend of Freud: Expanded Edition*

Aris Fioretos, ed., *The Solid Letter: Readings of Friedrich Hölderlin*

J. Hillis Miller / Manuel Asensi, *Black Holes / J. Hillis Miller; or, Boustrophedonic Reading*

Miryam Sas, *Fault Lines: Cultural Memory and Japanese Surrealism*

Peter Schwenger, *Fantasm and Fiction: On Textual Envisioning*

Didier Maleuvre, *Museum Memories: History, Technology, Art*

Jacques Derrida, *Monolingualism of the Other; or, The Prosthesis of Origin*

Andrew Baruch Wachtel, *Making a Nation, Breaking a Nation: Literature and Cultural Politics in Yugoslavia*

Niklas Luhmann, *Love as Passion: The Codification of Intimacy*

Mieke Bal, ed., *The Practice of Cultural Analysis: Exposing Interdisciplinary Interpretation*

Jacques Derrida and Gianni Vattimo, eds., *Religion*